EMPLOYMENT AND WORK RELATIONS IN CONTEXT SERIES

Series Editors

Tony Elger
Centre for Comparative Labour Studies
Department of Sociology
University of Warwick

Peter Fairbrother
School of Social Sciences
Cardiff University

The aim of the *Employment and Work Relations in Context Series* is to address questions relating to the evolving patterns and politics of work, employment, management and industrial relations. There is a concern to trace out the ways in which wider policy-making, especially by national governments and transnational corporations, impinges upon specific workplaces, occupations, labour markets, localities and regions. This invites attention to developments at an international level, tracing out patterns of globalization, state policy and practice in this context, and the impact of these processes on labour. A particular feature of the series is the consideration of forms of worker and citizen organization and mobilization in these circumstances. Thus the studies address major analytical and policy issues through case study and comparative research.

RESTRUCTURING IN THE SERVICE INDUSTRIES

Management Reform and Workplace Relations in the UK Service Sector

Gavin Poynter

Routledge
Taylor & Francis Group
New York   London

First published 2000 by Mansell Publishing Limited.

This edition published 2013 by Routledge

711 Third Avenue, New York, NY 10017
2 Park Square, Milton Park, Abingdon, Oxon OX14 4RN

Routledge is an imprint of the Taylor & Francis Group, an informa business

British Library Cataloguing-in-Publication Data
A catalogue record for this book is available from the British Library.

ISBN 0–7201–2341–0

Library of Congress Cataloging-in-Publication Data
Poynter, Gavin, 1949–
        Restructuring in the service industries: management reform and workplace relations in the UK service sector/Gavin Poynter.
        p.   cm.—(Employment and work relations in context series)
        Includes bibliographical references and index.
        ISBN 0-7201-2341-0
        1. Service industries workers—Great Britain.   2. Service industries—Great Britain—Management.   3. Service industries—Great Britain—Personnel management.   4. Industrial relations—Great Britain.   5. Financial services industry—Great Britain—Employees.   6. Insurance companies—Great Britain—Employees.   7. Health facilities—Great Britain—Employees.   8. Insco—Employees.   9. Credit UK—Employees.   10. Great Britain. National Health Service—Employees. I. Title. II. Series: Employment and work relations in context.
        HD8039.S452G757   2000
        331'.0941—dc21
                                                                99-37177
                                                                CIP

Typeset by Kenneth Burnley, Wirral, Cheshire

CONTENTS

PREFACE

Books on industrial restructuring and workplace relations have tended to focus on manufacturing industries. Theoretical debates have, in turn, been dominated by explanation of transitions – from mass to lean production or from Fordist to post-Fordist paradigms. Less attention has been paid to the transformations taking place in the service sector of the advanced industrial economies. Some authors have written about particular industries but few have attempted to offer theoretical frameworks for understanding the complex changes taking place within the sector. Ritzer's (1998) recently developed thesis on 'McDonaldization' is an interesting exception. The author's analysis, however, is primarily based upon a sociological explanation of broad cultural and structural change (particularly in the nature of consumption), involves excursions into the writings of, among others, Mannheim and Bourdieu and heavily relies upon Braverman's deskilling thesis to describe the emergence of 'Mcjobs' and routinized labour processes. This book takes a different approach.

It draws on the academic literature whose focus is the non-manual labour process (e.g. Smith *et al.*, 1991), while also taking stock of the explanations and projections of changes in service work from authors and practitioners drawn from the world of management and business. These sources provide useful insights into industries that have experienced rapid change over recent years. A complex process of transformation in work organization, technology, labour and product markets and skills and occupations has occurred in sectors, like the financial services, where previously conservatism, stability and tradition were the watchwords. Understanding this complexity, however, requires analysis to move between a broad appreciation of structural developments within the economies of the advanced industrial nations and an in-depth focus on the enterprise and workplace.

The book divides into four parts. Part 1 reviews the theoretical issues and debates raised by the growth of service industries in the advanced industrial economies. The definition and role of services are contested issues in contemporary literature. To some they provide the panacea for a decisive break with the past, the development of a new post-industrial society. For others the growth in services is the outcome of the continuing development of capitalist industrialism. Chapter 1 examines the change/continuity debate and explains the role of service industries in the advanced industrial economies of the late twentieth century. Chapter 2 argues that a business revolution has taken place in services industries, with new management practices being codified by leading enterprises and institutions into what might be called an 'American model'. Chapter 3 focuses on labour and suggests that many workers have experienced the adverse consequences of the business revolution in services through the intensification of work and the adoption of approaches aimed at achieving the real subordination of service labour.

Parts 2 and 3 explore these themes through detailed case studies of developments in two UK service sectors: the financial services and the National Health Service (NHS). Drawn from private and public service industries, the case studies provide evidence of an acceleration in the process of restructuring in the last decade of the twentieth century. In both sectors organizational and technological change combined with new developments in market relations to create an environment in which workplace relations shifted from centralization and stability to decentralization and instability. The case studies illustrate the main contours of restructuring in the two sectors and highlight the problems that trade unions must urgently address if they are to maintain an independent role as the voice of organized labour.

The case study fieldwork was conducted over periods of slightly varying length. The NHS studies were conducted over a period of two years between 1995 and 1997. The insurance company, Insco, was studied over a similar timescale and the author's analysis of Credit UK took place over several years, commencing in 1990 and concluding in 1997. The research relied primarily upon interviews with approximately eighty key informants: senior and executive managers, trade union full-time and lay officials and union members. Interview data were supported by published documents, including collective agreements and management and union policy and position statements. In each case, the author attended formal and informal meetings of union representatives and members as well as observing, in two cases, discussions and negotiations between management and union sides. Several informants were interviewed more than once, with formats varying between small group discussion and structured, individual sessions.

Part 4 provides an assessment of the trends evident in the case studies and relates these to a broader appreciation of the developments in work organization and management/workforce relations occurring in the service sector. With its focus on two industries, the book cannot claim to offer a comprehensive picture of developments within services as a whole. However, it aims to provide some useful propositions and arguments that might be deployed to inform the development of further comparative research on services industries within the UK and other advanced industrial nations.

ACKNOWLEDGEMENTS

Inevitably, a book that uses a case study approach builds up a considerable debt of gratitude along the way. Several senior managers provided access to their workplaces and offered sharp insights into developments in their institutions and enterprises. None of the four studies would have been possible without the help and support of the many trade unionists who provided contacts, set up meetings and spent many hours in discussions about their work, their aspirations and their concerns. In particular, I would like to thank Geof Luton, Pauline Ortiz and Alan Piper of BIFU and Phil Thompson and Mike Jackson of UNISON for facilitating the access necessary for the conduct of the workplace studies. The research for the NHS case studies was supported by a Nuffield Foundation Small Grants Award (SOC100/1429).

My colleagues in the Department of Innovation Studies, University of East London, provided me with the time and encouragement to undertake this project. Sally Wyatt took on many additional tasks to enable me to take sabbatical leave. Alvaro De Miranda offered insights and arguments as well as his constant support to complete the book.

A long-time colleague and friend, John Thirkell, University of Kent, provided invaluable help in getting me through the doctoral thesis which provided the raw material of sections of this text. Howard Gospel also gave excellent advice while supervising the doctoral thesis. Michael Fitzpatrick commented on the early chapters and shared with me several hours of late evening discussion, particularly on recent developments in the NHS. Several colleagues from other universities, including Jeremy Waddington, Bob Carter and Al Rainnie, gave very helpful comments and criticism. Finally, Peter Fairbrother guided me through the whole project and provided comments and encouragement when they were most needed.

ABBREVIATIONS

ABI	Association of British Insurers
ACAS	Advisory, Conciliation and Arbitration Service
AEEU	Amalgamated Engineering and Electricians Union
AEU	Amalgamated Engineering Union (now AEEU)
APAP	Association of Professional Ambulance Personnel
ATM	automated teller machine
BDA	British Dental Association
BIFU	Banking, Insurance and Finance Union (now UNIFI)
BMA	British Medical Association
BPR	business process re-engineering
CAC	Central Ambulance Control
CAD	computer aided despatch
CBI	Confederation of British Industry
COHSE	Confederation of Health Service Employees (now UNISON)
CWM	clerical work measurement
DHA	District Health Authority
DoH	Department of Health
EAP	employee assistance programme
EETPU	Electrical, Electronic, Telecommunications and Plumbing Union (now AEEU)
EFTPOS	electronic funds transfer at the point of sale
ERM	Exchange Rate Mechanism
EWC	European Works Council
G7	Group of Seven (leading industrial nations)
GDP	gross domestic product
GMBATU	General, Municipal, Boilermakers and Allied Trades Union
GP	general practitioner
HMO	health maintenance organization

HRM	human resource management
IT	information technology
LAUTRO	Life Assurance and Unit Trust Regulatory Organisation
MCA	Management Consultancies Association
MMC	Monopolies and Mergers Commission
MSF	Manufacturing, Science and Finance Union
NALGO	National Association of Local Government Officers (now UNISON)
NHS	National Health Service
NHSME	National Health Service Management Executive
NUBE	National Union of Bank Employees (now BIFU)
NUPE	National Union of Public Employees (now UNISON)
OER	operational effectiveness review
PACE	Performance Appraisal and Competencies Evaluation
PC	personal computer
PRP	performance-related pay
PTS	patient transport service
PUL	percentage utilization of labour
RCN	Royal College of Nursing
RHA	regional health authority
ROSE	Rest of South East (allowance)
TGWU	Transport and General Workers Union
TUC	Trades Union Congress
TUPE	Transfer of Undertakings (Protection of Employment) Regulations
UNISON	UK public services union

PART 1

RESTRUCTURING: THEORIES AND ISSUES

1 UNDERSTANDING SERVICES

Introduction

Service industries have been neglected over recent years, while researchers have engaged in heated debate about transformations taking place in manufacturing. This neglect contributed to the construction of a partial picture of the transformation of work in the late twentieth century. It allowed the analysis of industrial restructuring to be dominated by a narrow theoretical focus on shifts in production techniques and led to a disproportionate significance being given to these as the catalyst of social and economic change (Piore and Sabel, 1984; Hirst and Zeitlin, 1989; Womack *et al.*, 1991). The neglect of services is particularly surprising given that the vast majority of workers are now employed in what official statistics refer to as service industries. While authors (Martin and Rowthorn, 1986; Allen and Massey, 1988; Crompton *et al.*, 1996) have charted the changing patterns of employment between industrial sectors, relatively few have undertaken research into workplace change within services. As a consequence, our understanding of the role of services and the workplace relations within them is less developed by comparison to that of the manufacturing sector. Researchers have focused upon specific industries, like the financial and public services (Beaumont, 1992; O'Reilly, 1994; Fairbrother, 1994, 1996), but there has been no attempt to develop a comparative analysis across service industries with a view to constructing a broader perspective on workplace and sectoral change. There has been no debate on service sector restructuring comparable to that which took place around, for example, the model of lean production in manufacturing. This book attempts to open up such a debate.

In doing so it is necessary to identify the role played by service industries in the economies of the advanced industrial nations. This is not a simple task. Much of the discussion on services has been poorly theorized. Service industries have been loosely classified to incorporate a wide range of economic activities and occupations that simply do not belong to the sector. Riddle, for example, in her discussion of the various definitions of service industries, classifies utilities (gas, electricity and water), which are basic production industries, as services (Riddle, 1986). As a consequence of weak classification and too great significance given to such factors as employment change, many authors have misinterpreted their role in advanced industrial economies. Services, so the argument goes, have eclipsed production industries as the driving force of modern economies. They have become the 'mantra of national progress' (Roach, 1991: 83). Hence we are entering, or have entered, a new type of post-industrial society in which service industries and occupations have displaced manufacturing industries and manual employment (Fuchs, 1968; Bell, 1973). This myth of post-industrialism arises from a perception that services are detached from and overshadow production industries rather than being intimately linked to them. Arguably, this widely held perception has militated against the deepening of our understanding of the transformation of work within contemporary society.

The real task for the sceptic of post-industrialism is to define services clearly and illustrate the connections between them and the wider economy. Without this understanding it is difficult to explain the conditions under which the restructuring of service sector workplace relations has taken place. That is a central aim of this chapter. While acknowledging that service industries have expanded over recent years, the argument here is that the importance of this growth has been exaggerated. Government and academic classifications of services have included activities which should be located within the category of production industries. Services have become a catch-all for many occupations that have emerged as a result of what Sayer and Walker (1992) have called an expanded social division of labour. Furthermore, within the services sector, it is necessary to distinguish between the different roles played by the 'leading edge' industries. Financial services, for example, have a different economic location within society to those associated with the provision of social welfare. The former are concerned with the sphere of circulation, while the latter remain largely funded through deductions from the total revenue of capital. These distinctions are significant in determining the nature of the external economic conditions which have shaped their restructuring.

The chapter commences with a brief description of the prolonged nature of the contemporary restructuring process in the advanced industrial nations. It locates the growth of services within the context of an expanding social division of labour. It suggests that the growth in service sector employment has been over-emphasized, particularly by those who argue that we are witnessing a transformation from an industrial to post-industrial society. The catch-all title of services accorded to so many economic activities is not merely the product of loose definition but is, more fundamentally, associated with theories that proclaim the end of industrialism and of the class relations upon which it was based. This ideological perspective rests on a weak empirical foundation that is well served by the woolly conceptualization of service industries. Following a brief consideration of this ideological dimension, the chapter proposes a different framework for defining services which enables us to identify more clearly what has changed and what remains as an underlying continuity within capitalist societies. Finally, the chapter closes with an outline of the main themes and structure of the book.

Restructuring since the 1970s

Restructuring is a word widely used in business, management and academic publications in the 1990s. Its origin as an economic concept, however, is relatively recent. It first appeared in the literature of the late 1970s (Beauregard, 1989: 8). It described the broad changes in economic policies designed to enable nation states to adjust to the new conditions of reduced growth rates, rising inflation and high unemployment that arose in the wake of the 1973–5 recession. The concept was used more specifically in the 1980s to refer to the changes in the relative importance of industries within the advanced industrial economies, what is now called the manufacturing–service shift. In the 1990s, it has been widely used to refer to the strategies adopted by enterprises in their attempts to restore profitability and competitiveness. In its broad and more specific uses, the concept of restructuring has become closely linked with analysing the decline of old and the emergence of new industries and explaining the policies adopted by governments and enterprises in their attempts to cope with the experience of a protracted period of international recession.

Since the early 1970s the world economy has never been far from crisis. The conditions which guaranteed the sustained growth of the kind experienced during the golden age of the post-war period have long passed (Maddison, 1991). The specific changes in the international economy associated with the end of the boom have been widely identified, although their causal connections are still a matter of debate among economists. The 1970s saw the end of the dominance of a single industrial power over the world economy. The end of US hegemony was signalled by the break-up of the Bretton Woods agreement that had guaranteed international financial stability for two decades. The oil crises of 1973–4 brought huge increases in fuel costs and accelerated the rise in other prices. These, in turn, created inflationary pressures and a massive rise in the debt burden of less developed nations. Underlying all these developments was a significant slowdown in the economies of the advanced industrial nations. National governments moved towards policies designed to curb domestic inflation, dampen consumer demand and reduce public expenditure. A painful process of adjustment commenced in the latter part of the 1970s, accelerated as a result of the 1980–3 recession and continued into the 1990s.

The post-war boom saw shifts in employment patterns occurring under favourable circumstances of growth in output, trade and employment. Conversely, since the mid-1970s, industrial restructuring has taken place under conditions of reduced levels of output growth, low investment in manufacturing and rising unemployment in many of the advanced industrial nations. The underlying feature of the past two decades has been the slowdown in the growth of industrial production in the relatively strong and relatively weak advanced industrial nations. This slowdown gave rise to recessions in the early 1980s and 1990s. The recessions were the consequence rather than cause of the economic malaise (Magdoff, 1992), with each being longer and deeper than the one preceding it. This is a characteristic of a stagnating international economy, a condition reached in the early 1990s when even the most dynamic industrial nations, such as Japan and Germany, suffered domestic economic crises from which they are yet to recover. Indeed, the economic crisis in Japan was a central feature of a wider Asian crisis that afflicted the 'Tiger' economies of nations like South Korea. The Asian meltdown was followed by crisis in the fledgeling Russian market economy in 1998, increased problems for the economies of Latin and South America and, as a result of these global developments, downward projections for economic growth for the advanced industrial nations, including the USA. By late 1998 all the evidence pointed to a global economic slowdown and the continuation, therefore, of a process of industrial restructuring well into the new millennium (Wolf, 1998).

Over the past two decades the advanced industrial nations have found increasing difficulties in identifying new mechanisms to counter recession. A variety of government policies and business strategies have been used in an attempt to restore economic stability and respectable levels of growth. The mechanisms used to counter recessionary trends included new forms of state intervention (including privatization and the shift away from direct ownership to regulation), the increased export of capital, credit expansion and labour market reform. Timescales for the implementation of policy changes in each of these areas varied between states, depending upon the location of their domestic economies within the accumulation cycle (Maddison, 1991). Nevertheless, each of the leading capitalist nations undertook reforms in these areas in an attempt to restore competitiveness and economic growth.

While governments have adopted the rhetoric of the free market, the policies introduced in nations like the USA and UK have, paradoxically, often led to more direct forms of state involvement in the domestic labour market and in specific industries (Healey, 1993; Fairbrother, 1994, 1996; Jones, 1996). The overall weakness of economies like that of the UK was revealed by the trade gap in manufactured goods, the continued sluggishness of manufacturing investment and the reliance upon inward investment as a key source of innovation and change. The expansion of credit by the governments of the advanced industrial nations provided a useful means by which to avoid the deepening of crises in the mid-1970s and 1980s, but also contributed to the general instability of the world financial system, leading to the crash in October 1987. The export of capital by business, designed to offset the problems of sustaining profitability within domestic markets, served to increase competitive tensions on a global scale. The area in which, arguably, most success has been achieved, labour market reform, enabled business and governments to pass on the worst effects of recession to their own domestic working classes. Whether this strategy generated the conditions for sustainable economic growth remains to be seen. The relative failure of the mechanisms used to offset the tendencies to recession suggests that the current process of restructuring still has some distance to run. The policies and programmes adopted have created an uneven pattern of structural change and renewal.

Theories of Social Transformation

The historical development of capitalism has been widely presented as a linear progression. This perception was codified by authors like Fisher and Clark (Fisher, 1939; Clark, 1940), who presented the trajectory of capitalist development as one based upon sectoral change in which employment moved from a primary sector (agriculture) to a secondary sector (manufacturing) and then on to a tertiary or service sector. The Fisher/Clark 'thesis' emerged in the 1930s and 1940s. This influential analysis defined manufacturing as the making of tangible goods and commodities, while services were associated with the provision of the intangible or non-material. This 'thesis' was subsequently reworked in the post-1945 period by authors like Bell (1973), for whom the shift to the post-industrial society was characterized by the replacement of goods-producing activities by those concerned with the provision of services. Service work involved all those employed in activities such as information handling and the knowledge-based industries. Bell argued that since most workers employed in advanced economies fell within these broad categories we were seeing the emergence of a new post-industrial society. Over the past two decades many authors have jumped on to the Bell 'bandwagon'. In various forms, this perspective has had a significant impact on the contemporary theorization of social and cultural change.

At the centre of Bell's theory of social transformation lay the new technologies, particularly the computer (Kumar, 1996: 8). In his earlier writings Bell's argument concerning the creation of a post-industrial society rested primarily upon the growth of service industries and the emergence of new types of technical and professional occupations (Bell, 1973). By 1980 the advances in information technology enabled him to add the information dimension, so that the concept of the post-industrial was reworked into a theory of the information age (Bell, 1980). This new age was founded upon the convergence of computing and telecommunications industries, which broke down the distinction between the processing of knowledge and its communication. As a result the information technology revolution undermined the traditional boundaries of time and space. It was possible to create real-time links across the globe, providing the basis for the emergence of a new kind of global society. Earlier societies were structured by the spatial constraints of national territories and the confines of time measured in hours, minutes and seconds. The new society was not bound by the constraints of national governmental and institutional structures and operated in nanoseconds, thousandths of microseconds. The transformation of the infrastructure of modern society impacted upon the social and cultural sphere and was not merely confined to the techno-economic 'base' (Kumar, 1996: 13). This pattern of systemic transformation, encompassing all the activities of society, is a characteristic feature of the writings of the enthusiasts of the new information age (Toffler, 1981; Masuda, 1985). For the enthusiasts the evidence to support their claims was derived primarily from statistics that revealed the emergence of vast numbers of workers whose employment rested upon the use and manipulation of knowledge. According to Bell, the traditional classical economists' preoccupation with labour as the source of value was surpassed by the proposition that knowledge was the new source of value (Bell, 1980).

Theories that started from an analysis of the growth of employment in service industries took on new dimensions when fused with the theorization of technological change, particularly the convergence of information technology and telecommunications. By the 1990s the post-industrial thesis was the dominant discourse, though not all writers shared Bell and Toffler's visionary zeal. Academic writers focused upon different aspects of this transformation. Castells (1993) identified the consequences of the new global information age for the international economy, particularly the less developed industrial nations; Pakulski and Waters (1996) drew attention to the changing social composition of society, declaring the end of class as a useful sociological category of analysis; Lash and Urry (1987) identified the implications of the demise of industrialism for political and industrial structures, proclaiming the emergence of a new type of dis-organized capitalism and, in the cultural sphere, postmodernism was associated with the demise of rationalism and the progressive doctrines allied to the Enlightenment (Calinicos, 1989).

Elaboration of these varying strands need not detain us here except in so far as they served to distort analysis of the role of service industries within the advanced industrial economies. This distortion assumed four main dimensions. First, the growth in service sector employment was perceived primarily from a North American and North European perspective, which tended to ignore the growth of production industries and manufacturing employment in other regions of the world. From a global perspective, manufacturing production shifted location rather than experiencing significant decline and, in turn, created new patterns of uneven capitalist development (Dicken, 1992). Second, service work was assumed to contain many virtuous characteristics, although the evidence to support such a claim was limited. Those who processed and utilized information were attributed with skills and knowledge that did not match their experience of work (Robins and Webster, 1987, 1989; Webster, 1996). Third, as consumption conquered production (Kumar, 1996: 12) employers adopted a 'new' ethos, a customer orientation, that disguised the distinctive economic roles played by different industries in the accumulation process. In short, new management ideologies turned all workers into service providers, thus blurring the distinction between different types of productive and unproductive forms of labour. Finally, this service orientation was presented as a qualitative break with old forms of commodity production, when, in reality, it amounted to the extension of the capitalist imperative of 'commodification' to new areas through what Robins and Webster have referred to as the application of the principles of scientific management to those activities aimed at meeting consumer needs, desires and fantasies (Robins and Webster, 1989: 334).

As Kumar (1996: 34) and Slack (1984: 249–50) have argued, however, it is not sufficient simply to identify the theories of post-industrialism, the information society and their other variants as ideologies that serve the needs of capitalism. Several authors have provided compelling analyses that demonstrate this point with devastating effect (Calinicos, 1989; Meszaros, 1989, 1995; Clarke, 1992; Gough, 1992). What is more important is to indicate how these ideologies have had material effects on perceptions in the real world. This point may be illustrated by the way in which post-industrial theorists have exaggerated the significance of the shift to services through, for example, ascribing the demise of industrialism to the decline in manufacturing employment; ignoring the changing character of 'goods' production in advanced industrial economies and lumping together a diverse range of economic activities and occupations under a single generic title of services.

Employment growth in manufacturing has been overstated as an indicator of the development of industrial capitalism: the rise in total manufacturing employment being associated with the growth of industrialism and a fall in numbers being indicative of its demise. Taking a longer-term perspective, and presenting manufacturing employment in a relative context, a different picture emerges. In the USA, for example, even during the period of rapid industrial expansion in the 1890s, manufacturing employment stood at only 27 per cent of the total employed. A century later, in 1989, the percentage of the total labour force in manufacturing had declined by a mere 1 percentage point, to 26 per cent (Maddison, 1991: 32). A similar picture of relative stability in manufacturing's share of the total labour force emerges for other nations, like the Netherlands, Germany and Japan (Maddison, 1991: 31). More importantly, from the longer-term perspective, a more telling indicator of the continued significance of manufacturing industries has been the growth in output. This has maintained an upwards trajectory even in those economies, such as the UK, where the employment share of manufacturing has experienced a relatively sharper rate of decline. The strength in output growth relative to employment has merely indicated the capacity of manufacturing industries, with the exception of brief periods of cyclical recession, to produce more using less directly productive labour; a tendency of capitalist production that was identified by Marx over a century ago.

The character of industrial products has changed. The second half of the twentieth century has seen a dramatic rise in the production of 'white goods', or household goods aimed at an expanding consumer market. More recently this 'industrialization of household services' (vacuum cleaners, washing machines and so on) has been accompanied by the manufacturing of other commodities that would traditionally have been produced in the domestic sphere. The traditional distinctions between primary and secondary industries and those concerned with manufacture, retail distribution and hotel and restaurant 'services' has blurred. In short, the manufacture of hamburgers, chilled and other fast foods has taken on the same character as car production. Rather than witnessing the demise of industrialism we are observing its extension to virtually all facets of social life. This industrialization, or what some have called 'commodification' (Sayer and Walker, 1992: 88), of everyday life has, in turn, created difficulties for those who attempt to classify what constitutes service industries and occupations.

The categorization of labour that provides a diverse range of commodities, from meals in restaurants to films, books, software and other types of information, as service labour is simply wrong. Changes in the technical and social divisions of labour have given rise to the emergence of new occupations, such as software programmers, designers and information/database handlers. Many of these occupations provide intermediate goods that are essential to and part of the production process, but many have been erroneously classified as providers of business services.[1] Equally, the conflation of many non-production occupations under the generic title of services has led to those occupations associated with the sphere of circulation (financial services) being considered in the same way as other types of 'personal' services. Those engaged in circulation work undertake a specific form of service for capital, which is essential for its successful operation. This labour, in turn, creates profits for financial institutions through the redistribution between capitalists of the surplus generated within society. Circulation workers have a different relationship to the production process from other 'service' employees, and an effective classification of contemporary employment patterns should recognize this feature. It is these different relationships to the accumulation process that are essential to an analysis of the restructuring of workplace relations within these industries.

Finally, as Kumar (1996) and other critics have argued, a rejection of post-industrial theories of transformation is not at the same time commensurate with a view that nothing has changed. To the contrary, an effective critical perspective requires the development of an alternative approach to understanding the transformations that have occurred during the period of the rapid diffusion of information and communications technologies. These technologies have had the greatest impact in what official sources refer to as the service industries; so an analysis of service sector restructuring provides an effective opportunity to identify what has changed. To commence this task it is useful to situate the analysis of services within the context of changes in the social division of labour, before offering a different framework for understanding service work.

The New Social Division of Labour

The main argument here is that the growth in service industries and occupations should be more precisely analysed through a study of the changes taking place in the social division of labour. This view, while acknowledging the expansion of services industries, also suggests that the rate of growth of such industries has been exaggerated. The reason for this exaggeration lies in the weak theorization of the division of labour. Sayer and Walker (1992) have provided a fruitful perspective for understanding what is new about the division of labour in contemporary society. They identified the products of new sectors like the electronics industry as providing outputs that are atypical by comparison to more traditional industries. While the material form of the automobile typified the visible output of traditional manufacturing industries, the electronics sector has produced an increasing variety of products whose 'tangible material substratum diminishes radically whilst the meaningful content soars' (Sayer and Walker, 1992: 66). Processors, disks and operating systems may be small in size but their capacity has increased dramatically over recent years and their usage has extended to virtually all sectors of the economy. Traditional manufacturing industries have been joined by new ones to *widen* the social division of labour and increase the interactions between its various parts. Second, the social division of labour has *deepened* 'as the layers of the intermediate inputs have multiplied' (Sayer and Walker, 1992: 66). This deepening has taken place through the vast expansion in the production of unfinished goods and components which require the utilization of labour that might be remote from the production process but that, none the less, makes a vital contribution to it. The deepening and widening of the division of labour has been mislabelled as a growth of service employment in areas like business services, software design and development and in activities concerned with the servicing, repair and maintenance of machinery and equipment.

This misconception, according to Sayer and Walker (1992), is based upon the simplistic conflation of three different aspects of the division of labour within contemporary society. First, there is the extended social division of labour, which has developed in all areas of industrial production in which large amounts of necessary work is undertaken prior to, during and following the process of production. This extended division of labour has been increasingly 'formalized' in recent years by the rise in use of the modern version of the putting-out system of subcontracting and through the spatial and temporal disaggregation of the production process. Second, there has been a massive increase in the hierarchical division of labour, with management functions being separated and becoming ever more elaborate, and with the distinctions between those employed to control the labour process and those engaged in indirectly contributing to it being increasingly difficult to distinguish (Armstrong, 1991). Finally, Sayer and Walker argue that there have been significant developments in what they call the mental division of labour, a process involving the creation of specific and distinctive tasks involved in the 'application of knowledge and manipulation of materials' (Sayer and Walker, 1992: 68).

The late nineteenth and early twentieth centuries saw the rationalization of manual labour through the application of Taylorism. The mid-twentieth century saw management use materials (electricity, electronics and bio-engineering) to transform labour processes that went beyond the directly productive activities of labour, and the late twentieth century has seen the application of the same rationalism that was applied to manual labour and materials being applied to human knowledge and intelligence itself (Sayer and Walker, 1992: 73). Rather than being the triumph of ideas over practice, the information revolution, in the late twentieth century, represents the triumph of industrial capitalism over the processes that constitute the development of social knowledge: data collection, handling, storage and analysis. This development in the mental division of labour 'cuts right across the extended and hierarchical divisions of labour' (Sayer and Walker, 1992: 72) and, rather than creating a new elite, professional or middle class (a theme pursued by writers from Galbraith in the 1950s and 1960s to Lash and Urry, and Pakulski and Waters in the mid-1990s), brings the information worker directly into the 'service' of industrial capitalism. While many of these employees are pressed into the category of intermediate business services, the activities they perform are more akin to those of the productive worker. The technical and social divisions of labour have greatly increased, with their focus shifting from labour involved in the final assembly process to that engaged in the intermediate stages of production. It is this shift that has been obscured by the enthusiasts of post-industrialism. In short, rather than signifying the triumph of intelligence over industrialism, it represents a trend towards, what might be called the industrialization of intelligence (Kennedy, 1991).

This trend has been evident for most of the twentieth century and has been commented upon by many authors. Max Weber, for example, identified the tendency of capitalism to create new forms of rational bureaucratic structures in industry and political life. Burnham (1941) captured the changes taking place in the hierarchical divisions of labour with his analysis of the managerial revolution in the late 1930s, and the post-war boom years saw a plethora of writers commenting upon the emergence of industrial states in which a new technostructure was being forged (Galbraith, 1967: 69–80). The end of the post-war boom and the emergence of a protracted period of restructuring demanded a reassessment of these developments in the extended division of labour. Capital's achievement in improving productivity using less productive labour was also its problem. The growth in employment of intermediate labour could no longer be sustained. It was necessary to find new ways of rationalizing the organization of the extended and hierarchical forms of the social division of labour, while also subjecting those engaged in knowledge and information handling to a process, previously mainly associated with manual labour, of mechanization. It was these developments, that commenced in the 1980s and 1990s, that lend the contemporary period its unique character. The hierarchical division of labour was attacked by organizational reform, including delayering and downsizing, the extended division of labour was reordered via new contractual arrangements and the breakdown of traditional boundaries between industries and the mental division of labour was subjected to a 'ruthless' use of software technologies aimed at the routinization of knowledge and decision-making processes (Head, 1996).

Defining Services

The 're'-definition of service industries and occupations starts from the recognition that contemporary societies, even those displaying many of the traits of the post-industrial, are essentially industrial societies in which a new social division of labour has developed through the expansion of the range of activities that are not immediately concerned with the production process. This labour is often 'hidden' or remote. It may produce intermediate products or components, or contribute to design, development and manufacture via electronic networks or work stations some distance from the place of production. As with the case of software, for example, the knowledge content may greatly exceed the physical form of the good or commodity. Irrespective of its material form, the labour power expended on creating software is appropriated when it is used in production. The exchange between buyer (employer) and seller (the programmer) is merely the step that precedes the appropriation of the seller's labour in the act of production. Post-industrial theorists tend to focus only on the act of exchange and ignore the subsequent stages of appropriation and realization. Hence many business 'services' and the activities of, for example, utilities companies who supply essential 'services' like water, gas and electricity have been wrongly categorized as falling within the ambit of the service economy (Riddle, 1986).

Conversely, labour activities that do fall within the definition of services are those which are not realized in the process of production. These activities divide into four main categories. First, there are those occupations which contribute to the circulation of capital – what might be called circulation work. This involves the labour concerned with the money form of capital (financial services) and that which is engaged in post-production activities: retail, wholesale and transportation. Second, there are those activities which constitute a cost to total social capital. These are still primarily provided by the state and mainly take the form of health, welfare and educational activities. Third, there are those activities which consist of services directly purchased by the consumer. Here it is the service that is paid for and the seller of this service remains independent of the labour/capital relation. In contemporary society, childminders, domestic cleaners and other types of household labour usually fall into this category (though, as has been indicated earlier, this category is in decline as the 'conquest of household production continues with a vengeance' (Sayer and Walker, 1992: 88)). This type of labour service is different to that which is involved in the now highly commercialized leisure, travel and tourism industries. This is the fourth category of service work. In these industries direct labour services are minimal since they have become dominated by large-scale corporations that sell 'packages' to the vastly expanded market of ordinary consumers. While retaining the classification of service industries they have benefited considerably from the construction of whole branches of production industries that provide leisure goods, from trainers to travel goods and sports wear. This vast range of commodities symbolizes the industrialization of private consumption rather than the triumph of consumerism over industrial production. In brief, service industries involve those engaged in circulation work and post-production activities: retail, wholesale and transportation; the collective provision of welfare (provided typically by the state, particularly health and education); the individual provision of personal services; and, finally, the provision of leisure activities, like tourism.

The nature of these service industries has changed considerably in the second half of the twentieth century. Financial services, for example, has seen a significant growth in employment up to the early 1990s, an explosion in the range of financial products and services and a shift towards a more integrated, global financial system. At root, however, financial services has retained its essential character as the organizer of the money system and the facilitator of market exchange. Money performs a range of functions in the capitalist system. It is a means of exchange and a store of the value achieved in the process of commodity production, and, as money capital, provides the capacity for the entrepreneur to undertake investment. As a means of exchange and a store of value, money has contradictory purposes. As a store of value it may be hoarded or taken out of circulation when there are no opportunities for its profitable employment. This amounts to an interruption to the circulation process. On the other hand, it cannot remain idle in this way for too long, since it is only by pushing money into circulation that commodities may be bought and subsequently sold in order to realize a profit. This contradictory role of money lies at the heart of the recurring crises of capitalism, in which the accumulation of money wealth may take place at the same time as the collapse of industrial production (Clarke, 1988: 91). Managing this tension has been a central feature of the financial system over recent years. It has created new ways of conducting business transactions and provided for a massive extension in the range of financial services provided through the development of new credit and debt facilities, the creation of new money forms such as credit and debit cards and new ways of encouraging circulation through the development of futures and options markets. Circulation work has correspondingly seen an expansion in the division of labour, particularly within the banking system, where new industries have emerged engaged in processing paper and electronic transactions. These back office functions have increasingly displaced traditional types of banking activities conducted in the high street branch. In brief, the financial services sector has expanded in an attempt to oil the wheels of an industrial system faced with problems arising from a protracted period of restructuring.

Retail, wholesale and transportation are post-production activities that facilitate the trading of commodities. There is no realization of the labour used in a process of production. It is therefore a form of circulation work that facilitates the distribution and consumption of commodities. Recent years have seen this type of labour take on some of the functions of the labour employed in financial services. The growing range of financial services offered at the point of sale have served to blur the divisions between financial and retail labour. Accompanying these developments has been the consolidation of retail activities into large-scale retail parks and centres, with the corresponding advantages accrued in the development of the transportation infrastructure and facilities management . These developments have led to what some authors have called the emergence of a 'self-service economy' (Gershuny, 1978; Smith, 1983; Gregory, 1991). The self-service economy has extended to areas like leisure, tourism, sports and other recreational activities (Urry, 1990) and become dominated by large retail and leisure enterprises. By contrast, other personal consumer services, such as hairdressing and domestic services, have remained within the sphere of small-scale business, the self-employed and informal labour (Beynon, 1997; Brown, 1997).

The activities and occupations concerned with the provision of health and education remain within the sphere of public services in the advanced industrial nations (though the displacement of non-profit making by 'for profit' health institutions has taken place widely in the USA over the past decade). These services constitute a cost to revenue and their consumption is largely organized by the state or quasi-state institutions, with the principle being that such services are provided free at the point of demand. While the organization of consumption has remained firmly within the area of public service provision, the process of the production of health care has remained dominated by the major pharmaceutical companies. These have developed an extensive and direct link with consumers over recent years through the selling of goods in retail and pharmacy outlets, while also continuing to provide a wide range of commodities (drugs, machinery and equipment) to the state organized health services. As these services, such as the NHS in Britain, have experienced huge cost increases, their restructuring has led to the adoption of new organizational forms that attempt to emulate the operation of the private business world.

Education, like health, is a major pillar of the social provision of the welfare state and has, in the UK, for example, retained this position throughout the post-1945 period. It has not experienced the same level of industrialization as the production or input side of the health care industry. It has maintained a highly labour-intensive character. It has, however, begun to change in distinctive and complex ways. Education expanded with the development of industrial society by providing the social and intellectual skills required for employment and the effective participation in society. The benefits of mass education were always moderated by its other social function, that of differentiating between those who achieved and those who did not. This ambiguity has sharpened over recent years within countries like the UK. The expansion of higher education provision was accompanied by reforms in further and secondary education which provided government with the instruments necessary to make a significant impact upon the structure of the labour market (Rubery, 1996: 24). In the 1980s, for example, this was reflected in the development of Youth Training Schemes aimed primarily at reducing the level of youth unemployment rather than providing opportunities for developing the skills required for career development. More recently, training and educational provision in further and higher education has been used to reduce occupational identities and decouple the relationship between the achievement of educational qualifications and the expectation of obtaining a decent standard of living. These changes within the education system have enhanced its role in reshaping the domestic UK labour market by helping to keep the young out and focusing on the certification of the generic 'competencies' of those who remain within. Despite these developments, education has remained primarily within the public service sphere.

Productive and Unproductive Labour

Services perform a range of activities within advanced industrial nations. Some generate surplus value, while others do not. Labour power employed in service provision is not synonymous simply with the classical economists' category of unproductive labour. Its specific character continues to be determined by its relationship to the process of the creation and realization of surplus value. This relationship may change over time and in accordance with changes in the social division of labour. Contemporary changes in the social division of labour make the analytical distinction between productive and unproductive difficult to discern when, for example, managers combine production roles with those associated with the control of labour, and health and education professionals take on more private, for profit, activities. Such blurring does not detract from the importance of the analytical distinction but it does make the effort to categorize and quantify a relatively fruitless task.

Service theorists have tended to focus only on the exchange between the buyer and seller of the service, rather than enquiring as to whether this exchange led to a subsequent stage of realization. An absurd but logical consequence of this superficiality is that all labour power becomes 'service' labour and the question of definition is reduced to a matter of personal preference. This is the current state of affairs in much business and academic literature. The definition of services has been reduced to a debate about the material or non-material form of the service provided rather than being analysed in terms of its association with the process of the creation and realization of surplus volume. Post-industrial and service theorists cannot even claim originality in this deception. Their intellectual antecedents were the vulgar economists who '– like Bastiat – go no further than that first formal transaction *(between buyer and seller)* in order by this trick to get rid of the specific capitalist relation' (Marx, 1969: 407).

The trick, however, has assumed new and more complex dimensions in the late twentieth century by comparison to the conditions in which Marx first exposed the shortcomings of the classical economists' formulation. This complexity was revealed during the debates concerning the role of the public sector in the mid-1970s, when it became clear that the golden age of the post-war boom was at an end. Economists such as Bacon and Eltis (1976) argued that in countries like the UK, with a large public service sector, the economy contained too few producers and too many non-producers (teachers, civil servants, etc.). Britain's economic problems arose from a burgeoning public sector that could no longer be afforded. Hence public sector spending should be cut and unprofitable state supported industries rationalized. In response, left critics either claimed that under capitalism all labour was productive (Gough, 1973; Harrison, 1974) or argued that the crisis facing the unproductive public sector was indicative of a deeper malaise, an underlying crisis of profitability, that was initially expressed by an incapacity to sustain the activities of the welfare state (Bullock and Yaffe, 1979; Howell, 1979). The productive/unproductive labour debate that took place in the second half of the 1970s mainly concerned the role of the public sector and spurred a sharp political debate between left and right. Paradoxically, by the mid-1980s, the political debate had subsided as the expansion of private service industries had apparently provided the way out of the crisis for the UK economy. Writers from left and right traditions converged on to a common ground in which it was acknowledged that the UK economy had shifted to a new post-industrial phase (Stonier, 1983; Lash and Urry, 1987). In this sense, post-industrial theorists rescued the writings of the 'vulgar' political economists from their (deserved) obscurity. Their writings, however, were attempting to address a real problem.

The complexities of analysing the distinctions between productive and unproductive labour in the late twentieth century were compounded by the expansion of public and private service industries for a number of reasons. First, the identification of productive labour became a more difficult process as a result of the spatial and temporal break-up of the production process and the development of a vast range of intermediate products whose production could take place at some distance from final assembly. Second, the Marxist concept of indirectly productive labour – that which is engaged in facilitating the reproduction of directly productive labour in the form of health care, training and so on – is extremely difficult to distinguish in the contemporary world from that which is unproductive. Both forms of labour power coexist in, for example, the public sector health and education services within the UK, and while it is possible to establish a conceptual distinction it is more difficult, in practice, to disentangle those activities which contribute to the reproduction of productive labour from those which constitute merely a 'service' to those whose economic circumstances place them outside the labour/capital relation. Finally, welfare and training provision has assumed a purpose in contemporary workplace relations which goes beyond its material role in the reproduction of labour power. It has assumed an ideological dimension. Training schemes for the young, for example, have been questioned in relation to the extent to which they genuinely prepare them for work, as opposed to providing a convenient way of reducing unemployment levels, and employee care programmes provided by employers have a strong moral and ideological component which may be more significant than the benefits they claim to offer the employee (May and Brunsdon, 1994; Mizen, 1994: 99–121).

In brief, the practical distinction between productive and unproductive labour in specific sectors like business services, health and education in the advanced industrial economies, in which the social division of labour has assumed ever more complex forms, has become a relatively difficult task by comparison to previous periods of capitalist development (Carter, 1997). Only detailed case study analysis of, for example, management hierarchies in production industries or close analysis of the work undertaken by health teams in the NHS would reveal such distinctions. Despite the problems arising in relation to empirical verification, the conceptual distinction remains valid, for without it the world appears merely as a market-place peopled exclusively by the buyers and sellers of services.

Key Arguments

This chapter has argued that the 1990s has seen the extension of the restructuring imperative to all industrial sectors within the economies of the advanced industrial nations. Restructuring has taken place, alongside the extension of the tentacles of industrial capitalism to virtually all spheres of social and economic life, including those activities that were largely located within the area of private (household) consumption. The growth of services has been poorly theorized. Their growth is best understood from an analysis of changes in the social and technical divisions of labour. From this perspective, the role and growth of services may be demonstrated as being intimately linked to activities of the 'real' economy in which the conceptual distinction between productive and unproductive labour remains significant despite the difficulties associated with its empirical verification. Changes in the technical and social divisions of labour have been the subject of direct social intervention, the underlying feature of which has been a shift from the formal to the real subordination of labour. This uneven, contested process provides an underlying theme of this book. The key arguments and themes may be summarized as follows:

1. The restructuring imperative has extended to all sectors of the advanced economies in the 1990s, causing a loss of dynamism and business confidence within the entrepreneurial class in the leading industrial nations. This has been particularly evident in the period since 1989, when all sectors of the advanced industrial economies experienced recession. While the early 1980s witnessed a severe downturn in manufacturing industry, particularly in countries like the USA and Britain, service industries continued to expand in terms of employment and profitability. By contrast, in the early 1990s, the economic malaise spread to all industries and sectors, leaving no areas of economic activity untouched. Those industries that appeared to be the beneficiaries of restructuring in the 1980s became its victims in the early 1990s.

2. The decline in fortunes of leading service industries created a 'watershed' in relations between management and labour. The new management strategies and practices that arose from the imperative to restructure may be best understood from an analysis of those countries in which service industries were most developed – the USA and the UK. US companies took the initiative in developing new strategies to cope with rationalization and restructuring, which others, particularly in the UK, were to follow.

3. The new management strategies adopted in service industries involved a significant reordering of its relations with labour. This reshaping of workplace relations involved changes in work patterns and work organization as well as changes in the attitudes and values that informed the conduct of 'service' work. The new commercial and competitive orientation in public and private services industries disturbed traditional career patterns and beliefs in job security and constituted an attempt to achieve the 'real subordination' of service labour to new forms of management authority and control.

4. The challenges to traditional work practices and forms of work organization, coupled with new approaches to employee relations created significant pressures on the collective organization of labour in countries like the UK. Since a significant percentage of the unionized workforce in the UK is employed in service industries, labour's response to the changes taking place in these sectors, arguably, holds the key to the future prospects of organized labour.

In taking up these themes, the book moves between different levels of analysis. Part 1 is concerned with the debates on restructuring at the level of the national and international economy and their implications for management and labour. Parts 2 and 3 focus upon the workplace and industrial sector within the UK, drawing upon case study evidence to identify the 'messy dynamics' (Pollert, 1991: 30) of change in management/labour relations. The two industrial sectors from which the case studies are drawn are financial services and the National Health Service. Part 4 draws together the insights provided by the case studies and attempts to identify what is 'new' about workplace relations within UK service industries in the late 1990s.

The Structure of the Book

Service industries that were perceived by some as the foundation of a new and vibrant form of capitalism in the mid-1980s had, by the mid-1990s, experienced a rapid change in their own fortunes. Chapters 2 and 3 focus on the impact of what has been called the business revolution on management and labour in services. Chapter 2 examines the management strategies and organizational reforms that have been introduced to 're-engineer' business processes in the service sector, while Chapter 3 explores the implications for labour. Chapter 3 focuses on the development of a conceptual framework which provides insights into the changing character of work. In particular, it takes the concept of intensification, usually associated with the experience of work in manufacturing, and demonstrates the way in which it may be used to codify and explain the new forms of work organization that have arisen in areas of service sector employment.

Chapters 4 to 7 provide case studies of developments in two UK industrial sectors. The case studies illustrate key components of the business revolution. The two industries – health and financial services – have undergone significant changes in employment patterns over the past decade, experienced the growing pressures of 'commercialization' and, paradoxically, felt the impact of the new, more direct forms of state intervention that have accompanied successive Conservative administrations' ideological commitment to the tenets of the free market. The case studies identify the new climate that has helped to shape management strategies towards restructuring and provide insights into the experience of labour in working and organizing in difficult and often hostile conditions

The implications of management reform in relation to the organization of labour within the services sector are considered in Chapter 8. Drawing upon the evidence provided by the case studies, the chapter argues that while the institutional forms have remained relatively stable, the content of management/workforce relations has changed significantly. Chapter 9 examines these changes within the broader social context and considers, in the light of contemporary management strategies towards employment in the services sector, the potential for the further marginalization or renewal of organized labour.

Note

1. The case of software production is an interesting example of the problems associated with the classification of occupations. In 1998 the countries of the European Union adopted a new accounting mechanism, the European System of Accounting, which required software expenditure to be recorded as investment. This redefining of software as a 'good' should, logically, lead to the redefinition of the employment classification of those who write it, with many software designers and writers being shifted from the category of business services to a new category that reflects their 'productive' activity (see Whitaker, 1998).

2 MANAGEMENT AND RESTRUCTURING

Introduction

Twentieth-century literature on management has largely focused on the manufacturing enterprise. Relatively few studies have examined the role of management in the services sector (Smith *et al.*, 1991: 2). In the 1980s and early 1990s this situation began to change as a 'business revolution' took hold in the service industries. The revolution was precipitated by a number of factors. First, particularly in the USA and Britain, government became increasingly preoccupied with controlling the growth of the public services and developing within them a more 'commercial' orientation (Farnham and Horton, 1993; Fairbrother, 1994, 1996). Second, in key private sector industries, like the financial services, extensive technological innovation began to be associated with change in management organization and the labour process (Smith *et al.*, 1991; Cressey and Scott, 1992). Finally, the economic crisis that hit service industries in the 1980s in the USA, and a little later in the UK, concentrated management minds on the need for major programmes of rationalization and restructuring (Quinn and Gagnon, 1986; Roach, 1991).

These developments provided fertile ground for academic study and business analysis. While authors drew attention to the consequences for employment of these new approaches (Hakim, 1987; Pollert, 1987, 1991), demonstrating that many significant changes in work organization and employment patterns were occurring in the service industries, relatively few attempted to theorize or explain the management strategies and practices that lay behind them. There was no equivalent, in relation to service industries, of the debate that took place around Japanization and the 'end' of mass production in manufacturing.

This chapter attempts to address this imbalance. It identifies some of the main characteristics of the business revolution in the service industries. The chapter focuses on two main themes: the identification of a range of management practices that cohered into what is called an American model of service industry restructuring; and the appropriation of this model by institutions and enterprises in the UK service sector. The American model contains several features, including: the reform of management organization; the development of new customer-oriented approaches; the deployment of information technologies to re-engineer or reorganize work processes; the increased use of management consultants to facilitate change and the development of new approaches to employee relations. The proposition here is that these initiatives constituted a decisive break with traditional management practices within service industries, in effect creating a 'new managerialism' that has been strongly influenced by the business strategies adopted by American companies. Put simply, the past decade has seen the emergence of a US model that has had a distinctive impact upon service industries.

The Emergence of the US Model

The services sector contains a variety of activities which are amorphous and more difficult to define than those in manufacturing. Traditionally, services were bound by the need to meet specific local or national requirements. They were not considered to be a significant contributor to international trade and development. They were offered by local companies and local and national government, and tended to reflect their particular national and cultural settings. There were considerable cross-border barriers to the movement of service sector products in industries like banking and insurance and, in the public sector, the provision of welfare services was traditionally considered to be the task of national and local government, employing large numbers of staff directly. In recent years this situation has changed. Deregulation contributed to the internationalization of the activities of, for example, telecommunications, financial services and transportation companies. Privatization opened up previously publicly owned and operated services and basic production industries in areas like health, water and the energy sector to foreign competitors, and locational problems were reduced by the advent of technologies which facilitated the rapid transferability of services across time and space.

The American economy took the lead among the advanced industrial nations in developing an extensive service sector. The 1970s is regarded as the decade in which a significant structural transition took place. Manufacturing employment stood still at around twenty million, while employment in services steadily expanded. While charting the development of public and private services in the USA is beyond the scope of this text, it is useful to note that in the public sphere the expansion of welfare provision dates back to the New Deal and the 1935 Social Security Act. This legislation acknowledged the failure of the market as the mechanism to deliver adequate education and health provision for the whole nation. Welfare provision developed over subsequent decades to provide, by 1980, through a combination of contributory and in-kind payments, a system of medical care (Medicare and Medicaid), food stamps, free school meals, employment training schemes and grants for education and social services to around 24 per cent of the American population. This provision was costly, growing as a proportion of gross domestic product (GDP) from under 10 per cent in 1940 to over 20 per cent in 1980. This increased the public sector deficit and prompted demands for the reduction in size of the welfare bureaucracy. As employment in manufacturing stood still, federal, state and local government employment grew to a level of around 6 per cent of the national workforce by 1980 (Kemp, 1990). This expansion was complemented by growth in other service industries, particularly the financial services sector and communications (Riddle, 1986). Under increased competitive and financial pressures in each of these 'leading edge' service industries, American service sector management developed strategies for the rationalization and restructuring of employment and work organization, which others, particularly in the UK, would emulate within the context of their own social and institutional settings.

In his study of the productivity problem facing US industry, Thurrow attached much of the blame for falling US competitiveness on the services sector. Employment in services expanded through the creation of 21 million jobs in the period 1980–90, but productivity levels in service industries were much lower than the national average (Thurrow, 1993: 167). The growth in services was linked to the expansion of white-collar employment, the rise of white-collar 'bureaucracies'. The growth in these bureaucracies had not been checked by office automation. While real output from manufacturing companies had grown by 30 per cent between 1980 and 1990, blue-collar employment had expanded by only 2 per cent. Blue-collar productivity had risen during this period by 28 per cent. By contrast, white-collar employment had expanded by 33 per cent, while white-collar productivity had declined by 3 per cent (Thurrow, 1993: 168). Thurrow identified a number of reasons for the poor performance of service industries. First, people were cheaper than machines. Falling real wage rates, and low minimum wages relative to national average wages in many service industries, provided a disincentive for management to use new technologies as an instrument for reducing staffing levels. Second, Thurrow argued that where technologies were introduced they had been associated with the expansion of management information systems, enhancing and extending the role of middle managers rather than displacing them. Third, the growth in the white-collar bureaucracy had been encouraged by management structures in which individual managers received higher rewards if they were responsible for large numbers of staff. Middle management career prospects benefited from employment growth. Lastly, Thurrow argued, the growth of services like health arose from the political failure to grasp the need to control health care costs. Thurrow's critique was echoed by others in the USA in the late 1980s and early 1990s, and reflected the increased competitive pressures that service sector management faced. What has been referred to as a 'business revolution' in the service industries was the managerial response (Head, 1996).

To identify the strategies that may have informed the business revolution in services in the USA in the late 1980s and early 1990s it is most appropriate to commence from the specific economic conditions that affected these industries. From this perspective it is possible to begin to identify more precisely what was required to be 'restructured' and what emerged as the 'American model'. The key service industries in the USA in the late 1980s suffered from five interrelated problems. First, the leading edge industries like insurance, banking and health experienced acute economic 'crises'. The finance sector was under pressure from a rise in foreign direct investment, which enhanced competitive pressures, a credit crisis spawned by increases in domestic and international indebtedness and volatile market conditions caused by fluctuations in interest rates. The health sector found itself under increased financial pressures created by, for example, the rising costs of investment in new technologies and an apparently relentless increase in staffing levels. Many of these deficiencies became evident by the mid-1980s (Coddington et al., 1985). Second, service industries had experienced continuous growth in employment levels throughout the 1970s and 1980s, and that growth had not been matched by improvements in labour productivity. From the management perspective labour was attached to outmoded, traditional patterns of work (Drucker, 1991). Third, key service industries had made significant investments in information technologies that enhanced the range of products and services available but had relatively little impact upon the efficiency of work processes. Finally, service sector enterprises, from hospitals to banks and insurance companies, were integrated organizations with high costs incurred as a result of the continuous requirement to invest in information technologies. This burden adversely affected the potential for reaping the benefits from the provision of high value added products and services. These factors made restructuring 'an imperative' (Roach, 1991) and strongly influenced management approaches to the solutions to be found. The solutions had five main elements: the reform of management organization; the development of a more aggressive market orientation via the dissemination within enterprises of a client- or customer-centred approach; the use of information technologies to transform work processes; the employment of management consultants to create a new climate of change and organizational innovation; and the introduction of new approaches to employee relations (Kochan *et al.*, 1986; Hammer, 1990; Hammer and Champy, 1993). Not all these elements were evident in all institutions. Some were implemented in piecemeal fashion over time, while others were adopted as part of a more strategic approach to restructuring. They were particularly identifiable in large-scale businesses, such as insurance and banking institutions and information processing companies, and were adopted in public service institutions at state and federal levels as well as in the health care sector (Roach, 1991).

The US Model

Five elements – changes in management organization and structure; the use of information technologies to re-engineer work processes; the development of a customer orientation; the extensive use of external consultants; and the introduction of new patterns of employee relations aimed at creating a 'new worker' – were the main strands of 'Americanization'. Although they encompassed a range of management techniques that were not confined solely in their application to the service sector, it was service sector institutions, driven by the need to restructure rapidly, in which they were most readily developed and applied. In the course of this process, the American approach to the restructuring of service work began to be associated with specific management techniques such as business process re-engineering (BPR) and human resource management (HRM).

The US model encouraged the shift towards organizational agility, the re-engineering of work processes and the adoption of employee relations policies that attempted to secure control through commitment rather than commitment through control. Innovation in communications technologies enabled companies and institutions to maintain central management authority over devolved forms of management organization, while the new agility enabled company structures to respond rapidly to changes in market conditions. The re-engineering of work processes was designed to achieve significant increases in productivity, while also separating the qualitative work of the technical and managerial elite from the narrow competence-based skills and quantifiable activities of the majority of the workforce. Finally, commitment programmes were designed to sustain employee loyalty despite the adverse consequences of downsizing and its generation of fear among employees for their job security. The practices that were codified into a new model affected company structure and work organization as well as aspiring to create among employees a new set of values that informed their conduct at work (Table 2.1).

Table 2.1 *The US Model*

Company structure	Work organization	The new worker
Focus on core products/services	Process not task-oriented	Customer-oriented salesperson
Delayered/downsized	Software re-engineers work processes	Internalization of management values
Vertical disintegration: outsourcing product/supply chain	Competence displaces skill	Performance link to reward
Horizontal disintegration: outsourcing support functions	Polarization between qualitative and quantitative categories of work	

Organizational Reform

The reform of management organization involved four main developments: the review of company structure, delayering, the cutting of middle management posts and the devolution of financial and other management responsibilities. The reorganization of company structures was prompted by a combination of external market pressures, including takeovers, mergers and acquisitions, and internal organizational pressures to redefine core business functions and redraw boundaries between those business processes that might be undertaken internally and those which might be outsourced. These strategic decisions impacted upon the degree of vertical and horizontal integration of the enterprise and generated visions in the early 1990s of the emergence of the 'virtual' corporation. In the finance sector, for example, vertical disintegration took the form of outsourcing key tasks in the product or service supply chain, like data processing, while horizontal disintegration involved contracting out support functions like facilities management, cleaning and security. In the credit card industry, for example, Visa and Mastercard decided to withdraw from processing customer charges and transactions. They outsourced these complex and expensive activities to a major competitor, American Express, and concentrated their efforts on developing their marketing activities within their extensive customer bases and retail networks (Quinn *et al.*, 1990). Such strategies, according to some authors, led to previously clearly formed company structures becoming blurred or less clearly specified. The company became a 'virtual' organization in which the provision of financial products and services was widely diffused within the activities of the wider economy (Cressey and Scott, 1992: 89).

These structural changes were accompanied by delayering. Delayering required a reduction in management levels and a shift from hierarchical to flatter forms of management organization. In effect, this meant shortening the management chains of command, alongside the introduction of new forms of management control that were located closer to the work process. Delayering was complemented by staff cuts, particularly among middle managers and, together, these activities were commonly referred to as 'downsizing' (Moore, 1996). The effect of this organizational reform was to shift managerial responsibility for financial and operational matters to lower grades of staff, thus incorporating them into the management structure, without necessarily increasing their rewards to match the additional responsibilities they undertook. Broadly, this pushing downwards of management responsibilities took the form of either devolution or decentralization. Devolution required the exercise of greater local management responsibility for areas like budgets, marketing and personnel issues, while real management power (over policy and strategy) remained at the centre of the enterprise or institution. Decentralization, on the other hand, involved a genuine enhancement of local management independence and control over the strategic business decisions affecting organizations' activities (Heskett, 1986: 119). Decentralization complements an organizational approach that emphasizes the need for a closeness of the enterprise to its local market and customer base, while devolved management organization operates within the clearly defined and commonly held rules and procedures set down by the centre. In this context, the devolved or decentralized management models have been the main feature of new management structures in service industries. In some cases, however, companies have adopted a combination of centralism and decentralization. For example, Marriott, the US hotel chain, allowed considerable discretion to local managers over the strategies for the development of their properties and the customer services provided, while retaining a tightly centralized system of control over the utilization of labour:

> the company has become one of the industry's most efficient by applying a tightly centralised system of policies and controls to the slightest operational detail. Every job has a manual that breaks down the work into a mind-boggling number of steps. A hotel maid, for instance, has 66 things to do in cleaning up a room, from dusting the tops of all pictures (Step No 7) to making sure the telephone books and bibles are in good, neat condition (Step No 37). 'The more the system works like the army', says Marriott, 'the better'. (*Business Week*, 18 January 1982, quoted in Heskett, 1986: 120)

Whether decentralization or devolution, company internal organization became an important feature of management reform within the US service industries. Internal organizational change was accompanied by institutions and enterprises reshaping their external structures, creating as a result what some commentators have referred to as the 'agile' enterprise (Baker, 1996).

Creating the 'Agile' Enterprise

The reform of the service sector in the USA took two apparently contradictory directions. First, there was a tendency, in sectors like financial services, towards the centralization and consolidation of capital in the hands of fewer large-scale organizations. This led to the elimination of redundant and under-productive capacity and was facilitated by partnerships, mergers and acquisitions. In the period 1985–90, for example, the number of US banks was reduced by 14 per cent. Second, within these enterprises there was a shift towards the decentralization or devolution of management responsibility and control, through the establishment of semi-autonomous business units and profit centres. This was accompanied by the identification of 'core' and 'non-core' activities, with a tendency for the latter to be outsourced, particularly those functions concerned with routine data processing and facilities management. This disaggregation of operational activities, in turn, created what business writers variously called the move toward the 'virtual' enterprise, the 'networked' or 'agile' firm (Baker, 1996). In practice, concentration of capital and the disaggregation or decentralization of operations were different sides of the same coin. In the US banking industry, for example, market conditions in the early 1980s generated mergers and take-overs, the development of 'bundled' together institutions, that by the late 1980s required 'unbundling' (Bryan, 1991: 76).

The process of unbundling had several specific characteristics that were 'codified' by consultants and academics into models of good practice. The starting point for the enterprise was to refocus on the attributes of its core business by identifying those products and services that were at the centre of its operations and that it had the skills and abilities to deliver better than competitors. The company would then reorganize around the processes involved in the development and delivery of its core products and services, enabling them to be packaged and customized to meet specific segmented markets. This approach had its intellectual origins in manufacturing strategies developed in the 1970s. A focused manufacturing approach involved the recognition that a manufacturing system was not capable of undertaking different manufacturing tasks simultaneously. It was necessary to develop manufacturing 'cells' that operated separately, providing the scope for one cell to, for example, make low volume, highly varied products while another made high volume, low variety products. This development, in turn, required the company to introduce, at the organizational level, different business units in which the specific cell form of production could reside (Skinner, 1974). The adaptation of this approach to services was called for in the early 1990s. In his assessment of the need for the financial reconstruction of the US banking industry, Bryan, for example, argued for the introduction of 'core banks' who would have government insurance and would:

> take deposits through savings accounts, checking accounts and money market accounts. They finance home mortgages, market credit cards, lend to small businesses to finance accounts receivable and provide other traditional banking services. After restructuring the core banking industry (that is the amount of deposits covered by federal insurance) would be at least one trillion dollars smaller than it is today, a reduction in scale of 25%. It would also be decidedly more profitable. (Bryan, 1991: 74)

According to Bryan's analysis, diversified large companies like Citicorp and Chase Manhattan would have to make judgements about their non-core activities, either by covering them with their own financial strength or by divesting them. In practice, a modified form of Bryan's projections took place in several service sector industries in the USA in the early 1990s.

The refocusing on core activities, in turn, required innovation to take place in the domestic organization of the company. The introduction of business units facilitated the removal of management hierarchies and encouraged the development of team working and a less specific task-oriented focus to work. Training shifted from a task orientation to broader based education programmes in which individuals developed competencies to undertake a range of tasks. The company became, in the jargon, a 'learning institution' (Baker, 1996). The final key feature of the agile enterprise was the shift towards organizational 'disintegration' involving the development of partnerships and short-term contractual relations with companies that took over the tasks associated with specific steps in the product or service supply chain. Parallel to this development was the extension of the process of outsourcing of support functions that were peripheral to the companies core activities. Together these developments ensured that previously well defined structures began to lose their edges, giving rise to the virtual company, which may be presented thus:

- Focuses on 'core' products and services.
- Devolves or decentralizes.
- Is process- not task-oriented.
- Is a 'learning institution'.
- Outsources stages in product/service supply chain – vertical disintegration.
- Outsources support functions – horizontal disintegration.

In summary, the agile firm had several advantages over its highly integrated and bureaucratic competitors. It could cope more effectively with rapid changes in market conditions as a result of achieving greater flexibility in product development, marketing and delivery. It could adopt new process and product technologies more rapidly and, most importantly, it could develop customized products for sale to its expanding client base. Customized product development reflected the agile company's close proximity to and understanding of its customer base. This closeness to the market, in turn, required the company to adopt a strong customer focus or 'orientation', a focus that influenced the way work was organized and the ideas and values of those who were required to carry it out.

'Customer Orientation'

The shift towards a customer orientation within service industries was a necessary consequence, according to business consultants (Hammer and Champy, 1993: 18–19) of the rising expectations of consumers and the increased choice that was available to them. In the 1980s power in the customer/seller relation shifted from the latter to the former. While there is truth in this, it is not the full story. The changing relationship between customer and seller was caused by a number of factors, of which market conditions was one. Competition within service industries increased sharply in the 1980s in the USA. In financial services, for example, a credit crisis coupled with fluctuating exchange rates contributed to the necessity for extensive restructuring. A central feature of this was the refocusing of banks on their core customer-oriented activities, the removal of back office functions from branches and the reorganization of work processes to ensure that customer service was the primary task of branch staff. This programme of reform usually entailed job cuts and the reorganization of work. The new customer-centred approach, often launched along with a restatement of the enterprise's or institution's mission and values, was designed to consolidate and extend the customer base, while also encouraging staff to consider themselves increasingly as salespersons who were required to identify closely with their company and its products. In this way, customer care policies helped to re-establish companies within fiercely competitive financial product markets and proved a useful means by which management could elicit worker commitment to the enterprise and to a process of restructuring that often entailed adverse effects on jobs and conditions. Restructuring, in turn, was facilitated by the deployment of technologies that reworked front and back office relations and enabled the development of new forms of marketing and the development of new approaches to service delivery.

Information Technologies and Re-engineering

For consultants and business analysts, a central task facing services companies was the re-evaluation of the role played by new technologies. Roach (1991: 82) expressed their views succinctly in the *Harvard Business Review*:

America's next wave of restructuring is at hand but this time it is crashing down on the vast service sector. Once sacrosanct services are undergoing in the 1990s the same difficult and painful shrinkage that manufacturing suffered in the 1980s. The enormous white-collar job losses in service companies over the last year – led by some of America's foremost banks, insurance companies, retailers and airlines – are not simply a reflection of temporary recession. These jobs are gone for good . . . The explanation for this restructuring is quite simple. Until recently services have been sheltered from competition and have had little incentive to drive out inefficiency. Shielded by regulation and confronted by few foreign competitors, service companies have allowed their white-collar payrolls to become bloated, their investment in information technology to outstrip the paybacks, and their productivity to stagnate. (Roach, 1991: 82)

The investment in information technologies was considerable. In 1991, the service sector owned over 85 per cent of the USA's installed base of information technology, with investment per employee rising from $6,000 in 1982 to $12,000 by 1991, yet improvements in productivity were negligible (Roach, 1991: 85). Companies embarking on restructuring programmes were advised not simply to use computers to speed up old work processes but to 'obliterate them and start over' (Hammer, 1990). It was this radical approach to the reorganization of work, encompassing a central role for information technologies, that provided fertile ground for the ideas associated with Business Process Re-engineering (BPR). Re-engineering service sector work processes involved the incorporation of specialist knowledge and skills into tailored software packages run on networked desktop computers. These, once implemented, increased dramatically the throughput of work and facilitated a reduction in staff levels. The dissemination of this pattern of work reorganization spread quickly among leading service sector institutions. Those who could ill afford the cost of adapting existing technologies and investing in new networks were likely to be forced to merge or close (Roach, 1991: 90).

Re-engineering Work Processes

While agility referred to the changing organizational boundaries of the firm, re-engineering related to the transformation of work processes within it. Its leading exponent, Michael Hammer, claimed that re-engineering was about reorganizing work and 'applies to any organization in which work is performed' (Hammer, 1995). He indicated that, within the USA, insurance companies had taken a leading role in re-engineering work processes, while public service institutions had tended to lag behind, primarily because of the rigid boundaries between government departments and the lack of yardsticks of performance, such as profitability. Despite these obstacles, public service institutions had begun to focus on their operations, with revenue collecting departments taking the lead (Hammer and Champy, 1993: 219). Interest in re-engineering was prompted, as indicated above, by concerns about productivity and the experience within service industries of increasing investment in new technologies being coupled with a seemingly relentless rise in staffing levels. The financial crises experienced by many service industries in the late 1980s led to the search for more efficient ways of organizing work. BPR appeared to offer solutions.

The BPR model contained five broadly identifiable elements. First, it was concerned with the work process, even though the concept of process was relatively loosely defined. Second, it emphasized the importance of 'discontinuous thinking' (Hammer, 1990: 107), breaking away from the traditional rules and assumptions about the organization of work. Third, it stressed the role of information technologies as an enabling device in implementing drastic change. Fourth, it was conceived as a process which was undertaken from the 'top down', initiated by leaders or 'czars'. Finally, it required decision-making to be devolved to where the work took place and management control mechanisms to be built into the work process. The emphasis on the work process focused on the need to replace organizational forms, like departments, in which work was traditionally organized. Hammer provides a simple illustration involving the processing of a credit claim at IBM Credit, a subsidiary of the computer firm. In traditional organizations the claim may be processed by people located in several different departments: logging the claim, checking the client's credit rating, identifying the appropriate rate of interest, establishing the repayment period, identifying if any special conditions should apply and, finally, completing the quote letter. While this work at IBM Credit took only 90 minutes for each claim, the process took six to ten days to complete. Through re-engineering, IBM replaced the specialist credit checkers, pricers and administrators with a single generalist called a 'deal structurer', who, supported by a new computer software program, was able to process all standard credit applications, leaving only the more complex ones for specialists to handle. The change in work process created, according to Hammer, a transformation in productivity, with the number of deals within the same amount of time increasing by 10,000 per cent and the company also achieving a small reduction in staff levels. Re-engineering revealed that processing a credit claim did not require specialist knowledge in the vast majority of cases, so one generalist could replace four specialists once the new software program was in place.

The IBM case demonstrated how information technologies could be used to replace obsolete information systems, providing the leaders of the re-engineering process were willing to start with 'a clean sheet of paper' and were prepared to abandon the 'familiar and seek the outrageous' (Hammer, 1990: 185). Discontinuous thinking was a strong element in re-engineering. It required firm leadership from above and a clear identification of the processes that were most in need of change. Within this context the enterprise or institution could run a single or several re-engineering projects at once. This required the establishment of project teams who devised their 'case for action'. The case brought together the identification of the problem and the diagnosis of cause, and spelt out the costs of inaction. The re-engineering project was overseen by a senior executive and enacted by a senior manager, or process owner. Through re-engineering, according to Hammer, a team identity emerges, as does the empowerment of individuals and a team spirit. Rather than these being imposed externally through shifts in personnel or human resources policies, they become an organic part of the re-engineering process. Finally, at the centre of BPR was the role played by new technologies, not in making old processes work better, but 'by breaking with the old rules and creating new ways of working . . . it is this disruptive power of technology, its ability to break the rules that limit the conduct of our work, that makes it critical to companies looking for competitive advantage' (Hammer, 1990: 9).

Technological change impacts upon the work process and the management system devised to control and supervise it. For Hammer and Champy (1993), the task of supervision was built into the new work process via the development of software that incorporated performance measurement and checks on quality. As a result, lower supervisory grades of managers may be displaced, the management hierarchy flattened and specialist staff replaced by those with generic, relatively low level skills or, more accurately, competencies. There was a recognition that employees may be fearful or even opposed to this pattern of change, particularly middle managers and unionized workforces. Here Hammer and Champy presented the case for early 'involvement' in the re-engineering process as an antidote to opposition. If, however, opposition persists, a hard line was pushed:

> When union resistance develops, however, a strategy of firm commitment is a company's only choice while it continues to keep employees – unionized or not – engaged in the process. Union leadership that understands re-engineering and why it is being done is unlikely to push its unhappiness with re-engineering as far as a strike. (Hammer and Champy, 1994: 222)

In *The Reengineering Revolution*, Hammer (1995) presented the same case but in starker terms. Where opposition arises to re-engineering, 'slapping people's wrists' instead 'of breaking their legs is another sign of weakness . . . making it clear that termination is the consequence of their behavior is a very valid technique' (Hammer, 1995: 142–51). This employee relations aspect of BPR has received relatively little analysis in the recent texts on the subject.

In their book on BPR, Burke and Peppard (1995), for example, have managed to collate a series of articles, none of which addresses the implications for workers of the introduction of BPR at workplace level. It is useful, at this stage, to draw attention to three key consequences of the BPR approach for the workforce. First, there is an implicit tendency in the BPR approach to reshape the division of labour by polarizing the workforce between a majority who carry out lower level clerical functions at the computer/human interface and a minority who design and develop the technical systems and manage the work process. The majority are engaged in processes which mainly require the use of a range of narrowly defined skills and basic competencies that may be provided by the company within its training programme. Alongside these, there is a much smaller group of technically proficient staff, with systems knowledge, who devise and develop the sophisticated software programs that are tailored to meet the specific needs of the re-engineered work process. Second, an important consequence of re-engineering is the reduction of staffing levels through delayering and the 'mechanization' of work processes. Finally, management control over work is enshrined within the process itself, combining elements of worker 'self-discipline', including self-checks on the quality of their own work, and the introduction of software systems which contain in-built measures of performance, quality and efficiency. This approach challenges the traditional role of middle managers and facilitates significant change in hierarchical management structures (Keen, 1995) and, as a consequence, may meet with resistance from within management itself. To nullify this resistance, enterprises and institutions within both public and private services have tended to use management consultants as external agents of change. Recent years have witnessed a significant expansion in the use of management consultants, particularly by public and private services industries (Management Consultancies Association, 1995).

Enter the Gurus: the Role of Management Consultants

The management consultancy industry first developed in the USA at the beginning of the twentieth century. Anderson Consulting, now the largest global firm, started in 1913 and McKinsey and Co. in 1926. The rise of the large-scale corporation was closely associated with the development of new approaches to the organization of production, including the dissemination of Taylorism and scientific approaches to business management. Science and business reached new levels of interaction through the Second World War, as Locke (1996: 26) has recorded:

Examples of science gone to war are legion: the economists Stacy May and
Robert Nathan applying statistical analysis to war production programmes;
F. L. Hitchcock elaborating transportation theory to deal efficiently with the
complicated problems of moving vast amounts of men and material; Kurt
Lewin working on human relations at his new research Centre for Group
Dynamics. They covered the spectrum of hard and soft management subjects.

This relationship was underpinned in the post-war period by the professionalization of management via the rapid growth of masters in business
administration (MBA) programmes. From under 5,000 MBA students in US
universities in 1960 the number increased to over 200,000 by the mid-1990s.
This process of professionalization was reflected in the growth of management consultancies, as Locke wryly commented: 'doctors open[ed]
consultancies to help sick people, managers consultancies to help sick firms'
(Locke, 1996: 29). As American industrial dominance was subjected to the
Japanese challenge in the late 1970s and 1980s, many sick US firms, their
business confidence undermined, turned to consultants to diagnose the
problems and identify solutions. The golden age for the consultant 'guru'
had begun. Those, like W. E. Demming, with direct knowledge and experience of Japanese techniques, were particularly sought after by US
manufacturing companies. By the mid-1980s academics and consultants were
warning of the threat that foreign direct investment posed to US service
industries, but there was time, they argued, to save these industries through a
combination of strategic management, investment in new market opportunities and improved use of information technologies (Quinn and Gagnon,
1986). Financial institutions, government departments and the health care
sector made extensive use of external consultant advisers. Management consultants were used as facilitators of organizational and technical innovation.

Employee Relations

The final strand in the restructuring of the US service sector involved
companies developing new approaches to employee relations. The white-
collar service sector in the USA was traditionally acknowledged as one in which
employers had a strong commitment to avoiding unionization (Kochan et al.,
1986: 53). It provided fertile ground, therefore, for employers to experiment
with new approaches to employee relations. The new management techniques
varied between 'hard' and 'soft' approaches. The hard approach emphasized
the necessity to raise productivity through the radical reorganization of work.

It was commonly associated with downsizing and was an approach that dominated the reform of employee relations in the service sector for the first half of the 1990s. By 1996, however, downsizing became 'dumbsizing' (Jackson, 1996). Corporate America was criticized for hollowing-out policies that created a sense of job insecurity and impeded, so critics argued, subsequent attempts by companies to expand. Within the service sector, downsizing had an adverse affect on employee morale and loyalty. Low levels of employee loyalty led to low levels of customer loyalty (Riley, 1996). To avoid this downward spiral, companies engaged in employee commitment programmes aimed at reducing staff turnover and restoring staff confidence. This soft approach encompassed a wide range of new recruitment, training, empowering and employee care techniques, aimed at encouraging staff to adopt and internalize management values. Commitment, rather than control, became the key phrase of the soft approach. While, in practice, many leading service companies in the USA adopted combinations of hard and soft approaches during the 1990s, arguably the former predominated in the early years, while the latter came increasingly to the fore by the middle of the decade. The securing of employee commitment led to the widespread diffusion of HRM approaches. These engaged with the task of creating a new worker who identified closely with the aspirations and values of the enterprise for which he or she worked.

'It's My Company': the Emergence of the 'New Worker'

US service sector management aimed at the creation of a 'new' kind of worker who could readily adapt to the pressures associated with the provision of services within a highly competitive market-place. This involved the adoption of new human resource approaches to recruitment, training and employee motivation/commitment. Schlesinger and Heskett (1991: 80) summarized the new approach to recruitment in 'pioneering' service companies as being based upon 'how people think, not on what they are'. Commenting on the recruitment policies of leading services companies like ServiceMaster, Dayton Hudson and Marriott (health care, educational and management services), the authors illustrated their point. In these companies:

> they prefer to interview ten candidates to find the right person for the job rather than hire the first warm body who comes along – and then have to fill the job ten times over. . . . Interviewers at Dayton's for example favour applicants who see retail sales as a career. Suitable candidates for housekeeping

jobs at Fairfield Inn (the Marriott Corporation's new chain of economy inns) are not only people with good work habits and a passion for cleanliness but also people who are willing to be evaluated and compensated on the basis of their performance. (Schlesinger and Heskett, 1991: 80)

This outlook on recruitment was underpinned by the companies' careful analysis of 'entry level' employees for whom attitudes towards customer relations were more important than the ability to use a personal computer. Training programmes engaged with individual attitudes and morality, as well as providing the means for enhancing employee performance. At Service-Master new employees received:

talks from medical professionals about basic health issues such as how diseases are transmitted from one person to another. The talks contribute to the company's ability to provide good service because they emphasise how important it is for everyone to be scrupulous about cleanliness. But they also add to the hospital workers' stock of knowledge as well as their pride in themselves and the importance of their work. (Schlesinger and Heskett 1991: 80)

These induction programmes were typically supported by a continuous programme of training in which 'employees commit themselves to the company and its service expectations'. At Dayton new salespersons joined established staff in two-day 'celebrations' in which the key theme was 'it's my company' (Schlesinger and Heskett, 1991).

In addition to recruitment and training schemes, a 'commitment strategy' involved a range of other techniques through which direct management supervision and control was replaced by the employee's internalization of management values. Delayering removed traditional, hierarchical status relations, creating circumstances in which companies redefined 'status' in relation to active commitment rather than passive deference. For example, at the airline company, People's Express, all permanent employees were called 'managers' and were expected to rotate tasks within their spheres of competence. The company limited management levels to three and organized the workforce into groups or teams of three or four persons (Walton, 1985: 79). A further common element of the commitment strategy was to develop performance measures aimed at evaluating the level of the employee's engagement with the company's customer orientation. Most often this involved linking pay to the strength of conventional financial results, such as sales gains, individual sales per hour or customer response times In many cases companies developed new performance standards to measure what previously went unmeasured. This was particularly the case in the health sector and revenue collecting government departments.

Finally, the commitment strategy was linked to the development of employee assistance programmes (EAPs). US companies began to adopt EAPs in the 1970s to tackle, in particular, alcohol-related problems. In the 1980s and early 1990s these programmes expanded to incorporate a wide range of professional counselling support and advice on problems of a 'personal' nature (May and Brunsdon, 1994: 150). The underlying philosophy of such programmes was the assumption that non work-related difficulties impeded a worker's productivity or work performance. Schemes involved personal rather than work-related counselling and focused on the individual, emphasizing the importance of physical and mental fitness and the improvement of personal lifestyles. There were considerable variations in the content of EAPs but many included opportunities for self-referral for counselling, the introduction of health screening programmes and the development of 'customized' schemes designed to help individuals 'adjust their behaviour' (May and Brunsdon, 1994: 153). EAPs were adopted mainly by large US companies and were particularly prevalent in areas like financial services and the public sector, where staff were facing a combination of rationalization programmes and pressures to raise productivity. EAPs were designed to address the increased anxieties and uncertainties that accompanied these changes, and some companies, such as Ethicon Ltd, part of Johnson and Johnson, went as far as to offer employees their own 'lifestyle risk analysis' (May and Brunsdon, 1994: 153). These forms of corporate health care provision served purposes that went beyond the obvious desire of companies to raise productivity and reduce sickness levels and absenteeism. The practical purpose was complemented by an ideological dimension. As well as establishing a paternalistic bond between enterprise and worker, EPAs encouraged employees to perceive the consequences of increased competition, downsizing and work intensification in the same way as they experienced an illness or addiction, as either an act of god or a result of a personal imperfection. Either way, employees were the 'individual' victims and counselling provided the means by which they could learn to help themselves. EPAs were an important component in reconciling staff to the consequences of restructuring, while securing their commitment to programmes designed to improve work performance and productivity.

In his response to the productivity problem in services, Drucker (1991) argued that service work divided into three main categories. The first was where performance meant quality – where it was the new idea or the physician's diagnosis and its accuracy that was more important than the number of times it took place. The second combined quality and quantity and related to the work of a salesperson, nurse or claims adjuster, where 'customer satisfaction' or improved health was as important as the number of customers dealt with or patients seen. Here, for Drucker, the process of nursing, for example, combined quantitative measures and qualitative outputs and it was worthwhile analysing the process step by step to see if productivity gains could be achieved. The third category of service work was entirely quantitative or performance-based. This involved tasks like making hospital beds and filing and handling insurance claims, and could easily be subjected to the same process as real 'production' jobs to which Taylorist principles applied. Drucker argued that it was possible to go beyond Taylorist principles by ensuring that 'working smarter' was facilitated by continuous learning. This, for example, required service and knowledge workers learning most 'when they teach':

> The best way to improve a salesperson's productivity record is to ask her to present 'the secret of my success' at the company sales convention. The best way for the surgeon to improve his performance is to give a talk about it at the county medical society. We often hear it said in the information age, every enterprise has to become a learning institution. It must become a teaching institution as well. (Drucker, 1991: 78)

Drucker's perspective overlaps with that of the exponents of BPR. Their common cause was to subject service work to the underlying principles of 'mechanization' first expounded by Taylor; a process through which the knowledge of the individual worker is appropriated into the system of work. For Hammer, the means to achieve this was through the development and introduction of sophisticated software packages that substituted for the knowledge of the middle manager and lower level supervisors and clerks. This process enabled an increasing proportion of service employment to fall into Drucker's third category of work, which was entirely based upon quantitative criteria, and presented the possibility of the elimination of the second category, which previously combined quantitative and qualitative performance standards. Finally, the development of the 'teaching and learning' institution, in which employees continuously strive for self-improvement, has much in common with the *kaizen* approach, which, as Rinehart *et al.* (1996) have argued, has the effect of encouraging staff to develop new ways of intensifying their own labour.

Management Models and Practice

Explaining the relationship between management models and theories and management practice is a hazardous business. As Hyman observed in relation to the weaknesses of the 1980s debates on flexibility, it can lead to an emphasis on the production of theory rather than on a theorization of the process of production (Hyman, 1991). Business and academic writers have often fallen into this trap by focusing first on the explanation of the latest fashionable model or theory and then gauging the extent to which it has been adopted in practice. In effect, this approach puts cart before horse or, as Pollert has argued, 'it flattens complexity and unevenness into a reductionist dogma' (Pollert, 1991: 30). The tendency to adopt this approach has been increased in recent years by the emergence of various management 'gurus' or consultants, many of whom have made their names, and considerable fortunes, by promulgating particular techniques. BPR is a case in point. BPR is commonly associated with the writings of Hammer and Champy, and its origin is often traced back to a seminal article written by Hammer in 1990. As Jones has observed, however, the process-oriented approach that underpins BPR has a close affinity to industrial engineering, which, in turn, found its inspiration in the time and motion techniques of scientific management and, in particular, the work of F. W. Taylor (Jones, 1996). In this sense, all the 'new' or fashionable ideas and models that arise in the world of business have their origins in previous generations of management literature or practice. Their emergence as a new set of 'cohesive concepts' (Elger and Smith, 1996: 8) arises from their perceived relevance in addressing the real problems arising from the crises provoked by changes in social, political and economic conditions. The Japanese model, Toyotism, for example, developed in the context of the post-war reconstruction of the Japanese economy in which a quiescent working class was a particular feature (Schaller, 1985; Elger and Smith, 1996), while the American model of service industry restructuring emerged following a prolonged period of employment growth and in the absence of trade union organization in much of the service sector (Kochan et al., 1986). This social and institutional specificity tends to militate against the easy transfer of such models across national boundaries. The contention here is that Japanization travelled less easily to countries like the UK than did the American model. Emulation of the American model, particularly in the UK, was facilitated by broad similarities in the economic conditions faced by service sector enterprises and, in the public sector, there was clear evidence of the American experiments in health care and welfare reform having a real influence on UK government policy making (Enthoven, 1985, 1991).

Two important points should be made about the development and dissemination of the Japanese and American models of industrial restructuring. The first is relatively straightforward. Japanization refers to changes in company structure, work organization and employee relations primarily in the manufacturing sector, while, Americanization refers to changes in enterprise organization, work organization and employee relations in service industries. Both contain a variety of management techniques whose contents and boundaries may be contested but, as their names suggest, they have come to reflect a broad range of work and employment practices associated with Japan – lean production, team working, quality management – and the USA – re-engineering, agility and employee commitment programmes.

The second point raises more complex issues about the economic conditions in which each of these models emerged and was disseminated. The Japanese model emerged under a specific set of relatively stable state–capital–labour relations. Under these conditions the model contributed to, and was shaped by, a dynamic process of industrial growth and expansion, illustrated by the domestic and subsequent international success of such companies as Toyota and Nissan (Elger and Smith, 1996: 43–4). By contrast, the American model, which refers to the transformation of services, developed under different conditions in which there were significant changes occurring in state–capital–labour relations and an economic context in which key service industries had lost their earlier dynamism. The Japanese model emerged under favourable domestic conditions of economic growth and expansion, while the American model emerged during a period of domestic economic recession which particularly affected key service industries like banking, insurance and health. These contrasting economic circumstances necessarily had an impact upon the characteristics of the models. For example, the Japanese model embraced a pattern of stable long-term contractual relations between producers and suppliers, while the American envisaged a redefinition of core business activities and encouraged the growth of short-term contractual relations that, in particular, facilitated horizontal disintegration. The Japanese model envisaged a 'job for life', while the American emphasized 'downsizing' and led to feelings of risk, uncertainty and job insecurity. These contrasts were reflected in the patterns of diffusion of the two models outside of their countries of origin.

Diffusion of the Japanese model occurred in two ways, through the Japanese plants established in countries like the USA and UK and via emulation by the British, American and European companies located within the 'transplant's' host nation. In companies like Ford Europe, 'after Japan' strategies were developed to emulate the dynamic successes of Japanese firms. The 'adopters' engaged in a complex process of reinterpreting and repackaging Japanese production methods, often using the threat posed by Japanese competition to revisit old battles with their workforces over job demarcation, work organization and work practices (Elger and Smith, 1996: 46). Paradoxically, the model that represented a dynamic form of corporate capitalism was adapted to the needs of companies that were engaged in processes of rationalization and restructuring, with the effect that the 'positive' attributes of the Japanese approach, such as job security, took second place to those changes in work organization and work practices that were designed to expand job rotation and task flexibility. Emulation of the Japanese model involved, therefore, the pragmatic and often piecemeal introduction of elements which appeared to meet management's objectives in reconstituting its relations with labour. By contrast, in the service sector, the American model was developed in response to recessionary conditions in the US service industries and was emulated within the context of broadly similar recessionary conditions in countries like the UK. In this sense, the American model of service sector restructuring could be more readily assimilated into the thinking of those UK enterprises and institutions that were seeking new ways of addressing the acute problems they faced.

'Americanization' in the UK

In their evaluation of UK economic performance in the 1980s several economists have identified the underlying weaknesses of the UK economy. The economy suffered from high levels of unemployment, largely resulting from the shake out of jobs in the manufacturing sector. Manufacturing sector investment stagnated for much of the decade and improvements in productivity were mainly a result of job losses (Glyn, 1992: 86–7), and the prosperity enjoyed by some primarily arose from the redistribution of income away from those made unemployed towards shareholders. This shift was 'complemented by changes in the tax and government expenditure systems . . . and papered over in the late 1980s by the illusions fostered by the credit boom' (Glynn, 1992: 87). In the public services, Conservative government expenditure had risen in real terms, with some sectors doing better than others. The National Health Service (NHS) did relatively well, with the volume of inputs rising by 13.7 per cent over the period 1979–90, while other areas like housing and education fared badly. With the exception of the NHS, most of the rise in real expenditure took the form of increased salaries for public service employees (Rowthorn, 1992: 268–9). Capital expenditure in infrastructure suffered badly. Overall the growth rate in government consumption in the 1980s declined. By the late 1980s public services faced renewed pressures to cut expenditure arising from the recession that followed the credit boom. These conditions prompted government to press on with its attempts to reform the NHS through the introduction of trusts and the internal market, extend its privatization programme and develop further policies aimed at the 'commercialization' of service provision (Fairbrother, 1994, 1996).

In the 1980s private service industries in the UK followed a similar path to those in the USA. Employment levels rose, investment in information technologies expanded and productivity growth remained sluggish. The share of service sector employment in the UK compared to the share of employment in manufacturing rose from the mid-1960s. By 1981 the service sector accounted for 61 per cent of total employment in the UK, with over three million new jobs being created in the sector between 1965 and 1981. Between 1979 and 1989 service sector employment expanded by a further two million, creating a total number of employees in services at around 15.5 million, or 71 per cent of total UK employment. The growth in services employment in the 1980s had other, now well documented, characteristics, including a significant increase in the proportion of women employed in the sector, an expansion of part-time employment, a pattern of regional variation in the creation of service sector jobs and a significant growth in self-employment (Hakim, 1987; Healey, 1993). This pattern of employment growth was not mirrored by improvements in productivity in the service sector. Growth in output per head in non-manufacturing over the same period was slow. Non-manufacturing productivity growth remained at 'barely half that achieved . . . between 1964–73' (Blackaby and Hunt, 1993). While this weak performance was due to some extent to the growth in part-time employment, this does not account entirely for the poor performance of particular service industries. For example, while distribution, hotels, catering and repairs showed an improvement in output per head of over 3 per cent in the period 1979–88, education, health, finance, insurance, business services and leasing recorded a fall in output per head of 0.5 per cent over the same period (Blackaby and Hunt, 1993: 113).

This poor productivity record arose despite huge investment in new technologies. The 1980s, for example, saw a massive growth in capital investment in financial services in the UK. The composition of investment went through a remarkable change. While manufacturing investment remained flat for much of the 1980s, investment in the financial services rose dramatically. The composition of UK investment by industrial sector significantly altered, as Driver (1993: 89) observed: 'In Britain in 1979 the combined share of chemicals, engineering and metal goods, food and motors amounted to 20.5%, twice that for financial services. By 1989 the ratio was reversed, with a 30% share for finance and half that for the industrial sectors.' This contrast between the huge expansion in capital investment in financial services and stagnant manufacturing investment took place only in the UK and USA among the advanced industrial nations in the 1980s. It seems, therefore, that Thurrow's criticism of the US services sector applied equally to the UK. In an increasingly competitive market-place, and under conditions in which profitability had been squeezed as a result of the financial and economic crises of the late 1980s, key UK service industries had rising employment and investment levels, alongside very poor levels of labour productivity. Arguably, the main difference between the USA and the UK was that, in the latter, the average annual growth rate in earnings in industries like financial services remained relatively strong throughout the 1980s, while, in the USA, the average annual rate of earnings for service sector employees actually fell (Michie and Wilkinson, 1992; Head, 1996). These conditions created the circumstances in which UK service industries began to experience a similar process of restructuring to that which had already begun in the USA. As Cressey and Scott (1992) argued, the 'honeymoon' between management and labour in industries like retail banking was over.

The Restructuring 'Imperative' in UK Services

The early 1990s represented a 'watershed' in management organization, work practices and workplace relations in the key UK service industries. While many of the changes that took place had their roots in the 1980s, arguably, the early 1990s represented a qualitative break with the past in key service sector industries. In the public sector, for example, the changes that arose in the 1980s through privatization, contracting out and the commercialization of service provision were mainly confined to the civil service and manual employees in areas like local government. The early 1990s saw these reforms extended to other areas of the public sector, and, in particular, the NHS. The NHS and Community Care Act (1990) created a new set of institutional relations through the introduction of the internal market, the development of general practice fund-holding and the introduction of trusts. Within months of the implementation of the reforms hospitals begun to announce redundancies (Mohan, 1995: 210). At the same time the utilities – water, gas and electricity –

were established as private companies and began to embark upon new market strategies and employment practices. Extensive public sector reform was matched by a unique development in the banking sector. The four main UK clearing banks, between 1991 and 1992, began to close branches and cut staffing levels. Approximately 800 branches were closed and over 25,000 redundancies announced during 1991–2. Companies in the insurance sector began a similar pattern of rationalization around the same time. The UK service sector began a process of restructuring that was to continue over a number of years. The process affected middle management and professional occupations, as well as less skilled administrative and clerical posts, creating a climate of 'job insecurity' within public and private services that was perhaps disproportionate to the number of jobs that were lost. Insecurity was fostered by a combination of policies, which included outsourcing, the growth of fixed term contracts and management reorganization that tended to undermine the status traditionally accorded to professionals such as health service consultants and bank managers. Arguably, it was the impact upon the middle-class professions that generated a sense of risk and uncertainty that spread across society as a whole. Sympathy for the plight of the victims of 'downsizing' generated, by the mid-1990s, a growing literature that was critical of restructuring policies that appeared to place short-term expediencies ahead of longer-term considerations for the well-being of the committed and loyal workforce. 'Softer' employee commitment programmes began to displace the 'harder' policies aimed primarily at raising employee productivity. Several UK firms began to adopt American style employee care programmes (May and Brunsdon, 1994).

The close affinity between developments in the US economy and that of the UK provided the basis for the American model to offer management techniques that could be emulated by their UK counterparts. In the USA, management consultants played a significant role in codifying and developing the practices which brought about significant change within the service industries. In the UK, management consultants, often partners in, or employed by, US companies, played an equally significant role as external catalysts of the restructuring of service sector enterprises and institutions. In so doing they often acted as transmitters of the American model, and its accompanying jargon, to British shores (Trapp, 1993).

The management consultancy industry started in the UK in the 1950s and 1960s. The latter part of the 1980s was its period of most rapid expansion. The Management Consultancies Association (MCA) is the main UK trade association. In 1980, MCA members had fewer than 5,000 UK clients. By 1994, MCA members had nearly 20,000 UK clients. MCA membership expanded in the 1980s from 25 to 33 firms and included most of the UK's largest consultancy companies. By 1994, the MCA's affiliates employed 7,267 staff. The majority of these were employees of the main global companies. Andersen Consulting, for example, employed over 2,000 UK staff in 1994. In addition to these major players, the total number of businesses registered as management consultants rose dramatically in the late 1980s. Between 1988 and 1990 the number of businesses registered in the UK rose from 12,000 to 20,000; of these approximately 8,000 were sole proprietors (Efficiency Unit, Cabinet Office, 1994: 28).

The public sector and the financial services in the 1980s and 1990s were significant users of management consultants. In 1994 and 1995, for example, they were the two main sources of income for MCA members, despite the fact that fee income from the public sector had fallen by £71 million to £181 million. (Over the previous decade fee income from the public services had constituted 30 per cent of total fee income for MCA members.) Together the two sectors accounted for just under half of the total income received from UK industries (MCA, 1995: 2). The income was derived from activities related to financial and administrative systems, information technology and corporate strategy/organizational development as Tables 2.2 and 2.3 indicate.

Table 2.2 *MCA members' management consultancy activities in the UK – clients classified by industry 1994–5*

Industry	1994		1995	
	£ million	Percentage	£ million	Percentage
Agriculture, forestry, fisheries	1	0.1	0.2	0.0
Energy and water supply	60	6.0	62.1	5.5
Extraction of minerals and ores other than fuels, manufacture of metals, mineral products and chemicals	99	9.8	118.8	10.4
Metal goods, engineering and vehicles	76	7.5	67.2	5.9
Other manufacturing	143	14.1	157.3	13.8
Construction	7	0.7	10.5	0.9
Distribution, hotels, catering	40	4.0	66.9	5.9
Transport and communication	88	8.7	125.0	11.0
Banking, finance and insurance, business services and leasing	243	24.1	314.8	27.4
Private sector non-profit making bodies	–	–	7.2	0.6
Public sector	253	25.0	210.0	18.4

Source: MCA (1995)

Table 2.3 *Analysis of MCA members' fees earned by principal activities (£ million)*

	1993	1994	1995
Information technology	328	471	471
Corporate strategy/organization development	58	98	138
Financial/administrative systems	97	81	115
Production/services management	90	84	82
Human resources	64	40	61
Project management	67	44	50
Marketing/corporate communications	14	14	48
Economic/environment studies	29	20	23
Facilities management	66	79	116

Source: MCA (1995)

Management consultants played an important role in supporting the re-engineering of work processes, as the MCA's Executive Director commented in his 1995 Executive Director's Report: 'Earnings from information technology work remained static in the year with a continued shift away from systems development towards consultancy work, thus underlining client focus on the use of information technology as an integral part of business transformation, rather than as a tool' (MCA, 1995: 2). At the same time that the focus on IT switched to 'business transformation', so outsourcing also became an important activity on which consultants advised. In 1995, revenue from advice concerning outsourcing rose by 47 per cent to £116 million (MCA, 1995: 2). From the evidence provided by the national data collected by the MCA, by the mid-1990s the activities of management consultants were very much focused on re-engineering work processes, using IT as a facilitator of internal organizational reform, and assisting clients to identify core activities and develop outsourcing strategies for non-core functions. In this sense, management consultancy activities in the UK tended to follow many of the tenets of the US model. Management consultants played a significant role in its adoption by UK enterprises and institutions, in effect facilitating the diffusion of the model within, in particular, the private and public services industries.

The illustration of this process of emulation is one of the central themes considered in the case studies contained in Parts 2 and 3 of this book. This approach is informed by Elger and Smith's view that the transmission of models of 'good practice' can only be effectively assessed through what they call middle-range analyses based upon case studies (Elger and Smith, 1996: 56). This type of analysis requires an examination of developments at sectoral and workplace levels. The case studies discussed in this text focus on two service industries, health and financial services. These sectors provide scope for the commencement of a cross-sectoral analysis of the patterns of development and diffusion of the new management techniques. It is at the sectoral and workplace level that particular patterns of management style and practice may be identified. It is also at this level that specific institutional and social influences on the development of management behaviour may be assessed.

This study also adopts Smith and Elger's approach to the analysis of the process of transmission of management models. In their analysis of 'Japanization' the authors argue that the concept: 'had become a label for a fairly open-ended investigation rather than a set of strong claims about the scope and character of the spread of Japanese techniques' (Elger and Smith, 1996: 7). In their summary of the debates around Japanization, Smith and Elger pointed to some useful characteristics of this investigative label. First, they suggested that Japanization was often used to justify a variety of changes in work organization and practices demanded by the sharp rise in competition between companies. It provided an 'ideological' argument for changes that might have relatively little in common with the Japanese approach, which often resulted in job losses and a rise in labour intensity. Second, they suggested that new production approaches required the development of new sets of institutional relations between workforce and management in order to accommodate the social tensions and conflicts that arise. Finally, they indicated that companies 'modify or convert' those new management techniques associated with Japanization in order to meet their own priorities and circumstances (Elger and Smith, 1996: 23). These insights into the ideological, institutional and adaptive constituents of the Japanization label informs the approach developed here to the concept of Americanization. Such a perspective recognizes that while there were close parallels between the dynamics that informed US and UK service sector restructuring, there were also important social and institutional differences that undoubtedly influenced the process of emulation.

Summary

This chapter has argued that the latter part of the 1980s and the first half of the 1990s saw the commencement of a business revolution in service industries. The revolution started in the United States, where adverse economic conditions, poor productivity, rising staff levels and the high costs associated with the introduction of new technologies were the catalyst of a restructuring process. Management adopted a variety of new techniques aimed at organizational innovation, the transformation or re-engineering of work processes and the creation of new patterns of employee relations, in which employee commitment and a customer orientation were essential components. Americanization refers to the variety of techniques adopted by management that were aimed at creating a more agile enterprise, while also raising productivity through the extensive re-engineering of work processes and the creation of a 'new' kind of worker.

In contrast to the extensive debates around the development and diffusion of the Japanese model in manufacturing industries, there has been relatively little analysis of the new management approaches adopted in the service sector. This is despite the fact that a far higher proportion of the workforce was affected by these changes by comparison to those employed in manufacturing industries. While the Japanese model emerged under relatively favourable domestic social and economic circumstances, the US model developed as a response to a sharp downward turn in the fortunes of the US service sector. The nation with the closest affinity to the USA, in terms of the growth of service industries and employment and investment patterns, was the UK.

It is suggested that UK public and private sector institutions emulated the American model at the same time as adapting it to meet specific local conditions. The UK shared with the USA several common problems, including low productivity, a high utilization of new product and process technologies, a sharp decline in profitability in the private sector and a growing financial crisis in public service provision. In this sense, there was a closer correspondence between the objective conditions in which the American model emerged and those faced by its emulators in the UK. On the other hand, there were, of course, real social, political and institutional differences between the USA and Britain. The latter, for example, had a higher level of trade union membership density in industries like the financial services and the NHS, and the NHS was a uniquely British institution. Despite these differences, it is argued here that there was a rapid adaptation and subsequent diffusion of many of the characteristics of the US model in UK service industries, particularly the financial services sector and the NHS. In the former, the influence of the US model was exercised in a variety of ways. Information technology (IT) systems, such as customer-oriented databases, were provided by companies like IBM and required UK banking and insurance institutions to adapt management information systems to meet the requirements of operating the new technologies. New approaches to the organization of front and back office operations facilitated the development of business practices which were strongly influenced by the experiences of US companies and were transmitted into the UK by leading firms of management consultants. Likewise, the reform of the US health care system and the views of authors, such as Enthoven, played an important part in stimulating policy debate and discussion in the UK.[1] There were, therefore, several different factors which contributed to the adoption of the American model in the UK. There were broadly common experiences in relation to changes in market conditions and patterns of customer and patient demand; technical innovations, mainly inspired by US IT companies, encouraged institutions along new organizational trajectories, and in both the financial services and the NHS management consultants provided important contributions to policy and strategy debates, while also acting as vehicles for the infusion of new business ideas and practices.

The US model combined technical innovation, new forms of business organization and new approaches to employee relations, and appeared to offer the UK government and finance institutions new insights into tackling the problems they faced. The case studies in Parts 2 and 3 explore the theme of Americanization in detail by examining the extent to which the elements of the model identified above have been adopted in the course of sectoral and workplace restructuring. The case studies explain the process of restructuring in four institutional settings and identify the management reforms introduced in the course of the past decade. Four cases studies drawn from two industrial sectors cannot provide sufficient evidence in themselves to support a contention that the American model has been widely emulated within UK service industries. They do, however, provide evidence of some of the main contours of service sector restructuring and offer an interpretation of the key social and organizational trajectories of management reform. The case studies focus on the workplace level and analyse the specific character of management approaches to restructuring, as well as examining the implications for labour of attempts to create within the UK the model of the committed, customer-oriented, 'new worker'.

Note

1. In 1984, Alain Enthoven, a Stanford University professor, was invited by Gordon McLaughlan, Director of the Nuffield Provincial Hospitals Trust, to spend one month in the UK studying the NHS. At the end of his stay, Enthoven provided the board of trustees with a report on the future direction that the NHS should take. Enthoven's report was published in 1985 and contained the argument for the development of an 'internal market' at the centre of which was the

purchaser/provider split. Enthoven's recommendations drew upon the experience in the USA of attempts to establish a more competitive, lower cost system of health care provision through the introduction of, among other institutions, health maintenance organizations (HMOs). In their review of the reform of British health care, Day and Klein (1991) commented that 'Enthoven's notion of an NHS "internal market", to allow District Health Authorities (DHAs) to buy and sell services, looks remarkably like the solution adopted by the government four years later' (Day and Klein, 1991: 46).

3 LABOUR AND RESTRUCTURING

Introduction

Chapter 1 argued that the management approaches designed to achieve the routinization of manual labour in many production industries in the first half of the twentieth century were adapted, developed and applied to service sector labour processes in the 1980s and 1990s. Chapter 2 suggested that an important and distinctive component of the new management techniques accompanying the routinization of work in service industries was the creation of a new 'customer-oriented' worker whose experience of work was increasingly dominated by the requirement to absorb and internalize management values. These themes were significant elements in management attempts to ensure the reconciliation of labour to the restructuring process in service industries. In this sense, Chapter 1 suggested that the traditional distinctions between manual and non-manual labour were breaking down in the last decades of the twentieth century as a result of the adoption within service industries of techniques designed to achieve the routinization of work. Chapter 2, however, acknowledged that the trend towards the homogenization of work was modified by new management techniques which, for example, emphasized the customer-oriented nature of many service sector occupations. This chapter explores these themes further. In so doing it touches upon some complex issues concerning the definition and role of labour in service industries.

Service labour cannot simply be described as non-manual or non-productive labour (Smith *et al.*, 1991: 1–12). Some service work involves the generation and realization of surplus value and is, therefore, productive labour. Most service work, however, is located in the spheres of circulation, distribution and consumption. Circulation work is typically associated with the financial services. Distribution involves post-production activities like transportation and consumption divides between the provision of individual and collective personal services. Individual personal services include, for example, hairdressing, and collectivized services are those typically provided by the state in the form of welfare provision, education and health, as well as those activities involved with the maintenance of the state apparatus itself at central and local government levels (Carter, 1997). Public sector services are not directly part of the labour/capital relation and the activities involved in circulation and distribution, as post-production activities, are not engaged in the process of creating and realizing surplus value. In short, the specific character of service work is defined by its relationship to the productive constituents of the capitalist economy and much service work is both essential to the maintenance and functioning of this economy and parasitic upon it (Meszaros, 1995: 533). This point is further developed later in the chapter. The main argument summarized here is fourfold.

First, key public and private sector services (like health and financial services) have been subjected to a process of restructuring which has absorbed the principles underpinning management/labour relations in the productive constituents of the capitalist economy. Recent developments in the management of the labour process in service industries have involved the adoption of values and approaches akin to those associated with the real substantiation of labour in production industries. Second, this process has generated a drive towards what might be called the real subordination of service labour. Management has intervened in and reshaped the organization of work in ways that have reduced discretion and instilled practices aimed at strengthening management authority and control. Third, the new work patterns have often been represented by management as empowering and enabling labour, while, in reality, they have tended to achieve the opposite. Finally, at the centre of this transformation of work has been a significant rise in the intensity of service labour. Each of these arguments is explored below through a focus on the concept of intensification.

The Intensification of Work

In the economy as a whole, productivity rose slowly during the 1980s. Set against both historical and international comparative standards, an average growth rate of 2.0 percent is not impressive. However, the story in manufacturing is different. The average rate of growth in manufacturing productivity throughout the 1980s was 5.25 per cent per annum, and for all but the early 1980s it has averaged nearly 6 percent (Metcalf 1988, 1989). It is the figures for productivity growth in manufacturing that are usually cited to illustrate the success of Thatcherism at work. . . . Productivity growth in the service sector may be nearer 1.8 percent . . . between 1980 and 1987. It is, therefore, misleading to focus too much on manufacturing industry; indeed, leaving aside the obvious problem of measurement, it may be pertinent to ask why the low productivity growth in the expanding and increasingly important service sector has received so little attention. (Guest, 1990: 295)

Guest's article asked the question 'Have British workers been working harder in Thatcher's Britain?' His answer was a qualified no. Drawing upon an analysis of manufacturing industries, Guest argued that there was no clear evidence of the rise in UK manufacturing industry productivity in the 1980s being related to a rise in intensity or work effort. His main criticism was directed at the methods used to measure effort or intensity and his conclusion was that there was no real proof that increased worker effort was 'a significant component' in explaining the rise in manufacturing productivity (Guest, 1990: 319). If Guest's argument is accepted, then the examination of the relationships between productivity and labour intensity in service industries appears to be a daunting task. If finding objective measures of labour intensity is difficult for manufacturing, then it is doubly difficult to discern ones that may be applied to industries in which outputs vary considerably and are often 'intangible'. As Guest observed in his aside concerning the productivity problem in services, relatively little attention has been paid to this issue (Guest, 1990: 295). Arguably, the problem of methodology is one of the reasons for the oversight.

What follows addresses this oversight. The chapter examines the implications of service sector restructuring for labour and argues, contrary to Guest's view, that the concept of intensification is a useful tool for understanding the effects on workers of the transformation of work that has taken place in many service and manufacturing industries in the 1990s. This is particularly the case because the process of restructuring in service industries has occurred within a context in which advances in the social and technical division of labour have created a complex set of issues relating to the categorization of service work. Necessarily, operationalizing the concept of intensification requires some clarification of these categories so that the character of the intensification process for different forms of labour may be outlined. In short, the concept requires clarification and development. To date, authors have used intensification to convey a sense of the adverse consequences for labour of many of the changes at workplace level that have taken place over recent years, but the meanings associated with it have remained vague and often poorly defined.

Some authors have used a relatively narrow definition related to the measurement of effort (Guest, 1990: 296–7), while others have adopted a broader, more inclusive, approach that encompasses a rise in intensity resulting from changes in work organization and work methods (Elger, 1991). The concept of intensification developed below adopts a broad, inclusive approach. It suggests that labour intensification combines the techniques associated with objective, quantifiable improvements in output/productivity, as well as more subjective elements associated with, for example, the taking of greater responsibilities and commitments by employees. It is this subjective, or ideological, dimension through which there is an internalization of management goals and values. It is called here the 'internalization of intensification' and is an important feature of the contemporary experience of work.

There are several advantages in focusing on services. First, with its origins in the study of the valorization process in production industries, the analysis of labour intensification may help to shed light on the complex developments in the social division of labour in contemporary capitalist society. Second, many service industries have adopted a wide range of performance measures. Techniques used for measuring labour performance have been incorporated into process technologies, thus emulating management approaches that hitherto have been mainly confined to production industries. Third, services have played a leading role in developing those techniques associated with the internalization of intensification. This has been achieved, for example, via the widespread adoption of customer care programmes, employee commitment strategies and employee care policies. Finally, the reorganization of work within services has given rise to changes in patterns of working time, skills mix and occupational structure which have, arguably, created a polarization between specialist and generalist jobs, with the latter being increasingly susceptible to management attempts to 'mechanize'. The service sector, therefore, provides fertile and challenging ground for clarifying and developing the concept of intensification. The chapter commences with a review of recent debates surrounding the concept. It then outlines a framework that identifies both the 'objective' and 'subjective' character of the intensification process and, finally, reviews the evidence to support the case that there has been a significant rise in work intensity in UK service industries over recent years.

The Intensification Debate

Recent debates on intensification have focused on two main themes: the impact of new management techniques on skills and job content and the problems associated with the measurement of worker effort or performance. The main contours of the debates and their weaknesses are outlined below, prior to an alternative interpretation of the concept of intensification.

The new management techniques

The enthusiasts of each new wave of management techniques have espoused their virtues in terms of the creation of workers with enhanced skills, higher motivation and improved job satisfaction, while, in response, many critics have argued that these new techniques have given rise to the intensification of labour. In the 1980s, for example, enthusiasts of flexibility (Atkinson, 1985; Cross, 1990) supported the introduction of forms of functional flexibility that broke down traditional demarcation lines between skills and created the 'multi-skilled' employee. Cross identified a series of pressures upon companies and institutions to change job content and organizational structures. External pressures included changing market conditions and increased competition, while internal pressures arose from the introduction of new process technologies which incorporated tacit skills and knowledge into the production system. Together these created the necessity for the construction of new skills mixes within the workforce, which led to what Renault, the French auto company, called the emergence of 'rainbow-collar workers' (Cross, 1990: 3).

In his analysis of changing patterns of work organization, Atkinson (1984, 1985) broadly complemented Cross's approach by presenting the case for the development of labour use strategies which consciously constructed a core workforce of highly skilled employees that worked alongside a semi-skilled and unskilled periphery. While the evidence for the introduction of more flexible forms of work along the lines recommended by Atkinson's flexible firm model has been widely contested, there is little doubt that many companies in the UK embarked upon changes in work organization and occupational structures from around the mid-1980s (Incomes Data Services, 1986). Critics suggested that, in practice, these flexibility deals achieved more modest outcomes than enthusiasts like Cross and Atkinson claimed. They largely took the form of increasing job and task rotation and resulted in a rise in labour intensity. Elger (1991: 63), for example, while recognizing that workers may experience higher job satisfaction from removing the frustrations caused by demarcation lines that stop them from completing jobs that they started, concluded that the piecemeal changes adopted in manufacturing firms 'delivered significant productivity and profitability gains to many employers, at the cost of increased effort and insecurity but with few non-wage gains for most workers.' In his review of the case study material used to support this claim, Elger provided a useful summary of the evidence for the intensification of labour. For example, collective agreements revealed management cutting out rest breaks, while workplace studies revealed the introduction of forms of team working designed to create enlarged operator responsibilities. Identification of these forms of management pressure for changes in work practices did not, however, amount to a comprehensive analysis of the underlying characteristics of intensification in manufacturing firms in the late 1980s.

In the early 1990s, in relation to the adoption of team working and continuous improvement programmes associated with the lean production model, some authors argued that lean assembly plants facilitated the creation of a workforce of 'highly skilled problem solvers' (Womack *et al.*, 1990: 102). The dynamic work team was at the

> heart of the lean factory. Building these efficient teams is not simple. First, workers need to be taught a wide variety of skills – in fact all jobs in their work group so that tasks can be rotated and workers can fill in for each other. Workers then need to acquire many additional skills: simple machine repair, quality-checking, housekeeping, and materials ordering. Then they need encouragement to think actively, indeed proactively, so they can devise solutions before problems become serious. (Womack *et al.*, 1990: 99)

By contrast, critics indicated that such empowerment techniques did little to reduce the routinized patterns of work associated with mass production and merely encouraged workers to strive constantly to increase the intensity of their own labour. Rinehart *et al.* (1996), in their study of a Japanese auto plant in Canada, suggested that the company made no real attempt to reunify manual and mental labour through the continuous improvement process. Management was rather more concerned with the rotation of easily learnt, repetitive tasks which required extremely limited levels of conceptualization. It was this process that provided the basis for team working (Rinehart *et al.*, 1996: 170). Williams *et al.* (1992) reached similar conclusions in their detailed critique of the efficiency and productivity gains associated with the lean production model, as outlined by Womack *et al.* (1990).

More recently, advocates of re-engineering linked the introduction of new work processes with the empowerment of employees and the development of technical skills and competencies (Hammer and Champy, 1993). Re-engineering focused upon the work process and encouraged project teams to develop new ways of working that cut across traditional forms of company organization. Despite being instigated from the top down, re-engineering projects offered an effective means for the organic development of new forms of collective working through which employees assumed responsibility for the improvement of the labour process:

> Teamwork and empowerment are abstractions and generalities around which it is impossible to get one's arms. They describe characteristics and attributes that one might want an organization to exhibit, but there is no direct way to achieve them. They are consequences of process designs and they can only be achieved in that context. (Hammer, 1995: 203)

The new job designs arising from re-engineering, according to its leading exponents, created the conditions for employee solidarity and the basis for the emergence of new jobs and skills arising from the innovative use of information technologies.

On the other hand, critics of the re-engineering process suggested that the approach, with its origins in attempts to subject work to greater mechanization, resulted in quite different outcomes from those claimed by its proponents. The knowledge and skills of employees were absorbed within the new software packages used to structure and control the work process (Jones, 1995; Head, 1996). This resulted in improved productivity at the expense of worker discretion and control. The consequence was an intensification of work, along with the creation of an alienated and insecure workforce rather than one that was inspired by the re-engineering revolution.

The debates on flexibility, lean production and re-engineering have tended to polarize around upskilling versus intensity, empowerment versus alienation and commitment versus acquiescence. While the enthusiasts of these models have provided 'authoritative' accounts of their development and diffusion, arguably the critics' response has not achieved a corresponding level of rigour in defining and explaining the key characteristics of labour intensification.

Productivity and performance: the problem of quantification

As suggested above, the definition of labour intensity may be considered from 'narrow' or 'broad' perspectives. The narrow approach focuses upon objective measures, such as the rise in output achieved per employee, or, in the tradition of work study, operative. It is grounded in the principles of scientific management and seeks to measure improvements in worker performance as indicated by the increased output achieved over a period of time, assuming a close specification of the tasks to be undertaken and no changes in work methods or the equipment used. This approach has traditionally been associated with the use of work study schemes in manufacturing industries. The spread of these schemes in the 1960s and early 1970s provided the basis for Bennett and Smith-Gavine (1988) to develop the percentage utilization of labour (PUL) index. This index amounted to an ambitious attempt to measure human exertion per hour by factory operatives and enabled an evaluation of changes in their performance over time. The PUL index was based upon the measurement of throughput using data compiled from the operation of work study schemes.

When it started in 1971, a representative sample of 171 factories and 131,500 operatives provided the basis for the compilation of the data. The index was based upon the use of standard work data. In each of the factories within the sample, standard performances were developed for specific operative tasks. These tasks were closely defined by being broken down into their various elements and 'standard' times were established for their completion. The times were 'synthetic'. They were based upon the observation of the actual time taken to complete a task plus the accrediting of allowances/contingencies for pauses in work flow, delays and rest breaks. The actual time, plus allowances (e.g. rest breaks) and contingencies (e.g. disruptions in workflow outside the control of the operative) equalled the standard time for the completion of the task (Grant, 1983). This form of time study provided the basis for establishing the output to be achieved by an operative over a standard hour or standard week. For example, if the target was reached within the given time the operative achieved 100 per cent on the PUL index; if only three-quarters of the output was achieved then the operative's performance was recorded as 75 per cent and if it was exceeded by one-quarter then the performance was recorded at 125 per cent. The PUL index was derived from a calculation of the performance achieved by all the operatives employed within the sample factories. The PUL score for 1971 (96.3 per cent) was converted to 100 to provide the basis for comparison with subsequent years. The PUL index provided some evidence of the intensification of labour in UK manufacturing industries in the 1980s, and this evidence was utilized in debates about the nature and sustainability of the UK manufacturing 'productivity miracle' (Metcalf, 1989a; Nolan, 1989).

It was in the context of this debate that the PUL index was associated with the concept of intensity and met with sharp criticism. Guest (1990), for example, drew attention to the problem of relating effort to output, suggesting that an increase in the former did not necessarily give rise to an increase in the latter and, more fundamentally, he suggested that Bennett and Smith-

Gavine attached too much significance to the 'scientific' nature of work study, in which, for example, the conversion of actual into standard times left considerable scope for, in his terms, 'errors' (Guest, 1990: 299), or, in trade union terms, negotiation. Guest also identified problems with the PUL index as a measure of effort or intensity over time. The sample of factories changed over the years during which the index was constructed. The concept of an operative was likely to have been redefined within the sample factories, as well as the nature of work organization, as a result of the introduction, for example, of new forms of team working in the 1980s. As a consequence, these 'underlying changes . . . may have influenced the PUL index independent of any changes in the intensification of work' (Guest, 1990: 300). In identifying these weaknesses in the PUL index, Guest provided a strong justification for a broader framework for the definition of intensification.

His search for such a framework took Guest towards psychological approaches developed within the context of expectancy theory, which, he argued, could help to identify the subjective dimensions of the relationships between effort-performance and rewards. In seeking more objective measures of effort, he identified research that focused on the development of measures of physiological and mental effort in a variety of occupational settings (Guest, 1990: 306–7). While acknowledging the value of Guest's attempts to identify both objective and subjective elements in the quantification of effort, his outline framework is open to similar criticisms to those he applied to the methodology used by the authors of the PUL index. The rating of mental effort is open to as many, if not more, questions of reliability and validity as are those used to measure physical effort. Further, Guest tends to conceive effort and intensity as interchangeable terms, ignoring the fact that labour intensity may rise independent of the exertion of greater or lesser effort. This may be achieved through, for example, changes in work organization and work methods (in scientific management terms, method study). It is precisely these areas, outside of the scope of Guest's analysis, that provide the basis for a more inclusive approach to identifying all those factors that contribute to a rise in the intensity of labour. It is also these factors that, as a result of their concern to collate the quantifiable data associated with work study, Bennett and Smith-Gavine tended to ignore. Being based upon the analysis of standard times for tasks, the PUL index did not differentiate or attempt to calculate the distinctive contributions made by time and method study to improving the performance of labour.

In short, the search for a more comprehensive definition of intensification lies initially in the identification of the wide range of techniques that may be used to fill the pores of the working day and not merely in the elaboration of more sophisticated techniques aimed at measuring mental or physical effort. In turn, the elaboration of these techniques may subsequently provide the basis for discerning what is, and what is not, susceptible to 'measurement'.

Summary

Critical analysis of the new management techniques has rested heavily upon the argument that management has used the new language of upskilling, empowerment and employee assistance programmes to thinly disguise changes in work organization that, consciously or otherwise, have led to a rise in labour intensity. Despite its centrality to the arguments of critical analysts, the concept of labour intensification has remained relatively poorly defined. A brief review of debates on intensification suggests that four main propositions underpin the framework required for the clarification and development of the concept.

First, labour intensity is not simply synonymous with work effort. A rise in labour intensity may or may not be associated with increased mental or physical effort by the individual employee. Second, while scientific management approaches, understandably from the management perspective, have attempted to quantify labour performance narrowly in terms of a direct relationship between time and task, a broader framework for understanding intensification should take into account the contributions made by, for example, changes in patterns of working time, work organization and work practices. Third, some aspects of intensification may be more susceptible to measurement than others depending upon the nature of the tasks and the social organization of the workplace. Finally, intensification incorporates a subjective dimension that relates to the ways in which workers internalize the values that facilitate a rise in intensification. This subjective element may be referred to as the 'internalization of intensification'.

Interpreting Intensification

The interpretation of labour intensification requires some clearing of the theoretical decks. The concept touches upon many debates concerning the nature of the labour process, the role of management, the distinctions between productive and unproductive labour and the categorization of different types of work or occupations within advanced industrial economies. It is necessary to address some of the issues arising from these debates in order to identify a framework that assists in the clarification of the concept. In revisiting the debates, it not the purpose here to argue that nothing has changed and that the concept of intensification developed in the nineteenth century is, in itself, adequate to analyse the character of work in the late twentieth. On the contrary, by identifying the essential continuities which have sustained capitalist society over the past century, it is also possible to establish what is distinctive about the current period.

The underlying continuity of capitalist society lies in the relationship between capital and labour. The primary purpose of capital has continued to be the purchase of labour power as a necessary prerequisite for the pursuit of profit. Since the employer is purchasing the potential of labour power and not the direct product of labour, it is the task of the former to ensure that labour power is used effectively. It is at this point that the relationship between capital accumulation and the organization of the labour process comes into play. In the nineteenth century this relationship was examined in relation to the most dynamic sector of the capitalist economy, manufacturing industry, and the development of the social division of labour within it (Marx, 1974: 476–501). Initially, the capitalist employer was primarily concerned to establish a basic control over the use of labour time, with the main aim being the employment of labour for the purpose of extracting a rising mass of surplus value. With the development of larger-scale production and the emergence of a more complex social division of labour, labour power was pressed into greater interdependence or cooperation. This, in turn, facilitated the loosening of labour's control over the organization of production and provided the potential for management to move towards the extraction of relative surplus value.

This took the form of a transition from the 'formal' to the 'real' subordination of labour. This was not, however, a simple or natural process of transition. The capacity for capital to achieve the real subordination of labour varied between industries and was subject to the accumulation cycle and the relative strength and organization of labour itself (Elger, 1979: 66). Equally, the shift to a pattern of real subordination did not necessarily bring with it a deskilled labour force, but instead required the development of greater interdependence between different categories of labour and the subordination of individual craft skills to a pattern which contained an 'uneven variety of narrow skills and specific dexterities' (Elger, 1979: 82). It was in the context of controlling and directing this transition towards a more complex organization of the social and technical divisions of labour that the modern role of shopfloor management was born. Its birth may be traced to the United States.

In his evaluation of the early contributions of US approaches to shopfloor management, Litterer, writing in 1900, argued that US manufacturers' superiority over their European counterparts was not based upon their use of superior manufacturing technologies, but upon the attention given to securing effective ways of getting the most from the machinery deployed:

> the skill and knowledge of Europeans . . . was the equal and sometimes superior of that of Americans. The difference was how this technical knowledge and skill was used. The European manufacturer used it to make a product. The American manufacturer used it to make a process to make the product. . . . The literature of the time frequently mentioned that American machine tools were superior to the European. This, however, should be understood to reflect not the difference in abilities as much as a difference in the thinking of European and American management. One appreciated the importance of, and understood how to obtain, the advantage of machinery; the other did not. (quoted in Locke, 1996: 17–18)

This concern with the organization of the process of production was subsequently formalized in the early twentieth century into the scientific management techniques of Taylor and Gilbreth. The diffusion of Taylorism took place initially in the USA. Its development was associated with the emergence of the automobile and electrical consumer goods industries. European manufacturers adopted modified forms of scientific management during the inter-war years, but the American approach only began to dominate management thinking in the aftermath of the Second World War. It was complemented in the 1930s by the development of another strand of American management theory, the human relations school. This approach eschewed the command and control structures implicit in Taylor's work study techniques, and focused upon the role of social psychology in helping to motivate the individual worker. In practice, the human relations school contributed to changes in American management style rather than substance (Locke, 1996). Improved productivity remained the goal, with the debate centred on how best to motivate workers to achieve it.

The development of large-scale production aimed at the provision of goods for a mass market, in turn, spurred the development of the modern 'corporation' – the multifunctional and multiproduct firm whose task it was to develop new structures aimed at coordinating manufacturing, sales, finance, purchasing, marketing and engineering (Locke, 1996: 21). It was the emergence of the modern corporation, with its multidivisional forms of organization (Chandler, 1962, 1977), that facilitated the development of an increasingly complex technical and social division of labour in the advanced industrial economies of the mid-twentieth century. For management, the expansion of the technical division of labour was complemented by the development of its role in other spheres of the economy. Commercial capitalists, for example, linked production and distribution, and their activities expanded significantly by the mid-twentieth century, creating new opportunities for the growth of jobs in industries that were remote from the process of production. This expansion of the division of labour within areas removed from the direct process of production gave rise to the '"false costs and useless expenses of production" which are nevertheless absolutely vital to the survival of the system: a contradictory determination from which they cannot be extricated' (Meszaros, 1995: 533). In short, the growth of employment within, for example, the expanding commercial sphere of the economy arose directly as a result of developments within the process of production, and the activities of commercial labour were essential to and, in many cases, parasitic upon it. By the mid-twentieth century these activities, allied with the increasingly important role played by the state in providing social and welfare services, gave rise to what some called the new service economy and what Sayer and Walker (1992) have more accurately referred to as a reworking of the division of labour, a reworking that embraced an expanded social division of labour.

Sayer and Walker (1992: 57) usefully identified the features of this expanded division by reference to 'a classical and systematic set of categories': production, labour process, circulation and consumption. In challenging the service economy thesis, Sayer and Walker argued that the production system retained its predominance in modern industrial economies and that the growth of service sector employment was much exaggerated. In the sphere of production, for example, the confusions over what constituted an industrial good as opposed to a personal service led to the mis-categorizing of much productive labour as service labour. Within the labour process, the expansion in indirect productive activities had wrongly seen the categorization of indirectly productive labour as service labour, and, in the sphere of circulation, involving the movement of commodities, money and property rights, those engaged in circulatory activities had wrongly been lumped together with other forms of labour and given the generic label of service workers. Finally, within the sphere of consumption, Sayer and Walker (1992: 58) indicated that the twentieth century had seen the 'industrialization of everyday life' rather than 'the shift from industrial production to the satisfaction of consumer needs' (Sayer and Walker, 1992: 58). This process involved the mass production of those household and personal goods that tended to replace the provision of, particularly domestic, forms of service.

While correctly emphasizing the importance of the interconnections between the underlying categories of advanced industrial economies, Sayer and Walker rejected the distinction between productive and unproductive labour primarily because they found Marx's categorization of circulation work as 'necessary but unproductive' as an uneasy and imprecise description. This unease arose because 'the interpenetration of circulation and production in a complex division of labour elides any hard and fast line between unproductive and productive labour, and makes the hasty dismissal of circulation functions a grave error' (Sayer and Walker, 1992: 84). Here the authors were right to argue that there is no hard and fast line between productive and unproductive labour, but they were wrong to dismiss the categories, since in so doing they unnecessarily blurred the analytical distinction between the spheres of production and circulation. This distinction is important in terms of interpreting the relationship between the expanded division of labour and the role of labour intensification in different industrial sectors in the late twentieth century. It was necessary for management to take those techniques exercised in the use of labour power in the direct production process and adapt them to meet the needs for raising the effectiveness of labour employed in indirectly productive and unproductive spheres of the economy. This was achieved, for example, via the commercialization and privatization of public services, a process which served to muddy the distinction between productive and unproductive labour. An example illustrates this point. In the UK National Health Service the commercial disciplines arising from the purchaser/provider split, introduced as a result of legislative reform in 1989, facilitated the creation of an 'artificial' market and the development of a plethora of measures of financial performance and labour productivity that were applied to a work setting in which labour retained its unproductive character. At the same time, the requirement that local units, such as pathology and haematology laboratories, secured new sources of income generation saw the emergence of contracts with private sector companies through which the laboratory workers were engaged as indirectly productive labour. This creeping process of privatization pushed labour power into a range of activities that crossed the productive/unproductive boundary in the course of an ordinary working day.

In summary, the last decades of the twentieth century saw an acceleration of the trend towards an expanded social division of labour within the advanced industrial economies. This acceleration was associated by many authors with the emergence of a new post-industrial or service economy, but this label tended to confuse rather than clarify our understanding. Changes in the forms of industrial organization and the technical division of labour saw the growth of employment in the sphere of circulation and other, often state organised, activities, such as the provision of social welfare, that were essential to, but often parasitic upon, the production process. It was precisely in these areas that management developed new strategies that emulated the move from the formal to the real subordination of labour that commenced a century earlier in production industries.

In short, the last two decades of the twentieth century have seen a concerted effort by management to move towards the real subordination of labour in those industries and occupations that are remote from the direct process of production. Emulation has not been a straightforward affair, since the activities of much service labour are not susceptible to simple measures of productivity and performance. None the less, management, often led by the state sector (Fairbrother, 1994, 1996), has adopted a variety of techniques designed to facilitate such measurement and parody the operation of market mechanisms, even in industries where they do not 'naturally' exist. The inter-war and post-war period witnessed early attempts at this process. Clerical work measurement (CWM), for example, represented an attempt by management to subject office work to the rigours of work study. It was unevenly adopted and primarily focused upon lower level office tasks. By contrast, contemporary approaches have tended to focus on a wider range of occupations, encompassing even middle and upper layers of the hierarchical management structure, and leaving very few employees untouched by the re-engineering process. It is this all-embracing character of the contemporary transformation of service work that distinguishes it from the earlier, piecemeal approach typified by CWM.

The Real Subordination of Service Labour

There are four main dimensions to management strategies aimed at the real subordination of service labour. These are the measurement of worker performance, the reorganization of working time, the application of new technologies in the re-engineering of the labour process and, finally, the 'internalization of intensification', a process by which employees are encouraged to internalize management values. These four elements constitute the basic pillars of the emulative model of labour intensification in the service industries. They have tended to be linked in their implementation. For example, in financial services industries, workplaces involved in direct-line links with customers have expanded significantly in the 1990s. Staff use networked computers to access customer databases and respond to customer queries using the software that structures the staff/customer conversation. Performance is evaluated via, for example, the automatic monitoring of the call-time; staff work flexible shift patterns aimed at facilitating 'out of hours' service provision; and training is primarily concerned with promoting the appropriate interpersonal communication skills demanded by the customer service orientation. The provision of direct-line customer services has been an area of spectacular growth within banking and insurance companies that have been rapidly shedding labour in other areas of business. In many respects, these white-collar factories exemplify the trend towards the real subordination of service labour.

Identification of this trend is not, however, a simple matter of spotting within the white-collar labour process those characteristics of work which allow us to make visible what hitherto has been an 'invisible' assembly line (Stamp, 1995). The task is more complex than this. The reordering of workplace relations in service industries amounts to more than a description of the ways in which Henry Ford's assembly line has been adopted. For example, in many UK financial services companies, while workplaces offering direct-line services may have adopted many of the features of the assembly line, other units and workplaces within the same company have established patterns of team working, or cooperative working, in which traditional specialists in, for example, pensions, motor and household insurance have been replaced by generalists whose skills are stretched across these areas. The new customer orientation has simultaneously generated an expansion of routine, factory-style labour processes as well as the development of more cooperative forms of working based upon the emergence of multifunctional teams. Furthermore, those engaged to undertake the routine direct-line jobs may be drawn from an external labour market in which part-time employment creates different work experiences and career expectations from those employed in full-time jobs, while the development of multifunctional teams has tended to focus on the reordering of the internal labour market, involving company-specific training programmes. In short, the shift towards the real subordination of service labour has not given rise to a single, dominant pattern of work organization or work experience; nor has it necessarily resulted in a straightforward confirmation of the deskilling thesis provided by Braverman and other labour process theorists. This point may be illustrated by a more detailed examination of the main pillars of labour intensification.

Measuring performance

The measurement of performance has become something of an obsession in service industries over the past decade. Management has adopted two main techniques: quantitative and qualitative. The quantitative approach largely rested upon attempts to measure throughput and output, while the qualitative approach relied upon the introduction of more subjective management measures of individual or team performance. Quantitative techniques may operate at the individual or group levels, or may be associated with the production of data that measure the achievements of whole-service groups or industries. The origins of the new management approach to quantifying performance in the public services in the UK may be traced back to the civil service in the early 1980s. It was in central government departments that management experimented with the introduction of a wide range of performance measures. These measures were designed to reduce overstaffing and increase efficiency. Their introduction commenced with the Rayner Scrutinies. Sir Derek Rayner, of Marks and Spencer, was given the task of introducing 'good' management practices associated with the private services into the public sector. His Rayner Unit undertook around 300 scrutinies between 1980 and 1985. The Unit set down the timing and procedures to be adopted to raise efficiency within departments, while allowing local level managers discretion over the methods to be used to achieve this goal. The effect of these scrutinies was to create a new culture among officials which shifted the focus of their activities away from a traditional administrative approach, based upon well established rules and procedures, and towards a managerialist outlook that emphasized efficiency and 'value for money' (Horton, 1993: 134–5). The Scrutinies set the scene for the subsequent introduction of local cost centres, the extensive use of competitive tendering and the identification of the most efficient local departments and offices whose performance provided a benchmark against which the activities of other comparable departments and units were measured. By 1987 it was estimated that over 1,800 performance measures had been introduced in the civil service over the preceding five years (Greenwood and Wilson, 1989: 132). These techniques were emulated by other public services. With the introduction of the internal market within the NHS in the early 1990s, for example, the efficiency of local units were measured via the widespread introduction of compulsory and voluntary competitive tendering, market testing and the setting of profit targets, referred to as percentage rates of return.

Measures were introduced to evaluate the efficiency of the work process, as well as to estimate the outcomes of these activities in private as well as public service industries. In financial services, for example, traditional estimates of individual performance based upon sales achieved per employee were complemented by the development of other measures aimed at evaluating the effectiveness of the employee–customer interface. Financial institutions introduced methods designed to check on, for example, the speed at which employees responded to customer enquiries or the time taken to process electronic and paper-based transactions. Many institutions established checks upon error rates and the interactive performance of staff who dealt directly with customers. In public services, performance measures became enshrined in service standards agreements and the output-oriented performance tables for hospitals, schools, colleges and universities. While performance measures were not unknown to many service institutions prior to 1980, their range expanded dramatically in the early 1990s.

Qualitative approaches to performance assessment were mainly introduced in public and private services via the development of employee appraisal schemes. Typically, schemes were based upon annual interviews between managers/supervisors and individual members of staff. The system required appraiser and appraisee to undertake a joint evaluation of the latter's performance in relation to a range of core competencies concerning, for example, the skills, attitude, knowledge and expertise required to undertake a job. For each competency, schemes might identify up to five levels of performance within a spectrum ranging from exceptional to unacceptable. In the course of the appraisal interview the appraisee would agree areas of strength and weakness and identify ways of achieving improvements over the future appraisal cycle. In practice, such schemes served to clarify managerial roles at workplace level and establish clear responsibilities among supervisory and line management staff for the performance of those under them. The schemes usually incorporated an appeals mechanism that could be used by staff if they considered their appraisal to have been unfair. In practice, such schemes have proven to be extremely complex to operate, time consuming and paper-generating and there has been uncertainty about their contribution to improving the efficiency of institutions and enterprises. On the other hand, they have been useful as a technique designed to legitimate the idea of performance measurement in areas where none previously existed. The linking of performance appraisal to rewards or payments systems has spread extensively within the private services, particularly the financial services sector. In public services, with some exceptions, the linking of appraisal to pay has been mainly confined to senior and middle management grades. In the public services, performance measurement has also been introduced as a means to reward or punish whole institutions financially. In education, for example, further and higher education institutions have received financial rewards or penalties related to their capacity to recruit to target student numbers or achieve levels of excellence or satisfactory performance in teaching and research activities. In the health service, the achievement of performance targets (usually quantitative measures such as the number of consultant episodes or the number of outpatient visits to an accident and emergency facility) by specific medical units has been used as a means to determine their income for the subsequent financial year.

Performance measurement has been linked in many service industries to the evaluation of the quality of service provision. In this way, the client or recipient of services has been brought into the evaluation process via, for example, surveys, questionnaires and complaints procedures, whose effect has been to increase the pressures on service providers to become more client- or customer-oriented. This process has tended to work more effectively in areas where quality is easier to define, say in terms of the percentage of trains or buses that arrive at their destination on time. Where quality is related to other less clearly defined outcomes, as with medical interventions aimed at curing disease, the evaluation of the quality of provision has been less easy to determine (Dent, 1991: 72–3).

In brief, performance measurement has contributed to labour intensification in service industries in a variety of ways. First, efficiency targets have been met by trading in jobs, so that costs may be reduced relative to income in order to keep within budgetary limits (particularly in public services like health, education and central government). Second, performance measurement has strengthened and clarified in many service industries the supervisory role of line-management, enhancing its control over the daily conduct of work. Third, performance measurement has been linked to financial rewards and penalties for good or poor performance. Arguably, in private services these have been more closely related to wage payment systems, while in the public services they have tended to be linked to the financing of institutions like universities, colleges, schools and hospital trusts or specific units and departments within them. Finally, performance measurement schemes have widened to incorporate professional as well as administrative and clerical functions, often reducing the discretion traditionally exercised by professionals over the character, pace and conduct of their work (Miller, 1991: 109–35).

Reorganizing labour time

Studies of the productivity 'miracle' in UK manufacturing industries in the 1980s revealed how employers achieved 'a closer filling up of the pores of the working day' (Marx, 1974: 386) by cutting staffing levels, requiring those who remained to work more flexibly and using overtime to extend the length of the working day (Elger, 1991: 64). These approaches achieved an uneven pattern of labour intensification across a variety of industrial sectors. In the absence of investment in new plant and machinery, there was strong evidence that overtime was used to increase the rate of utilization of existing plant and machinery. A study undertaken in 1988 revealed, for example, that 'Latest figures from the Department of Employment show that in April this year 13.22 million hours of overtime were worked in manufacturing industry. A larger proportion of the workforce is now working overtime than at any time since records began in 1950' (Income Data Services, 1988).

Increased overtime working accompanied by cuts in rest breaks and downtime served to raise the intensity of labour and achieve 'piecemeal and uneven restructuring' in UK manufacturing industries (Elger, 1991: 64). By contrast, changes in the patterns of working time in service industries have taken a more complex course during the period of restructuring for a number of reasons. First, and most obviously, service industry activities involve greater variety than manufacturing, and the organization of their delivery has undergone significant change over recent years, through, for example, customer-driven and legislative changes that led to the extension of opening times in areas such as the retail sector and financial services. Second, restructuring in leading edge service industries, like the financial services, has been accompanied by significant investment in new technologies that have transformed the work process (creating 24-hour banking) and facilitated the introduction of new product ranges. Finally, while manufacturing industry experienced a general decline in employment levels, services have undergone a more varied pattern of change in the structure of employment. New jobs created have tended to be part-time, while the proportion of permanent full-time posts has fallen in specific sectors like retail banking and insurance. There has also been a shift of jobs from the public to the private sector, accompanied by changes in employment contracts and terms and conditions. This shift has resulted in the expansion of what has been called precarious employment, in which the length of contract between the service purchaser and provider builds in job insecurity and often brings with it the reorganization of jobs and hours and the loss for many staff of redundancy, sick pay and pension rights (Allen and Henry, 1996: 65–82).

While precarious forms of employment have expanded, it would be inaccurate to characterize management approaches as being primarily driven by a commitment to create insecure work. Enterprises require a relatively stable skills base, even in areas like contract cleaning, to ensure the effective execution of contractual obligations; case studies have revealed that many part-time (sometimes characterized as 'peripheral') employees are often regarded by management as essential or 'core' staff; and there is evidence that more varied patterns of working time have resulted from employers' attempts to cope with shortages in local labour markets (Rainnie and Kraithman, 1992: 64–5). Problems of labour supply and workforce stability have been important factors in influencing management approaches to the use of labour time. These may, however, be regarded as secondary factors. Most importantly, management's approach to working time has been influenced by its concern to maintain competitiveness through the utilization of labour time in more efficient ways. In this sense, consciously or otherwise, the management response to increased competition (whether through market testing and contracting out in public services or via the invention of new products and services in the private sector) has been to experiment with ways of changing working time arrangements to raise the intensity of labour.

The increased intensity of labour has been linked to attempts to match the hours worked with fluctuations in the demand for services. In turn, fluctuating demand has been fuelled by the process of technological change. In this sense a rise in intensity has taken place, along with an increase in the productiveness of labour. Under these circumstances working hours per employee may be reduced (or broken down into short shifts), while the intensity of work increases. This is particularly evident in those areas of work that require the performance of routinized responses to customer enquiries (direct line services) or where work has assumed the character of an electronic or paper-based assembly line (cheque processing and clearing). By contrast, in areas where work rhythms are less prone to fluctuation, management has adopted flexitime arrangements which allow employees to determine how they fulfil their contracted hours as long as the work gets done. This pattern of organizing working time has much in common with those techniques associated with the Japanese model of lean production. Case studies of North American auto plants have suggested that the introduction of greater autonomy in organizing patterns of working time and the pace and sequence of work tasks through team working and quality circles has contributed to a climate within workplaces in which employees have been encouraged to take initiatives that have the consequence of raising the intensity of their own labour (Graham, 1996; Rinehart et al., 1996; Waddington and Whitston, 1996).

The willingness of employers to experiment with different approaches to the organization of working time is more evident in service industries than in manufacturing, and not just in relation to the expansion of part-time and more casual forms of employment (BIFU, 1995). New working time arrangements have tended to enhance the employer's discretion over the utilization of labour time. An extreme example of this is the 'zero hours contract', through which the employee has no guaranteed hours of work during a week or payment period but is required to be available for work for as few or as many hours as business demand requires. Such contracts have been adopted by some fast food chains in the USA and UK. Within financial services, however, an alternative approach to enhancing employer discretion over the use of labour time has been considered in terms of the introduction of annualized hours. By 1995 several companies in the finance sector in the UK had introduced annualized hours schemes and several others, including Midland (now HSBC) and the Co-operative bank, were considering doing so.

Annualized hours schemes average working time over a 12-month period rather than on a weekly basis. Schemes move away from the concept of a standard working week and provide the opportunity for the employer to match working time with business needs in order to maintain a higher level of productivity. Annualized hours may be calculated in a variety of ways, depending on whether holidays are included. Some schemes establish work rosters which incorporate committed hours, while leaving a number that are 'banked' or uncommitted. These hours have been paid for by the employer and are, therefore, 'owed' by the employee. It is these uncommitted hours which provide the employer with considerable discretion over how labour is utilized. The uncommitted or banked hours may be used to cover absenteeism, staff holidays, public holidays or unanticipated periods of high demand for services from the public (BIFU, 1995: 4-5). In practice such arrangements can remove unsocial hours and overtime payments, creating a more pliable workforce to meet the needs of employers who seek greater flexibility in the utilization of labour. A similar effect has occurred in the health service through the operation of bank nursing systems, in which a register of available nursing labour may be kept at local level by management to be called upon at times of staff shortage. Many of the nurses registered with a local trust may be employed full-time elsewhere or even with the same trust. The bank nurse would receive no overtime and work extra hours often at a reduced rate, a system, as Lloyd and Seifert's (1993) research has suggested, that is 'OK for a few months, but then they go off sick with exhaustion'.

By contrast with annualized hours arrangements, another form of flexible working has been piloted in service industries, such as the financial services and telecommunications, which appears to be more worker 'friendly'. This is variously called teleworking or remote working. Typically, this form of working is associated with the use of information and communications technologies, which allow an employee to work from home or from a place away from the office or workplace. Electronic communication allows staff to undertake their work and communicate with the enterprise via e-mail, fax and telephone. Teleworking has been introduced in several insurance and banking institutions, particularly for data processing undertaken by relatively junior and unskilled staff (Smith and Anderson, 1992: 170–86). More recently, pilot schemes have extended the use of teleworking to middle and more senior levels of staff in such companies as the Co-operative Bank. The use of mobile phones and other forms of electronic communications has helped to establish new patterns of work organization for many other groups of employees in service industries, particularly those whose employment requires them to work within the community or travel extensively to sell, repair or maintain products and services. It has been estimated, for example, that the number of remote workers in the UK had reached two million by the mid-1990s (Ackers *et al.*, 1996: 12). The benefit to the employee arises from not being tied to a specific office or workplace and therefore having more influence over the pattern of a working day. On the other hand, this form of work organization has the consequence of isolating individuals from work colleagues and tends to break down the traditional distinction between work and non-work time, creating circumstances in which staff are rarely free from the demands of their employment. In this sense, direct forms of management control have been replaced by virtual forms that may, in fact, have a greater impact upon the worker–employer relationship, since fewer opportunities arise for labour to establish collective ways of mediating or influencing the employment relationship.

Changes in patterns of working time in service industries provide a sharp illustration of how management has pursued the shift from the formal to the real subordination of labour. In some cases this has involved the use of 'traditional' approaches to the ordering of working time, such as in information processing plants, where in many workplaces clocking on and off has been introduced and rest breaks have been subjected to close management supervision. In other cases 'new' approaches have been piloted using electronic technologies as a way of establishing more flexible patterns of work. The reorganization of working time in industries like the financial services has been driven primarily by competitive pressures, particularly in such areas as direct line services, and by the necessity to reduce labour costs. At the same time, more flexible forms of working – shorter shifts, homeworking, flexitime – have often been presented by management as meeting the needs of staff, particularly women workers. There is strong evidence that more flexible forms of working have benefited young married women of child-bearing age, many of whom are employed in data processing and direct line workplaces which have been consciously located within areas in which the local labour market has provided this type of labour in abundance (Fincham *et al.*, 1994; BIFU, 1988).

Such workplaces, often created on greenfield sites, provided opportunities for institutions to rethink the banking process, as one author has argued

> By moving this banking operation out of its traditional setting onto a greenfield site, it has been possible to reorganise or re-engineer the banking process. The substitution of female clerical workers for skilled male professionals has reduced costs and increased flexibility. The demand for women's labour has arisen from the deskilling of previously professional work. (Equal Opportunities Commission, 1996)

Call centres, located on greenfield sites and in reconstructed offices, also provided the physical or spatial environment in which experiments in work layout could be undertaken. Some were structured like vast factory-like assembly lines, while others, particularly more recent in design, established delineated spatial areas for work teams. Whatever their design, these workplaces provided management with a physical environment and a choice of technological systems which facilitated the monitoring and measurement of performance at the human–computer interface, including the means by which staff could evaluate the quality and efficiency of their own activities. In this sense, the design and development of the physical space and the technologies used within it consciously incorporated a variety of techniques associated with intensification, creating what Baldry *et al.* (1998) have called the 'bright satanic office'.

Re-engineering work processes

The introduction of new technologies has traditionally been associated with a rise in the productivity of labour. New machinery enables each commodity produced or task undertaken to embody less labour time than was required when using the old equipment.

The rise in productivity gained by the introduction of new machinery is greater than that which may be achieved by varying the length of the working day, since the former improvement does not confront so immediately the limitations inherent in the finite capacities of human labour. In the 1980s and 1990s the re-engineering of labour processes in service industries, particularly those concerned with circulation work, emulated those practices in production industries which sought to raise the productiveness of labour as well as its intensity. In Marxist terms, the combination of new management approaches to the organization of service work was aimed at 'simultaneous variations in the duration, productiveness and intensity of labour' (Marx, 1974: 494–5).

Changes in patterns of working time were linked to the introduction of new technologies and the development of new work practices. This process occurred unevenly across service industries, with, arguably, private services like the retail and banking industries taking the lead. Put simply, the face of the high street was changed as bank branches closed and financial products and services were delivered in more varied ways, and supermarkets shifted from the high street to new, out-of-town, hypermarkets. Re-engineering changed patterns of consumption as well as the processes by which services were organized and delivered. The definitive characteristic of re-engineering rested upon the way in which new technologies were introduced. Previous generations of new technologies served primarily to automate traditional manual administrative and clerical activities. The introduction of mainframe computers in the 1960s and 1970s enabled financial institutions, for example, to automate data processing and facilitated the electronic storage of vast amounts of paper-based information. The second generation of computer technologies served to distribute these data around the organization through the use of minicomputers at branch level. Re-engineering of whole work processes was only made possible by the convergence of telecommunications and computing technologies, which facilitated the development of local networks and new forms of customer–staff interaction. This third generation of technological change provided the capacity for enterprises to change their organizational structures as well as work processes, as one senior executive in a UK insurance company described:

> Generations one and two replicated what they found. They were based upon the old administrative and policy systems serving a devolved branch structure. The third generation of systems has become the driving force for rearranging past processes with administration being concentrated in regional centres. In these a combination of Adam Smith and Henry Ford take over. (Interview with senior management executive, UK insurance company, 1997)

In financial services, the third generation of technological systems facilitated a reorganization of work processes, and changes in the mode of service delivery and in skills and occupational structures. Location no longer determined whether staff would be in contact with the customer. Back office staff were as likely to deal with customers as those situated in high street branches. All staff who engaged with the customer were required to become salespersons, even though their work environment varied according to whether they were located within a call centre/direct line operation or within a traditional department or branch setting.

Typically, call centre and direct line operations took on the character of the white-collar factory. The work process was broken down into specific functions like cheque processing, customer enquiries and data entry, with the majority of staff required to concentrate on specific, narrowly defined tasks that were routine and repetitive. While staff may have been encouraged to rotate between tasks, the workplace contained many of the characteristics of the assembly line, as this description of the Bank of Scotland's Visa Centre revealed:

> Work organisation at the Centre resembled a computer-based assembly line. Several hundred dumb terminals were linked to the mainframe for the entry of customer data and answering customer queries through the FDR package. [First Data Resources (FDR) was a subsidiary of American Express that specialized in providing the software and machinery required for processing centres.] The majority of staff worked on the terminals in a large open-planned space subdivided at intervals by screens to separate off different functional areas. Except for the handful of women who directly supervised the labour process, all the work was screen-based; and all the pressures of cost and volume characteristic of highly intensive work systems were much in evidence . . . efficiency reflected the operators' speed in putting through work as applications handlers and payments clearers. For example, the Centre management opted for a local telephone exchange system and a payments processing system, both of which made the women's work easier to monitor. (Fincham *et al.*, 1994: 90)

The tendency in these white-collar factories was for skills to polarize between the unskilled tasks done by women employed at the computer terminals and the 'career jobs' (Fincham *et al.*, 1994: 91) which involved developing the IT systems and planning and overseeing the work.

While the white-collar factories tended to be established in greenfield sites, those financial service employees who continued to work in more traditional departmental settings were no less prone to changes in work organization and skills mix. In both banking and insurance industries, traditional skills, such as underwriting, claims and loans evaluation, largely disappeared with the development of software which could process most standard types of application. These skills traditionally provided the basis for career development within management structures. Their disappearance affected, therefore, the fundamental basis of the hierarchical management order. Companies shifted towards the establishment of functional teams who dealt with financial and insurance 'packages' which crossed the traditional discipline boundaries. For example, insurance staff who previously specialized in pensions, life, motor or household insurance were forced to develop a 'generic' skills base which enabled them to piece together customized packages for individual and corporate clients. Staff were reorganized into teams which cut across traditional departmental boundaries, and the management function was no longer based upon specialist knowledge but upon broader operations management skills. This shift facilitated the recruitment of non-specialist management staff from outside the financial service industries whose skills were derived from experience in commerce and industry (Interview with insurance company senior executive, 1997). The differentiation between different types of financial service activities provided the opportunity for institutions to revise their organizational structures, with many establishing separate business units whose performance could be more closely monitored. This pattern of organizational change enabled companies to identify profit and performance targets which cascaded down the organization to the workplace and team level.

In financial services, restructuring embraced the phasing out of traditional skills, the polarization of the workforce between a majority of unskilled and semi-skilled staff and a minority of skilled technical staff and managers, and the introduction of new work methods that emphasized either the routinization of tasks or their clustering into cooperative and interdependent forms of working undertaken by multifunctional teams. This pattern of change was not confined to financial services. It was also evident in such sectors as the health service in the UK. In the NHS, a minority of nursing staff, for example, had their skills upgraded, while a new type of less skilled health care assistant was introduced in the early 1990s. While this process should not be analysed as merely 'deskilling', it represented a move by the state, as employer, to 'play on the nebulous character of skill in nursing, and by redefining grades and grade boundaries was able to substitute cheaper labour for the more expensive grades, a process which can be described succinctly as "grade dilution"' (Thornley, 1996: 165). Like the financial services, the NHS experienced significant change in management personnel and organization. The Department of Health (DoH) sought changes in the skills mix and required local managers to identify the 'most cost effective use of professional skills' (DoH, 1989: 15) and the Dyson Report of 1992 suggested that trusts could reduce costs by cutting the proportion of skilled to semi-skilled and unskilled staff. Secondary care (provided usually by hospitals) developed new approaches to the labour process which in many ways emulated those developments within processing centres – with the emphasis on improving patient throughput – while primary care (general practice) was consolidated into health centres consisting of teams whose skill boundaries had been redefined.

In summary, the re-engineering of service industries has encompassed significant changes in occupational structures, skills mix and work organization. In turn, particularly in industries such as the financial services, these developments have been facilitated by technological change. While there have been important differences between sectors and an uneven process of workplace restructuring, it is possible to identify some common themes. First, technological change, particularly in financial services, has not merely sought to automate what were previously manual processes. It has incorporated decision-making and intellectual activities that have impacted upon traditional skills and professions (whether of the physician or the underwriter). Second, the disturbance of traditional professional skills has served to change the form of the hierarchical division of labour, enabling management functions to be undertaken by 'non-professional' staff whose primary concern has been to improve business efficiency. Third, changes in the skills mix have tended to cause a polarization between a minority of skilled and a majority of unskilled staff or employees whose skills (particularly in the caring professions) have been devalued. Finally, these developments have contributed to an uneven pattern of labour intensification in which the activities of staff have been increasingly subjected to performance measurement.

The internalization of intensification

The restructuring of service industries has involved widespread changes in skills, occupational structures and patterns of working time. Change has occurred at a relatively rapid rate. Within a decade in the UK many sectors have moved from situations of employment growth and record levels of profitability to conditions in which employment levels have fallen in, for example, retail banking, insurance and public service professions like nursing. Profits have been squeezed and institutions subjected to increased competition via competitive tendering, deregulation and privatization. Staff no longer expect to hold a job for life and are constantly reminded of the precarious nature of their employment. Given these conditions, it is important to consider why management–labour relations have remained relatively stable and why employees have tended to participate in changes which have contributed to the intensification of their own labour. What have been the essential ingredients of the glue which has bound employees to management strategies designed to raise labour intensity? It has three main aspects: the individualization of benefit/reward systems; the absorption of a customer-centred service orientation; and the marginalization of collectivism. The first two elements constitute the ways in which labour is encouraged to perceive itself and its experience of work, and the third refers to the wider social institutions and contexts which may influence or modify these individualized perceptions, depending upon the strengths/weaknesses of labour's own collective organization. In the absence of a countervailing union influence on the employment relationship, the more likely it is that individuals are susceptible to those techniques designed to achieve the internalization of management values.

Traditional payment systems in the public and private services tended to be based on salary scales which rewarded professional qualifications and length of service. By contrast, new approaches have required individuals to participate in the evaluation of their own performance. In this context, performance appraisal has incorporated criteria aimed at evaluating attitudes and values as well as those capacities associated with the more specifically defined capacity to 'do the job'. New reward systems have also contained symbolic as well as financial elements, with the symbolic reflected in the recognition of the individual's contribution to the well-being of the company or service. In this context, the role of reward systems has shifted from being based mainly upon the use of financial payments as a means of motivation to a broader one which defines individuals' perception of their own worth in relation to their contribution to the goals of the institution or service for which they work. In their study of employees in a life insurance company, Knights and Morgan (1996: 222) succinctly illustrated this shift:

> In our case study managers as well as sales staff are transformed, through the disciplines and mechanisms of power, into subjects whose self-definition or identity demands that they work hard at meeting targets, earning large commissions, competing for prizes so as to secure a sense of themselves as both competent and successful.

The traditional mechanisms underpinning management authority and power were complemented by techniques through which employees' self-identify was related to their contribution to the company's mission, values and needs. In turn, these values and objectives were reinforced in the company's internal communications and training programmes. The individualization of the employee's contractual relationship with management has also been underpinned by changes in the forms of non-financial benefits offered by enterprises. The social benefits awarded to employees have tended to reaffirm individual rather than collective forms of protection and advancement. Companies have introduced private health and medical insurance schemes and encouraged staff to opt into counselling for a wide range of employment and non-employment related problems.

The second element contributing to the internalization of management values has been the development of a strong customer service orientation through which the contractual relation between employer and employed has been overlaid by a relationship between purchasers and providers of services. The traditional management demands received 'from above' for quality and efficiency are represented as arising from the needs of the market, whether it is an internal market, as in the NHS, or an external one driven by competition between enterprises. In this way, all employees become sellers of services and this sales orientation is reinforced in their daily experience of work. For example, the pressures experienced by service providers in local government, health and other parts of the welfare state are increasingly perceived by staff as arising from the potential or actual threat of privatization, contracting out or market testing, which themselves impose pressures to contain costs and improve productivity and encourage staff to collude with local management in attempts to 'prove' their efficiency.

Trade union membership density in service industries remained strong during the first half of the 1990s in the UK. Most sectors retained higher density levels than manufacturing and higher average levels of density than existed across the economy as a whole. Despite this numerical strength, several analyses have suggested that unions often exercised relatively little influence over the restructuring process and were often by-passed or marginalized by management. In their evaluation of union responses to the new management techniques, Ackers *et al.* (1996) drew attention to the failure of British trade unions to develop a practical response to the new management strategies associated with human resource management (HRM). Bacon and Storey (1996) argued that the union response to new employee commitment programmes was to adjust or accommodate to the individualizing of workplace relations. Cave (1994) went as far as to suggest that, under conditions in which collective organization had weakened considerably, it was necessary for unions themselves to adopt the new customer service orientation towards their own members and forsake the posturing that often accompanied the traditional adversarial approach to management.

Some authors suggest that unions have been relatively unsuccessful in challenging the shift towards the individualization of employment relations or providing alternative perspectives through which the internalization of management values could be checked or countered. Indeed, some unions have even begun to adopt the terminology of the individualist agenda (Bacon and Storey, 1996: 43). On the other hand, other authors have argued that there is no automatic connection between the application of the new management techniques and the marginalization of union influence (Fairbrother, 1994, 1996), and there is some justification in the view that the new techniques may have created at workplace level new types of collective responses which may have little in common with the traditional forms of collective industrial action. The suggestion here is that such a proposition has not been extensively tested, particularly since change in workplace relations in service industries has not received the detailed attention it deserves. The case studies in the following parts begin to address this oversight.

Summary

This chapter has argued that the past decade has represented a watershed in management–labour relations in service industries. Management has adopted new approaches designed to achieve what might be called the real subordination of service labour. At the centre of this emulation of the labour process in production industries has been the intensification of labour. While critics of the new management techniques have widely reported their application as leading to an increase in intensity, the specific character of intensification has remained poorly theorized. Here four main characteristics of intensification have been identified: the widespread introduction of performance measures, the re-engineering of work processes through the utilization of new generations of technologies, the experimentation with new patterns of working time and the introduction of new practices aimed at the internalization of management values that encourage labour to participate in the raising of its own intensity. The extent to which labour has been able to resist or moderate these trends towards intensification is an important theme in the chapters that follow.

PART 2

FINANCIAL SERVICES

Restructuring in the UK Finance Sector

The 1990s has been a period of transformation in the financial services sector. Traditional patterns of employment, work organization and customer relations have been swept aside. New market conditions and technological and organizational innovation have combined to create a pattern of irreversible change in the sector. The traditional image of a workplace in the financial services sector is a small, high street branch of a bank, building society or insurance company. Work centres on face-to-face contact with the customer and transactions occur through the exchange of cash and paper. The branch employs a small number of staff whose roles are clearly defined and conform to a well established pattern of career progression. This image persisted to the late 1980s. It is has been displaced within a decade by a new one in which cash and paper transactions are displaced by electronic exchanges, staff are engaged on a range of permanent and casual contracts, and are required to work flexibly, and customer links are geographically separated by hundreds of miles. The typical workplace is likely to be large, with the branch being displaced by the 'white-collar factory'.

Two key factors have been the catalysts of this transformation. First, there has been a significant change in the market conditions prevailing in the financial services. This has been fuelled in the UK by a combination of economic recession and deregulation. The recessionary conditions that prevailed in the late 1980s and early 1990s created pressures on profit margins. Banks, for example, were required to cover a rising burden of bad debt and insurance companies were forced to meet a significant growth in claims from personal and corporate customers. These adverse and volatile market conditions were exacerbated by the increased competition between banks, building societies and insurance companies arising from the deregulation of the sector in 1986. Deregulation enabled companies to cross the traditional divides between the banking, insurance and mortgage industries, encouraging each to compete with the other in presenting new combinations of financial services or 'packages' to personal and corporate customers.

Second, the financial services have been at the centre of technical innovation, initially through the introduction of new process technologies and subsequently through their use as a means to deliver new products and services to customers. Up to the late 1980s, technological change had relatively little effect on employment levels and traditional patterns of work organization. As companies began to experience lower profit margins, increased competition and rising pressures on costs, technical innovation was used increasingly as a key weapon in the implementation of rationalization programmes.

Rationalization has involved a combination of changes in employment patterns, management structures and work organization. Employment in the UK financial services rose steadily in the 1980s, but 1990 was the watershed. Employment levels have declined in each year since then within the financial institutions that dominate the banking, insurance and building society industries. There has also been a change in the gender composition of employment, with the proportion of part-time women workers increasing. Management grades have been cut as a result of the adoption of 'delayering' policies and new business strategies pursued, with the emphasis shifting to a more commercial approach to sales and customer services.

Changes in work organization have been closely associated with the introduction of new technologies. In the 1960s and 1970s technological change was used to support the traditional branch structures of banks and building societies. Mainframe computers provided the processing power required to ease the burden on branch-based 'back office' activities, which typically involved transactions processing of payrolls, customer accounts and other clerical activities. Computerization facilitated the centralization of administrative tasks within processing centres away from the branch back office. The growing range and complexity of financial transactions in the 1960s and 1970s prompted the development of specialized database systems designed specifically for use within the financial services sector. By the mid-1970s many of the larger financial institutions established on-line links between central mainframe databases and local branches. These enabled management to receive more accurate information on business activities within branches, and helped to provide more effective controls over the planning and monitoring of work. By the late 1970s computerization spread to most workplaces within the sector and was no longer the preserve of the processing centre.

The early 1980s saw the introduction of personal computers (PCs). PCs offered opportunities for the more flexible application of software packages to a range of front and back office tasks. A second development was the introduction of digital communications technologies which helped organizations to move towards the total integration of computer systems and enabled the introduction of automated teller machines (ATMs) and electronic funds transfer at the point of sale (EFTPOS).

Restructuring in the Service Industries

The integration of communications and computing technologies offered the opportunity for the financial services institutions to begin to offer new types of products and services to customers, though the rate of diffusion of these integrated systems varied within the sector. The larger clearing banks in the UK tended to innovate faster than the insurance companies (Fincham *et al.*, 1994: 154–6). By the late 1980s, technological innovation provided the opportunity for financial institutions to review extensively the relationships between back and front office functions. Technology could be used to by-pass completely the local branch, providing customers with opportunities to interface directly with an institution's 'back office' banking facilities. EFTPOS and ATMs enabled traditional branch-based activities to be delivered within the 'wider external economy' (Cressey and Scott, 1992: 89) and telephone banking services offered the opportunities for transactions to take place outside the branch and traditional office hours.

These developments provided the capability for a fundamental restructuring of work organization and service delivery. Branches were reorganized and their number dramatically reduced, particularly in the banking industry, with many of their functions being transferred to regional processing centres. The processing centre became the focal point of the operations of many institutions, providing opportunities for the displacement of labour-intensive branch-based activities by more highly automated, routinized processing factories. This shift involved significant changes in the composition of the workforce, its skills and career structures. It also facilitated important changes in the structure and organization of the division of labour within the financial services. The complex range of tasks involved in data processing have been either retained in-house by institutions or partly or wholly outsourced to specialist 'third party' processing companies. These companies have their origins within either the financial services or computing industries.

The financial services case studies in Chapters 4 and 5 provide insights into the restructuring process within the financial services. Chapter 4 analyses the emergence of a third party processor within the UK banking sector in the 1990s, while Chapter 5 looks at the changing character of a UK insurance company that experienced a major programme of restructuring between 1994 and 1997. The case studies illustrate how, during the 1990s, enterprises embarked upon a process of rapid change which undermined long established work patterns and traditional approaches to workplace relations. The 'white-collar factory' discussed in Chapter 4 was established in 1972 as a processing centre for a consortium of retail banks. While in its early days the factory was perceived as performing an unusual service within the banking sector, by the 1990s its systems of work organization began to assume a character that was increasingly typical of the sector. In this sense, Credit UK was at the cutting edge of new forms of work organization within the industry. Chapter 4 provides a unique picture of the history and development of the plant. By contrast, the UK insurer discussed in Chapter 5 epitomized the long tradition of the UK insurance industry. Founded in the eighteenth century, the company had long traded on its distinguished past, but by the 1990s what previously had been its strength became its weakness. Its weakening financial and market position created the necessity for a process of rapid restructuring that amounted to a traumatic period of change for management and workforce alike. While the case studies deal with enterprises with highly contrasting histories, the chapters reveal a pattern of change that contains many common features.

4 CREDIT UK: THE WHITE-COLLAR FACTORY

Introduction

The credit card industry first developed in the United States. Consumer credit usually took one of two forms: 'closed end' loans or 'open end' loans. Closed end loans were based on fixed term regular repayments and used for such things as home mortgages, car and major home appliances purchases. These repayments were for a fixed amount and were repaid over a set time period. Open end loans had no fixed payment amount or time period for repayment. The repayment arrangements were fixed by the customer within credit line limits, with the minimum repayment amount usually being fixed between 20 and 50 per cent of the billed balance which had to be repaid within a specific time period. In the USA consumer instalment credit expanded dramatically between 1946 and 1955 as family formation increased through soldiers re-entering civilian society and the backlog of consumer demand generated by war-time controls was unleashed. Consumer instalment credit growth exceeded 20 per cent per annum between 1946 and 1955, fell to a level of between 5 and 15 per cent between 1956 and 1975 and returned to an annual growth rate of around 20 per cent in 1984. The development of open end loans in the UK occurred later than in the USA, emerging on a modest scale in the mid-1960s and expanding significantly in the 1970s.

Credit UK was established in 1972 and expanded quickly, taking advantage of the growth in consumer demand for open end credit provision. The company was founded by a consortium of five UK clearing banks and existed primarily to process the credit card transactions of each of its parent institutions. The company situated its processing plant in a town located on the south east coast, within commuting distance of London. The volume of the plant's processing activities dramatically rose throughout the 1970s and 1980s. In the 1980s, however, increased competition between banks for a variety of customer services and rising public concern over the operation of UK credit card cartels caused the parent companies to distance themselves from their creation. In 1990 Credit UK changed its name to the Credit Consortium and was prepared for sale. In 1991 it was purchased by a major American company, Global Data Corporation (GDC). GDC incorporated the UK company within its data processing division and began to develop a strategy aimed at turning the company into a major third party processing concern. The following sections examine the historical development of the company within its sector and the evolution of management and workforce at workplace level, and explains the dynamics that shaped workplace relations at plant level. The concluding section draws together some analytical themes and issues that arise from the case study.

The Historical Context

From the early 1970s there were two main credit card retail networks in the UK. These were Barclays and Credit UK. Barclays established its Barclaycard in June 1966. It was the first Visa card introduced in the UK. Credit UK was established in 1972 to 'perform the retailer, marketing, general advertising and promotion and data processing functions, whilst the respective banks each individually retained responsibility for credit holder recruitment' (BIFU, 1988: 7). The new company provided the opportunity for its parent institutions to establish a sound base in the expanding market for credit cards. Credit UK pursued activities in marketing and data processing that were different from those found in conventional banking. In the marketing context the new credit card had to be sold positively to both potential cardholders and retailers, and a processing plant was required that could deal efficiently with the projected growth in the volume of credit-based transactions. Market growth for Credit UK occurred at a rapid rate throughout the period 1972–87. The growth was measured in two ways: the number of cards issued to customers and the number of retail outlets accepting the credit card. The number of cards issued to customers rose dramatically. Between 1978 and 1987, for example, the cards issued rose from just over three and a half million to over eleven million in the UK. During the same period, the number of retail outlets accepting the card more than doubled, rising from 123,000 to 286,000. In 1973 Credit UK joined Eurocard International, the European equivalent of Mastercard, and, in 1975, it became a principal member of Master Card International, thus providing the basis for its acceptance as an internationally recognized credit card. Through these developments Credit UK established itself as an effective intermediary between its founding institutions and the international credit card market, while also asserting an overwhelming domination, in conjunction with Barclaycard, over the UK credit card market.

During the 1980s the Monopolies and Mergers Commission (MMC) took a growing interest in the UK credit card market. In its 1980 report it expressed concern at the grip of the clearing banks over the market, but its findings were largely ignored within the industry. As retailers and building societies moved into the credit card market during the course of the 1980s, the MMC came under increased pressure from within the industry to undertake a further investigation into the role of clearing banks in the sector. The MMC began a second investigation of the credit card market in 1988. Its second report was published in 1989 and challenged many of the business practices adopted by the cartel within the industry. The report was, however, in many ways overtaken by events within the sector. Rapid changes in the competitive structure of the credit card market served to undermine the basis of the cartel's operations. The October 1987 crash, deregulation and the rapid development of global money markets sharpened competition between the UK clearing banks. These competitive pressures undermined the conditions that had given rise to the existence of the Credit UK company as the agent of its parent institutions. Between 1988 and 1990 the company adopted a new business strategy, a strategy that had been forced upon it as a result of pressures from three external sources: the MMC, the wider restructuring of the financial services sector and the changing business approaches of its founding institutions.

The company strategy was based primarily on moving towards greater independence from the institutions that had created it. The movement was reflected in two fundamental developments. First, the company relinquished its marketing functions and concentrated solely on its role as a data processing concern. Second, the company moved from being 'a cost centre not a profit centre, the creature of its constituent banks, to being a self standing profit centre with all the related changes in financial accounting that this shift required' (Interview with employee relations manager, 1989). The effects of the shift in accounting techniques from cost to profit centre were not confined to the financial management of the enterprise. Its introduction had important implications for management organization, employment conditions and work practices and prepared the way for the subsequent sale of the company to GDC in 1991.

The sale to GDC confirmed that the future role of the UK plant would be in third party transaction card processing. The UK plant was located within the company's card services group, which was a world leader in card processing. GDC's growth in the USA was associated with the development of processing hardware and software. Its headquarters was located in Omaha, Nebraska. The company's strategy for developing its UK acquisition had three main strands. First, it sought to expand the customer base of the UK plant by concentrating on securing contracts with financial institutions within the UK for the processing of credit and debit transactions. Second, the company undertook a programme of piecemeal investment aimed at upgrading the processing technologies through the introduction of new software and hardware. Third, the company sought to raise plant efficiency and productivity through reforming management organization, cutting staffing levels and improving work organization.

Within five years, several of these objectives had been achieved. By 1996, the company had attracted a number of new customers from the financial services and other industries. It had moved into new processing activities and was beginning to use its UK base to develop its core processing services into other markets in the Middle East, South East Asia and Australia. The US parent company had also, in 1995, merged with one of its main rivals in the USA, a merger that created a company of over 36,000 employees with around 75 per cent of its revenues coming from the expanding payments services and financial segments of it businesses. Following the merger, the new American company established eleven business units covering areas like transaction card services, database management, telecommunications, imaging systems, health care (a health care cost management organization serving the self-insured corporate market) and mutual fund processing. The UK operation was located within the transaction card services business unit and was the main European base of the global corporation.

In its first quarter century of operation, the UK processing plant experienced several phases of development in relation to business strategy and market conditions. In many ways the plant has been at the cutting edge of developments within the financial services sector, experiencing rapid expansion, the shift to a more commercial orientation, rationalization and, more recently, take-over and the restructuring of its core operations. The plant offers unique insights into the changing character of workplace relations within the financial services sector and useful comparisons between UK and American management approaches. Before we explore these in depth, it may be useful to outline some of the main characteristics of the management and workforce as these developed over the period 1972 to 1996.

The management

In 1972 the managing directors and senior management staff of Credit UK were either seconded or transferred to the new company from its founding institutions. The post of chairperson of the new company was rotated between senior management staff drawn from the parent banks. The management structure was hierarchical, based upon the style and ethos of the 'traditional' UK banking industry. This structure persisted throughout the 1970s and into the early 1980s.

In response to the changing market conditions in the card processing industry, the management style began to change in piecemeal fashion from the mid-1980s. Credit UK began to develop a more proactive approach to marketing and sales, and moved away from a management style that was largely informed by simply responding to the needs of the parent institutions. In 1988 an industrialist was appointed to the first permanent chief executive post created within the company. The chief executive had no background in the UK banking industry. His task was to oversee the shift within the company from cost to profit centre and facilitate the introduction of conventional measures of performance in relation to accounting and work organization. The years 1988–90 saw several changes in management structure and organization. The top tiers of senior management were cut and middle management layers reduced, while new supervisory grades were introduced on the shopfloor. The new management team consisted of staff mainly drawn from outside the banking industry, while the older managers brought up in the banking industry 'tradition' were retired or removed. These developments created the conditions for the company to be prepared for sale, finally breaking from the institutions that had created it.

The take-over in 1991 served to accelerate the shift in management style towards a more commercial, competitive operation. The plant was no longer able to rely upon its parent companies to guarantee its processing activities. Contracts had to be renegotiated and new customers found. At the same time, the wider sectoral conditions within financial services had changed significantly as a result of the world recession and its impact upon the credit card industry. The new American owners introduced a voluntary redundancy programme and established an approach to employee relations that combined elements of business re-engineering and human resource management. The plant's 'core' activities were defined, a mission plan was drawn up and work arrangements were reshaped to accommodate the introduction of team working. The period 1991–6 saw the introduction of an American-style management model that had profound implications for employment and workplace relations. An aggressive approach was established to securing contracts with new partners. This marketing strategy was linked to the implementation of policies designed to encourage the customer orientation of staff. Communications between senior management and staff were reviewed. The internal company magazine highlighted the performance of high achievers. Pay systems were progressively reformed to award performance and staff were provided with an employee care package which incorporated access to counselling and private health care insurance.[1] Many of these changes were imposed rather than agreed with the union, with the consequence that the influence exercised by the union over workplace affairs was severely weakened. In short, the case study provides insights into a process that exemplifies a management strategy aimed at union marginalization.

The workforce

The decision to locate in a south east coastal town was strongly influenced by the characteristics of the local labour market: 'Prior to our launch we identified suitable premises at acceptable costs for a location in the south east, together with a potential workforce of the right type and size. Those criteria have remained as the business has expanded over the last fifteen years' (Local Authority Business Brochure, 1987). The company identified a location in which the local labour market contained a higher percentage of young, married women than the national average. Other financial services companies had made similar judgements about the local labour market when deciding upon the location of their processing plants. Barclaycard found that Northampton fulfilled this requirement when it located there in 1966 (BIFU, 1988: 20) and the Bank of Scotland reached a similar decision when it decided to situate its Visa centre on a greenfield site near Dunfermline, where 'census and population returns for the area indicated a large supply of "married ladies who are really excellent workers"' (Fincham et al, 1994: 87). The availability of married women workers ensured a ready supply of labour that would be willing to work on a part-time basis. A second reason for the location of the UK Credit plant on the south east coast was because there was a sound telecommunication structure and spare capacity in telephone lines.

Employment at Credit UK significantly expanded throughout the 1970s and most of the 1980s, reaching a peak in 1988. The gender balance within the workforce was always tilted towards women being the majority of employees. Throughout the plant's lifetime, about two-thirds of the workforce were women, a significant proportion of whom were part-time employees on permanent contracts, most of which were located in the ranges 1–15 hours per week or 16–20 hours per week. The key feature of employment patterns in the 1990s has been the number of job losses, over 1,300 (38 per cent of the total workforce) since the 1988 employment peak (see Table 4.1). In addition, there has been a steady growth in the number of employees on fixed-term contracts. By 1996 these constituted about 11 per cent of the total workforce. There were two main workplaces that constituted the south east plant. The original plant, established in 1972, was located in the coastal town and the second, located a few miles away, was set up in 1986. It was established on an industrial estate close to a new town. The workforce in these workplaces was divided into production and non-production areas. The largest of these included telephonics, data capture, systems and programming, operations services, output services, data processing, client services and cheque clearing.

Table 4.1 *Employment at Credit UK 1972–96*

| Year | Men | Women | | Total no. of employees |
		Total	Part-time	
1972	150	300	100	450
1980	850	1650	595	2500
1988	1135	2288	828	3423
1996	716	1390	600	2106*

* Includes 222 staff on fixed-term contracts

Source: BIFU (1988), Company internal memorandum (1996)

The union

The Banking, Insurance and Finance Union (BIFU) secured a recognition agreement with Credit UK when it was established in 1972. BIFU membership covered all grades of workers. The recognition agreement and terms and conditions of employment were broadly similar to those pertaining in the partner institutions that founded the new company. Employees were encouraged to consider themselves as 'bank' staff, and many had relatives working in the banking industry in London and the surrounding south east area(interview with employee relations manager, 1989). In the 1970s membership density at Credit UK stood at around 50 per cent of the workforce. During the 1980s membership density tended to fluctuate between 40 and 60 per cent, though it did rise for a short period to around 65 per cent in 1988 following a recruitment campaign which primarily focused on the new town site. By the mid-1990s density had fallen back to a little over 20 per cent of the workforce. The union developed two branches, one at the coastal town plant in the 1970s and a second at the new town site in the mid-1980s.

Union representative roles were similar to those to be found in the main UK clearing banks. BIFU had a seconded representative, an employee of Credit UK, who undertook full-time trade union duties. The seconded representative was paid by the company and had an office on site. In addition, the union had a number of accredited representatives. These were elected from the membership and had responsibility for groups of members located in specific work areas. As accredited representatives they had the right to raise issues with local management and time off from their work for trade union duties. The number of accredited representatives rose to a peak of 23 in 1988. Since that time, as union density levels have dropped, so has the number of accredited representatives. By 1996 the number had fallen to 13. The gender balance among representatives was broadly consistent with that of the workforce as a whole. The majority have been women since the late 1970s. By 1996, however, the gender balance shifted decisively towards women. Of the 13 accredited representatives, 11 were women.

Union recognition rights and collective agreements were retained when Credit UK was sold to GDC in 1991. However, in the five years following the take-over, union organization suffered the affects of rationalization at the two workplaces. In 1993, the union lost the right to retain a seconded representative, paid for by the company. The company cited the decline in membership density as the main reason for withdrawing this role. In turn, the union, recognizing the importance of sustaining a union presence, appointed a 'secretary' who was paid by BIFU and undertook the task of administering union business at the local level. The secretary was appointed in 1994 but her role was contested by the company. The union secured modest office facilities on company premises for the secretary. In turn, the company sought to ensure that she did not adopt the role as an officer of the union. She was not recognized by the company as an organizer or negotiator, though in practice she provided essential advice and support to the union's representatives and members at workplace level.

The union's two branches held meetings on company premises and maintained a modest level of membership involvement throughout the 1980s and early 1990s. The accredited representatives played a 'dual' role as branch officers. In turn, these local activists were supported by BIFU full-time officers. Senior full-time officers played a leading role in negotiations with the company from its inception in 1972. By the mid-1990s this role had not changed. Both Credit UK and its American successor placed considerable emphasis on the protocols associated with negotiating with a senior full-time official of the union. In the mid-1990s, this officer was an assistant general secretary of the union. He was, in turn, supported by a full-time officer who provided advice and support for the local lay representatives, particularly in areas such as recruitment and collective bargaining advice. The officers and lay officials met bi-monthly at the union's institutional committee, which in practice was the committee that had responsibility for the union's activities within the company. The institutional committee met during company time and off company premises. Most accredited representatives attended regularly, though some had difficulties with local managers in securing release to attend meetings and others, particularly following the American take-over, found that the pressures of work often created problems for them when they returned to the workplace.

The Changing Context of Workplace Relations

During the 1970s, workplace relations at Credit UK mirrored those that prevailed in the banking industry, despite the differences in the form of work organization and patterns of employment that prevailed. Managers largely perceived themselves as 'a small group of bankers' working within the traditional norms and customs of the sector (Interview with senior industrial relations manager, 1989). Personnel policy and industrial relations practices adhered to sector norms. The collective agreement covering Credit UK was similar to that which prevailed in one of its leading parent institutions. Between 1975 and 1979 the union role was progressively institutionalized as written agreements were extended to cover consultation rights, time off for union duties, grievance handling and disciplinary procedures. The growth in the credit card market secured the role of the new plant, and this security, in turn, provided the climate in which the potential for conflict between union and employer was minimized. Another factor which influenced the conduct of workplace relations was the social contract legislation introduced by the Labour government between 1974 and 1979. The legal framework facilitated the institutionalization of the union's role on the 'greenfield' site and provided the foundation for the growth in the union's role in relation to representation and consultation between management and workforce.

The period 1980–8 was a transitionary phase in the process of workplace relations shifting away from the 'traditional' pattern established by the founding clearing banks and towards an independent commercially oriented outlook. Several factors created the opportunity for this shift towards greater independence. First, the accelerated growth in the customer and retail markets for credit cards required a significant expansion in the data processing function. This, in turn, created the need for high levels of capital investment and the shifting of the plant towards greater efficiency in managing and controlling the labour process. Market growth pressed the company into embedding work methods that had much in common with a continuous process plant, more usually found in the manufacturing sector than in financial services. Second, the company's relationship to its founding institutions began to come under pressure as a result of the interest shown by the MMC in the cartel operating in the credit card sector. The 1980 MMC Report provided a rationale for Credit UK to achieve a greater independence from the clearing banks. Third, the company found itself under pressure from the union to achieve greater legal clarity on the employment status of staff at Credit UK. In 1983 an industrial tribunal case was taken up on behalf of an employee who had been seconded to work at Credit UK from one of the founding institutions. Over time his employment conditions had changed and his employee status had become unclear. The case caused the company to review its attitudes towards secondments and provided the impetus for it to establish a more independent approach to its domestic employment policies. This was reflected in the adoption of new procedures in the mid-1980s for the recruitment of senior and middle management staff. As 'old-style bankers' retired, they were replaced by new staff drawn from outside the banking sector.

These developments had a significant impact upon the conduct of workplace relations in the 1980s, and were reflected in the negotiating positions adopted by management and union. In brief, the company sought to establish procedures, agreements and work practices more consistent with its views of 'good commercial industrial practice' (Interview with employee relations manager, 1989), while the union attempted to hold on to the employment status and practices that had traditionally prevailed in the banking and finance sector. Company personnel policy shifted in emphasis away from the joint management of institutionalized relations between company and union and toward managing the workforce as 'a staff resource' (Interview with employee relations manager, 1989). The operationalizing of this policy change was reflected in a series of new management initiatives introduced between 1981 and 1988.

A new procedure agreement was introduced in 1981, with union acceptance. The agreement brought to an end the automatic referral to arbitration on pay negotiations and saw the introduction of a new grievance procedure, designed, from management's perspective, to increase the direct role of line management in handling and resolving local disputes. A new payment system was phased in in 1982–3 following an extensive job evaluation exercise. The workforce was divided into three grades – clerical, data processing and technical services – with each being subject to a different job evaluation scheme. This enabled the company to introduce significant differentials into the payment system by, for example, acknowledging the market value of programmers and developers and giving them higher basic grade rates than other groups of workers. In practice, the introduction of the job evaluation system increased management's discretion over pay rates and differentials and encouraged workers to identify more with their pay grade than with the collective interests of the 'whole' workforce. The implementation of the job evaluation exercise was followed four years later by further developments that served to marginalize union influence over pay. In 1987 technical services staff were brought under the same job evaluation scheme as clerical staff. Harmonization ended the blue- and white-collar distinction and provided management with an effective way of overcoming the challenges presented by the Equal Pay for Work of Equal Value legislation (Interview with employee relations manager, 1989). At the same time, performance-related pay (PRP) was introduced via the adoption of a performance appraisal scheme that provided for an annually negotiated cost of living rise plus an additional increase based upon the assessment of an individual's performance. Performance was measured in relation to three levels – standard, merit and outstanding – and its linkage to pay provided the company with the pretext to develop a range of productivity and performance measures in each working area. The system was modified in 1988 to reduce the cost of living and increase the performance element. The changes in job descriptions, the adoption of new performance measures and the reorganization of work that arose from the search for new ways of raising productivity caused the union's seconded representative of that time to refer to this period as the one in which the 'white-collar factory' was created (Interview with BIFU seconded representative, 1989).

The changes achieved through the introduction of a new pay system, job evaluation schemes and procedural agreements reflected the company's success in pushing the workforce away from 'bank clerk' conditions during the 1980s. The company, however, did not succeed in all its endeavours. It was over the Rest of South East (ROSE) allowance that the workforce first signalled a hostile reaction to the loss of its bank clerk status. The ROSE allowance was paid by the clearing banks to staff who lived in the south east of England. It was a lump sum annual payment received in addition to the basic salary, and was initially designed to compensate staff for living in a more costly part of the UK. Credit UK inherited this agreement from the clearing institutions. In 1986 the company decided to end the payment of the ROSE allowance, making clear to staff its view that the allowance was an anachronism and that the company no longer adhered to employment practices that applied to the banking industry.

BIFU opposed the scrapping of the ROSE allowance and gained the support of members for its opposition at a well attended union meeting. There was widespread indignation at the company's decision to take away an allowance that other bank employees received. According to the union's seconded representative: 'the entire workforce was with the union. The company was visibly shocked. A thousand people were in the canteen for the meeting. Following that meeting management informally told us they would go to ACAS with a better offer' (Interview with seconded representative, 1989). The company was forced to negotiate. The Advisory, Conciliation and Arbitration Service (ACAS) was used to arbitrate.[2] A settlement was reached which involved the consolidation of a one-off lump sum of £750 into basic rates. The company had achieved the symbolic break from 'ROSEland' but the union had safeguarded earnings and provided for some groups of workers, who received bonus payments as a percentage of basic pay, a significant increase in earnings. The union had, at least temporarily, returned from the margins in its relations with the company and strengthened its credibility among the workforce. Union recruitment improved significantly during and shortly after the ROSEland allowance dispute. This success proved a temporary check on the company's aspirations to make a decisive shift towards independence from traditional banking industry employment conditions.

From 1988, management openly proclaimed its commitment to independence from its parent institutions. The pace of the move was accelerated by rapid changes in product and market conditions. The MMC second enquiry, published in July 1989, placed further pressures on the clearing banks' cartel and the banks themselves were drawn into greater direct competition as a consequence of deregulation. New credit card operators, like Halifax and other building societies, moved into the market, and banks like Lloyds moved to join both the major credit card operations. The consequences of these moves for the sector were far reaching:

Lloyds was the first to become a member of both payment systems, doing so in order to launch a Visa debit card alongside its Mastercard. Once the bank had a foothold in both camps, however, other marketing opportunities opened up. Lloyds was able to offer both Visa card and Mastercard handling facilities, and thus establish valuable commercial banking relationships.

Lloyds' rivals . . . responded swiftly to this challenge and all the leading high street banks are now members of both credit card organisations, and fighting for the affections of retailers. This competitive struggle places retailers in the happy position of being wooed rather than wooers and they will undoubtedly use their new power to drive down commission rates. The card companies' income from retailers will therefore fall. (Slaughter, 1989)

As a result of these rapid changes in market conditions, Credit UK quickly relinquished its role as the institution standing between the individual banks and the international credit card market. Its gave up its marketing functions and returned them to each individual bank. It became a third party processor and was forced to compete with other processing companies for contracts to handle all transactions concerning credit cards, including those transactions conducted by customers of the institutions that founded Credit UK in 1972. The change in markets and product portfolios occurred in 1988–9. This rapid change largely shaped the developments in workplace relations, accelerating the trends identifiable in the transitional phase that had commenced in the early 1980s. A further factor influencing Credit UK management's acceleration of the move away from banking employment conditions was the break-up of the multi-employer national bargaining framework in 1988. Each clearing bank went its own way, also causing the break-up of the non-TUC affiliated National Clearing Banks Union.[3] This fragmentation of the industry-wide collective bargaining arrangements strengthened the company's resolve to move quickly to restructure its operations.

By the end of 1989 the company had shifted its accounting approach from cost to profit centre. It closed its marketing operation and cut 150 jobs, including those of senior managers and clerical staff. Some employees took early retirement, others secured posts in the parent institutions and some left the industry. Lastly, the company began to cut its labour costs by subcontracting its security functions. It argued that in-house security was no longer required as the company had become a third party processor. Seventy-two security staff were made redundant. These were the first moves in an extensive rationalization programme that also saw the company reposition itself within the credit card market. Its objective was to establish itself as the largest processing unit in Europe. It was doing so at a time when transaction charges were being squeezed and other competitors were entering the market. Survival, and subsequent success, required Credit UK to cut costs, particularly labour costs. Management organization was reformed and middle layers cut, and a new, more commercial, image was created. The company changed its name to the Credit Consortium and was prepared for sale by its founding institutions. It was purchased by GDC in 1991.

Take-over and rationalization

In the 1980s Global Data Corporation (GDC) moved to achieve a leading position within the financial services in the United States. It acquired a major national brokerage company and several regional brokerage firms and purchased a leading investment bank. Through these acquisitions the company 'gained several important capabilities: enhanced retail distribution through 6,000 stockbrokers, investment banking, traditional brokerage, consumer and business advisory services, and many banking services including home mortgages and consumer and commercial lending' (Capon, 1992: 507).

The company sought to expand the range of markets and financial products it sold by establishing 'cross-selling opportunities'. This involved providing customers with new combinations of credit card services and outlets, including travel, medical, retail and fast foods, as well as providing more customary insurance, mortgage and banking services. By 1986 over 100 individual cross-selling programmes had been introduced and another 200 were being considered (Capon, 1992: 507–8). The company recognized that this vast expansion in financial services products required the support of information processing facilities. In 1983 it had sold a 25 per cent share of its own data processing company. In 1985 the company was repurchased. The company, Primary Data, was the largest third party processor of Visa and Mastercard transactions in the United States. In mid-1987 it had 25 million accounts; for 16 million of these it provided a full service, including distributing cards and issuing monthly statements. It handled merchant accounts for banks and transmitted retailers' credit card slips to proper banks and issued statements. It was a major player in the US financial services market and its parent company, through the repurchase of Primary Data, had recognized the growing significance of information processing as an activity to support product diversification and as an industry that was 'enjoying vigorous growth'. The purchase of Credit Consortium in the UK marked the company's commitment to breaking into the European credit card market as a processor.

Prior to the purchase in 1991, GDC had mainly concentrated on selling its credit card processing package to UK purchasers. In 1985–7, for example, the company sold a range of hardware and software equipment to the Bank of Scotland so that it could set up a new processing plant at Dunfermline (Fincham *et al*, 1994: 85–7). When it purchased Credit Consortium it brought with it a considerable knowledge of the industry. The UK company joined Primary Data in GDC's data based services division, one of four divisions within the company.

The take-over served to accelerate the restructuring and rationalization programme that had commenced in the late 1980s. The new US owners indicated their willingness to continue union recognition and collective bargaining arrangements with BIFU. This was a departure from the company's practices within the United States, where none of its employees enjoyed union rights or recognition status. The company was, however, strongly committed to achieving rapid changes in work organization and sought immediate improvements in productivity and efficiency. The new owners claimed that their US data processing workforce, compared to their UK counterparts, 'undertook triple the amount of business with half the staff' (Interview with BIFU accredited representative, 1996).

The period 1991–2 saw the company embark upon a significant restructuring programme. This had four main elements. First, the employee relations management team was reorganized and retitled, with the senior personnel officer becoming the human resources manager. Management organization was reshaped and further layers of middle management were removed. Second, in January 1992, the company announced a programme of 400 job losses to be achieved through voluntary redundancy, with most jobs going from the lower grades of unskilled staff. Third, the company introduced a new form of work organization called 'work schedule bidding', in which teams of employees were invited at six-monthly intervals to compete for new work hours contracts. This new system caused considerable concern among the workforce and the company was forced to modify the scheme, which was compared by one union official to those forms of contract bidding that once occurred at dock gates before the end of the casual labour system. Finally, the company extended the use of computer-based assembly line working in an attempt to raise productivity towards the levels achieved at its US plant.

Work Organization in the White-Collar Factory

The processing activities associated with the credit card industry involve five discrete elements. These are confirming the card's validity at the transaction point, collecting purchase statements from merchants, crediting the merchant's account, billing the consumer's account and collecting from the consumer (Capon, 1992: 477). Third party processors may undertake all these activities on behalf of clients or may undertake discrete parts (like cheque clearing, customer billing and collection). The system of work organization typically resembles an assembly line through which information passes as paper or electronically. The more highly automated the plant, the more likely it is that data are presented in electronic form. The development of image processing technologies provides the facility for paper-based data to be transformed into electronic data at the point of entry to the plant. Details, for example, about customer accounts and cheques may then be passed around for processing by computer rather than manually or by machine. The processing plant has the characteristic of a computer-based assembly line, with hundreds of terminals being linked to a mainframe. The key production areas are large open-planned spaces. The workplace is divided into specific functional areas. The GDC workplaces are typical examples of this pattern of work organization.

At GDC the workforce and work functions divided into production and non-production areas (Table 4.2). The majority of staff, particularly in the major production areas like telephonics and data capture, work at terminals. The key to efficiency is the woman–machine interface, and in many production areas this may be measured by inputting speeds. In some areas, like telephonics, it is possible to ensure the automatic distribution of customer calls and monitor response times and lengths of calls. All these checks on employee performance were in place at the two UK sites of GDC. The capacity to raise efficiency at plant level, however, relies upon a number of factors. The efficient processing plant requires sophisticated computer systems that facilitate high quality optical character recognition. This, in turn, needs effective IT support from programmers capable of developing and adapting software to specific processing needs. Second, the plant needs to develop the effective deployment of labour within work systems that need to operate on a 24-hour basis all year round. There has to be an effective use of labour to cover times of peaks and troughs in processing activities. Finally, the labour force mix requires a combination of unskilled staff operating at the terminal interface and a smaller number of skilled IT staff and managers whose task it is to seek

Table 4.2 *GDC workforce by job type*

Production areas		Non-production areas	
Area	Number	Area	Number
Telephonics	434	Personnel and education	66
Performance data	15	Sales and marketing	22
Quality	3	Client transactions	18
Data services	67	Products	30
Data capture	459	Client services	71
Systems and programming	191	Finance	71
Operations services	167	Legal	3
Output services	164	Audit	3
Data processing	142	Customer services	54
Plastics	34		
Cheque clearing	88		
Cardholder services	4		
Total	1358		748

Sources: Company document (1996); interview, BIFU secretary, 1996

incremental technical improvements in the work process, while also supervising the production process as a whole. The skills pattern at workplace level tends to polarize between the skilled IT staff and senior management team and the less skilled staff on the shop or 'factory' floor. This polarization also reinforces a gender divide, with women doing the less skilled tasks and men mainly dominating the IT and senior management grades.

Restructuring 'American-style'

In a short period of four years, between 1992 and 1996, GDC established its sites in south east England as the main third party processor in the UK. By 1996 it had over twenty main UK and European customers and offered a range of processing services mainly to other financial institutions, but also to companies operating in industries like printing and publishing. The company sought to develop its overseas markets and by the mid-1990s was using the UK as a base for extending its business into the Middle East, South East Asia and

Australia. This achievement in a highly competitive industry required the company to maintain a tight control on processing costs within its plants in order to maintain profit margins. It did so by introducing widespread changes in staff levels, work organization and employee relations.

The 400 job losses introduced in 1992 began a lengthy process of reducing staffing levels at the two south east plants. Over the period 1993–6, around 800 further jobs were lost through a voluntary redundancy programme, with most staff who left being drawn from the lower grades. Work reorganization took place between the plants, with several functions moving from the coastal town to the greenfield industrial site. Job losses occurred at the same time as there was an expansion of processing work undertaken. The increased workload was partly met by incremental improvements in the processing technologies deployed – especially the introduction of new image processing equipment – and through the improved utilization of labour. One accredited representative explained:

> The key development has been the introduction of more work alongside the reduction in staffing levels. There has been a loss of experienced people, people with knowledge. This has happened in particular areas. For those with experience who are left, they are required to cover a wider area of tasks and, therefore, work harder through rotation. (Interview with BIFU accredited representative, 1996)

Work reorganization also involved changes to shift systems in each of the main production areas. A complex pattern of shifts was in place at the plants. Shifts varied from relatively short peak time shifts of four hours, to permanent night shifts of 12 hours' duration. The company phased out 12-hour shifts and introduced a new eight-hour continental shift pattern for employees working in engineering and maintenance areas (operations services). Accompanying the change in shift patterns and working hours, management also introduced, in 1996, a clocking-in system for staff. It was initially introduced in the despatch area but was subsequently extended to other areas where staff were not on flexitime contracts. Alongside changes in the shift patterns and hours of work, staff were also given new performance targets, using performance measures that were appropriate to each functional activity or work area. In keying-in areas, for example, staff were required to achieve capability levels which related to those set down in the company's performance appraisal scheme, and in telephonics the number and duration of calls were monitored to ensure that staff adhered to target response and length of call times.

This system of work organization, which emphasized the importance of management control over the pace and supervision of work, was complemented by a series of initiatives aimed at changing the culture of employee relations. Many of the new practices introduced by the management team had similarities to the process 're-engineering' approach pioneered in the services industries in the United States (Hammer and Champy, 1993; Head, 1996). This approach emphasizes the adoption, or internalization, of management values by all staff. It requires 'a concerted effort by management to instil within the workforce the acceptance of change and the absorption of the company's vision of what it wishes to become' (Hammer and Champy, 1993: 148–9). This approach was reflected in GDC's policies on employee performance, rewards and communications.

GDC inherited from the Credit Consortium a range of performance measures designed to evaluate productivity as well as individual employee performance. Over the period 1992–6, the company systematically reviewed the performance targets to be achieved in each functional area. Team meetings were used to discuss ways of improving productivity and targets were constantly reviewed and revised upwards, particularly for staff working in jobs that required routine and repetitive processing operations, such as inputting and call answering. The drive to improve productivity was complemented by the introduction of a new performance appraisal scheme in 1995. The scheme, Performance Appraisal and Competencies Evaluation (PACE), established a system of twice yearly review of each employee's performance by his or her line manager. PACE gave each employee the responsibility to reach a performance agreement with his or her line manager. The agreement covered six core competencies and involved staff in setting their own objectives to be achieved over the coming review period. Managers were required to rate employees in each core competency, with each area containing different levels of performance that facilitated the evaluation of all grades of staff. Level 1 in the 'working with people' core competency involved the capacity to carry out instructions carefully. By contrast, a level 4 competency involved an assessment of the employee's ability to make recommendations to senior management that were often endorsed and acted upon. The scheme was given considerable publicity within the company, and staff were aware that poor appraisal results could lead to disciplinary action being taken against an employee under the competency or disciplinary procedures.

In spring 1996, during the course of the annual pay negotiations between BIFU and the company, management announced its intention to end the arrangement by which pay increases would combine both performance and annually negotiated across the board increases. From 1997, the annual appraisal scheme would be the sole basis upon which an employee's pay rise would be determined. This shift to the individualization of reward systems was underpinned by an extensive system of recognition for employees who made special contributions to the company's success. The company offered an elaborate system of annual awards for high achievers, or, as the company called them, the 'Royal Order of Fatcats' (Company employees' magazine, January/February 1996). This system was supported by departmental awards for staff who were identified as 'key players' and those who undertook tasks that were 'beyond the call of duty'. These reward systems were complemented by a raft of management techniques aimed at communicating directly with staff through the company magazine and via regular meetings with work teams and key staff. The year 1996 began, for example, with a 'Kick-off '96' meeting between senior managers and selected staff, at which the management team presented its goals and objectives for the coming year. In February 1996, management announced the introduction of a scheme called 'Employee Care', a counselling and legal advice service which was available for 24 hours, every day of the year.

The service was designed to enable employees to seek professional counselling advice on a 'wide range of personal and work-related problems in areas such as stress; bereavement; family worries; financial concerns; relationship difficulties; anxiety; alcohol and drug abuse' (Staff newsletter, 1996). The company assured staff that information provided to counsellors would be confidential and that only statistical information about the usage of the service would be made available to the company. The scheme represented a further step towards a form of paternalistic relations through which the company established its influence over employees' work and domestic affairs.

While the company introduced techniques designed to individualize relations between management and workforce, it also continued to recognize BIFU for collective bargaining purposes. A joint negotiating committee continued to meet at quarterly intervals throughout the early 1990s. Although the formal structure of industrial relations was maintained, the content of management–union relations changed. This was illustrated in several ways. The union, for example, was not included in the PACE appeals process that might follow from an employee's expression of dissatisfaction with an appraisal rating. The union was not consulted over the introduction of the 'Employee Care' scheme, and when management announced the pay settlement for 1995–6, no reference was made to the fact that the outcome was the result of negotiations with the union. While there were no overt attempts at derecognition, the union was, in effect, being pushed to the margins of workplace affairs.

Workplace Unionism in the White-Collar Factory

Over the period 1972–96, the union role at workplace level divided into three main phases. The 1970s saw a process of membership growth combined with the institutionalization of the union's activities within a set of formal, written agreements. The industrial relations traditions pertaining to the banking industry were extended to the new processing plant. Management perceived BIFU as the main form of employee organization through which the conduct of industrial relations would be carried out. The company provided time and facilities for establishing the role of the seconded and accredited representative system. The company benefited from the orderly operation of industrial relations, while the union was able to rely upon management, as much as its membership, for the legitimisation of its role.

The 1980s placed significant strains on this relatively stable and ordered relationship. External market factors created pressures upon management to push the enterprise into a more independent and commercial direction, resulting in clear differences emerging between union and company over the underlying assumptions that informed the conduct of industrial relations. Management sought to push its workforce away from the employment conditions associated with the UK banking industry, while the union attempted to resist this pressure. Management was broadly successful in achieving incremental changes in terms and conditions, but the union, despite the adverse legal and political climate, maintained respectable membership levels through its mobilization on specific issues such as the ROSEland allowance. The crisis that struck the UK financial services in the period 1989–92 served to accelerate the process of change at workplace level that had commenced in the 1980s. The take-over by GDC marked a significant turning point in domestic workplace relations.

While there was some evidence that the management of Credit UK was prepared to adopt a dualist approach to employee relations (Ackers *et al.*, 1996: 24–5), combining human resource management techniques with a significant role still to be played by BIFU, the new American owners tended to tilt the balance towards a model in which employee relations would be reshaped and the union pushed to the margins. The emphasis shifted to the individualization of employee relations, incorporating a strong element of personal recognition and reward and the adoption of techniques designed overtly to encourage, within the workforce, the internalization of management goals and values. The process of internalization was accompanied by changes in work organization that, paradoxically, tended to reinforce management control and authority, particularly over the work methods of staff employed in the more routine, assembly line tasks. This was achieved through, for example, changes in shift patterns, the introduction of clocking-in and the steady rise in performance targets. While the management literature associated with the adoption of HRM approaches emphasizes the enhancement of individual discretion and autonomy, the evidence provided by the GDC workplaces indicates that many employees experienced increased management authority, rather than individual empowerment, over their day-to-day work affairs. In short, the internalization of the company's ethos and values was designed to secure the cooperation of the workforce in the routinization and intensification of their own work. The company also endeavoured to ensure that the consequences of this process would involve the development of staff strategies aimed at individual survival, through, for example, the Employee Care programme, rather than provoking a collective response that might enhance or strengthen the role of the union at workplace level.

By the mid-1990s union membership density had fallen to its lowest level for many years and the number of active union representatives had declined. The union's capacity to influence or oppose management policies and practices was extremely limited, its role being confined mainly to that of the critical bystander. The US company had accelerated the process of marginalization through the aggressive adoption of an employee commitment programme, the expansion of more individualized forms of employment contracts and the piecemeal introduction of new forms of work organization that entailed greater staff mobility and job rotation, particularly in the areas of more routinized work. The union, however, while marginalized, was not inactive. Union organization changed in the 1990s. First, the leadership at workplace level shifted mainly to women representatives, drawn from the larger production areas of the two workplaces. Second, the formal relationship between management and union, through the joint negotiating committee, was supported by a significant level of day-to-day negotiating between union representatives and managers at workplace level. These local exchanges often involved minor disputes over work organization and operational matters, as well as dealing with the consequences of appraisal, disciplinary and grievance issues, the number of which had increased with the introduction of the new performance appraisal scheme (Union institutional committee meeting minutes, February 1996). Finally, the union attempted to develop its own agenda for improving organization and developing a critical outlook on management practices. It produced occasional newsletters sent to members' homes, and sought to expose the dangers of accepting company policies designed, for example, to link pay increases entirely to the performance appraisal scheme (Union institutional committee minutes, March 1996). Thus, the new American model of employee relations realized a reduction in the union's powers to influence workplace affairs through the formal negotiating procedures, but also provided a stimulus to local pockets of resistance to management practices that were aimed at tightening management control and authority over the shopfloor.

Evaluation

Data-processing plants have obtained an increasingly important role in the business activities of enterprises in the financial services sector. The 1990s saw such plants provide a growing portfolio of direct line services to customers, as well as expanding their role as a provider of back office services. The disaggregation of financial transactions into the wider economy, through the use of ATMs and EFTPOS, has been accompanied by a concentration of administration and customer service provision in plants that resemble factories in terms of their size and forms of work organization. The south east plant of GDC exemplifies this trend. From the late 1980s the plant faced increasingly competitive market conditions as it sought to establish itself as a leading third party processing concern. In response, management attempted to expand its customer base, while at the same time reducing operating costs, primarily through a significant reduction in staff numbers. This process commenced under the ownership of Credit UK and the Credit Consortium and accelerated rapidly under its new US owners, GDC.

The pattern of work organization at the processing plant has three striking features. First, there was a sharp polarization of skills and occupations, with those jobs associated with software development and other IT functions being relatively highly skilled, while those employed at the telephonic and terminal interfaces tended to be engaged in less skilled and more routinized work. Among the less skilled employees, however, job cuts contributed to a loss of knowledge among staff of the range of tasks associated with specific work areas. This led to those more experienced shopfloor staff with this knowledge experiencing a significant increase in job rotation. Second, the polarization of skills reflected a gender divide. A significant proportion of women staff were part-time and the majority of full- and part-time posts undertaken by women were regarded as unskilled. The main burden of intensification, arguably, fell on the shoulders of women workers, particularly those whose competencies required them to accept job rotation. Third, increased output was achieved via the reorganization of work, as well as through the piecemeal introduction of new process technologies. The reorganization of work took place via the introduction of new shift patterns and the development of performance measures, particularly in those areas involving the woman–computer interface.

Union–management relations also went through important changes. Although the institutional forms of workplace relations remained relatively untouched, the content altered significantly. Rather than complementing collective bargaining relationships, achieving a 'benign jointist approach' (Storey and Sisson, 1993; Ackers *et al.*, 1996), the human resource techniques adopted at GDC tended to displace them. This was evident in management's unilateral decisions to implement changes in work practices and the performance-related payment scheme, and in its decision to introduce the Employee Care programme without reference to the union. These events suggest that the HRM approach adopted at GDC amounted to a cocktail of techniques aimed at asserting greater management control rather than empowering those on the shopfloor. This cocktail contained both coercive and welfarist elements. The former was illustrated by the introduction of the clocking-in system, the continuous rise in performance targets and the linkage made in the appraisal scheme between poor performance and the threat of disciplinary action. The 'welfare capitalist' strand, much evident in many US non-union firms, was reflected in the introduction of the Employee Care programme and the recognition and rewards offered to those whose achievements were above and beyond the call of duty. In this context, while collective forms of employee representation retained a foothold within GDC, the 1990s saw the individualistic 'American model' gain the upper hand. Interestingly, the collectivist foothold was maintained primarily by women union representatives drawn mainly from work areas where changes in work organization had taken their sharpest form. It was at the local workplace level that sporadic conflicts arose, but these local incidents, the continuance of union recognition and the maintenance of the industrial relations institutions between management and union could not disguise a significant decline in the capacity of the latter to influence the course of workplace affairs.

Notes

1. It is worth noting that the form of 'individualization' encouraged within GDC through the implementation of its paternalistic welfare policies had a distinctive, contemporary character and had little in common with the strategies traditionally associated with the welfare capitalism developed by nineteenth-century employers. Whereas, a century ago, welfare benefits took a 'collective' form in the provision of housing and other services for a working 'class', contemporary welfare policies tend to replicate the individualization of the employment relation by taking the form of individual counselling and advice. Put simply, if you lived on an employer's housing estate in Saltaire in the nineteenth century, the very form that the employer's paternalistic policies took reinforced your identity as a member of a working class. In the late twentieth century the new forms of employer paternalism tended to reduce class identity and emphasize the individualization of social problems and solutions, with, as a result, the recipients of such benefits encouraged to consider themselves at best as 'patients' in need of help or at worse as 'victims' of events outside of their control.

2. The Advisory, Conciliation and Arbitration Service (ACAS) was established in 1974 by a Labour government in the wake of the crisis in industrial relations that arose under the previous Conservative administration. ACAS represented the first attempt in the UK to establish a role for an independent third party that could provide employers and trade unions with advice on the development of 'good' industrial relations procedures and practices and conciliation and arbitration services when disputes arose. Staff joined ACAS from the Commission on Industrial Relations, which was closed, and the policy and operation of the new body was overseen by a council consisting of three trade union, three employer and three independent members. For a more detailed explanation of the emergence of ACAS and the role it was designed to play in reducing conflict in workplace relations see, for example, Clegg (1978, Chapter 12).

3. Until the mid-1980s, industrial relations in the banking industry were highly centralized and stable. A combination of industry-wide and company-level bargaining relationships facilitated uniform pay and conditions, and staff worked in highly bureaucratic and conservative institutions. Employers in all the leading retail banks encouraged the formation of staff associations whose primary purpose was to keep independent unions, like the National Union of Bank Employees (NUBE), at bay. Staff associations were favoured by employers in the financial services as being more appropriate forms of staff organization for white-collar, professional and clerical employees. The associations were moderate in outlook and expressly ruled out industrial action to pursue the interests of their members. Staff associations were not affiliated to the Trades Union Congress (TUC).

    It was only in 1968 that independent unionism secured equal negotiating rights to those enjoyed by the staff associations at industry and company level in the financial services. The campaign for recognition had been fuelled by concerns among bank workers about the decline in real pay standards in the industry. Following the recognition battle, employers settled into a relatively stable relationship with staff associations and the National Union of Bank Employees (NUBE became the Banking, Insurance and Finance Union in 1979). NUBE sat with its staff association counterparts in the industry-wide negotiating bodies until 1977, when the union pulled out of the industry-wide negotiating committees and adopted an approach to collective bargaining that focused upon the company level.

There were very few industrial disputes in the 1970s and 1980s, and employee relations continued to operate within a paternalistic framework of company and industry-wide bargaining through such employers' organizations as the English and Scottish Banking Employers' Federations. The industry-wide framework broke down in 1987 when employer disagreement arose over London allowances. In truth, London allowances were not the real issue. The banks found themselves increasingly in competition with each other for business. This, coupled with deregulation through the Building Societies Act 1986, created the necessity for banks to review their approaches to industrial relations and employment practices and go their own separate ways. The break-up of industry-wide bargaining, in turn, affected the role played by staff associations. The main high street retail banks all had staff associations. Three of these – Barclays, Lloyds and NatWest – came together in 1980 to form the Clearing Bank Union (CBU), whose primary purpose was to conduct negotiations with the London Federation of Clearing Bank Employers. In the wake of the collapse of this structure in 1987, the CBU was dissolved. For a detailed history of trade unionism in the banking industry see BIFU (1992). For a broader analysis of the emergence of white-collar unionism in the UK see Jenkins and Sherman (1979). A detailed exploration of changes in employee relations up to the mid-1980s may be found in Morris (1986).

5 INSCO: INSURING SURVIVAL

Restructuring in the UK Insurance Industry

The insurance industry in the UK has experienced significant restructuring over recent years, fuelled by a combination of legislative reform, the expansion of product range, the opening of the European and global insurance markets, technological innovation and economic recession. This chapter examines the impact of these on one UK insurance company. It outlines the main elements of a restructuring process that took shape over a period of three years, between 1994 and 1997, and had a dramatic impact upon management structure, work organization and workplace relations.

The insurance industry has three main categories of activity: life assurance (long term); general or non-life insurance; and reinsurance. Life insurance covers pensions, annuities and permanent health insurance; general insurance covers the assets of individuals and businesses; reinsurance is the 'insurance of the insurers', the wholesale side of the business. The insurance industry is based in the rich countries, with over 80 per cent of the market dominated by the seven leading industrial nations (the so-called G7). Over recent years other market locations have emerged, particularly in South East Asia (South Korea and Taiwan) and South Africa, and companies have increased their interest in the so-called emerging markets like Eastern Europe and Latin and South America.

Long-term insurance (particularly life insurance) is considered by industry analysts as a key activity, with a company's performance in that sector being regarded as an important indicator of its well-being. Strength in the provision of long-term insurance provides the basis for companies to cover risks in other product markets. The contemporary insurance market is highly segmented and has experienced, over recent years, a significant rise in competition in each of its product areas. The long-term insurance market in the UK, for example, is highly competitive, with the top ten companies accounting for 62 per cent of the market in 1995. UK insurers' total world-wide net premium income from long-term insurance rose by 20 per cent between 1991 and 1995, reaching a level of £56 billion. Some 80 per cent of the UK insurers' income was written for risks based in the UK. Of this, life insurance accounted for nearly 50 per cent of business, up from 42 per cent in 1991. Of the 20 per cent of income gained from overseas, the European Union accounted for 40 per cent of business in 1995 (up from 30 per cent in 1991) and the USA was the second largest market, accounting for just under 20 per cent of overseas business in 1995 (Association of British Insurers (ABI), 1996).

The general insurance market is dominated by property and motor insurance. The motor insurance market was worth around £8 billion in 1995, and was dominated by the ten leading companies, which held a 63 per cent share of the market. The non-motor sector returned to profit in 1994 after four years of losses. In 1995, however, while remaining in profit, the sector was down 60 per cent on the 1994 result. UK companies developed their overseas business between 1991 and 1995 in an effort to offset domestic losses. The EU market expanded by 90 per cent (from a very low base) and overtook the US market in terms of relative importance. While UK insurers have been authorized to sell their products in overseas markets from their UK base, they have tended to purchase existing companies or set up subsidiary companies or agencies. The rise in overseas income has, therefore, been mainly derived from acquisitions and take-over activities. An important contributor to increased competition in the general insurance area has been the development of direct selling. The share of personal lines business accounted for by direct selling rose from 13 to over 23 per cent between 1991 and 1995. Direct selling was particularly effective in motor insurance, where it was estimated that over 50 per cent of business would be transacted in this way by the year 2000. In 1995, 30 per cent of business was transacted in this way (ABI, 1996: 18–19). Employment in the UK insurance industry reached its peak in 1991, with an employment total of 249,000 staff. Between 1991 and 1995, 37,500 jobs were lost to the industry. Women's employment fell from 120,000 to 103,700 and men's employment declined from 126,800 to 105,600 (ABI, 1996: 69).

A combination of factors has caused major changes in the UK insurance sector. The recession in the late 1980s caused declining profitability, particularly in the general insurance market. Insurance, like banking, enjoyed continuous employment growth up to the end of the 1980s, when the recession began to reveal a significant gap between the rate of growth in employment and the relative sluggishness of financial performance and productivity. The highly developed UK market became a battleground in which market share was increasingly important. Companies developed merger and acquisition strategies to maintain market position and profitability, at the same time as introducing new approaches to selling their products. This 'customer-oriented approach' placed increased pressures upon companies to introduce new technologies and replace old systems. Together these factors prompted insurance companies to engage in restructuring programmes that bore close similarities to those adopted a few years earlier by many leading UK banking institutions. Insco, a company with a distinguished history in the UK insurance sector, was no exception to this trend.

Insco: the Historical Context

Insco is a large UK composite insurer dealing in both life and general insurance products. Approximately two-thirds of Insco's profitability in 1996 was derived from general insurance and the remaining third from the sale of life or long-term insurance products. Insco was established through the merger of two prominent UK insurance companies in the late 1960s. It sustained a position as a leading composite insurer until the late 1980s, when two events raised doubts about its reliability and integrity. The company made a poor judgement when purchasing shares in three Italian insurance companies. These purchases led to the writing off of a £67 million investment within a period of two years and were accompanied by a significant cut in share dividend in 1991. Second, the company was found to have used unlicensed insurance sales staff over the period 1989–90, and was considered to be in breach of the unit trust and life assurance regulations, eventually being fined by the industry regulator, LAUTRO, in 1994. These events occurred at the same time that economic recession hit the insurance industry. The recession exposed the company's weakness in the UK market in terms of its relative dependence upon general insurance, rather than the safer long-term life insurance side.

The 1989–92 recession revealed a number of problems concerning the company's market position and internal organization. These problems were not effectively addressed until 1994. In the following three years the company embarked upon a major rationalization and restructuring programme that had a huge impact upon management organization, patterns of product development and delivery, work organization and management–workforce relations. This chapter describes the main features of the restructuring that took place within the company between 1994 and 1997. It identifies the characteristics of the company's business and labour use strategies, as well as exploring the changes in management–union relations. The final section identifies the main contours of the restructuring strategy and examines the extent to which it encompassed several of the features of the model outlined in Chapter 2.

The problems facing Insco may be grouped under 'external' market pressures and 'internal' organizational weaknesses. The externally derived pressures were threefold. First, the company had a weak UK life insurance profile and was, therefore, over-dependent upon its general insurance business. The general insurance market experienced considerable volatility between 1991 and 1994 as a result of the collapse of the UK property market and low premiums arising from increased competitive pressures. Second, the emergence of direct selling increased competitive pressures, particularly in the UK motor insurance market. In effect, the UK general insurance market had reached saturation point in the early 1990s, and companies were primarily concerned with maintaining market share. Direct sales sharpened competition in key segments of the market for general insurance and prompted Insco to move rather belatedly into direct selling. Finally, a merger of two key rival companies, Royal and Sun Alliance, in 1995 increased market pressures on Insco. The company found itself wrong-sized in relation to its market position. Two competitors had created a single enterprise that was set to overshadow Insco in the UK insurance sector.

These externally generated problems revealed and exacerbated several internal weaknesses. First, the company's UK life insurance business was relatively undeveloped following a period in which poor investment decisions had been made and serious errors of judgement reached over the provision of private pension schemes. The weakness in long-term insurance products created too great a dependence on the more volatile general insurance side and called into question the company's image as a sound insurance institution. Second, Insco used inefficient technologies that were designed to service a network of local branches whose role was no longer central to the company's operations. The closure of local branches created the necessity for developing a new strategy for the introduction of those technologies required for the company to deliver a more customer-oriented service, primarily from a smaller number of regional centres. Third, the company had inadequate management information systems for monitoring and evaluating its performance in different product markets; such information was essential for the company to begin to improve staff performance and productivity. Finally, the events of the late 1980s and early 1990s revealed to industry analysts that the company had been poorly managed for some time. The combination of these externally generated problems and internal weaknesses created an urgent need for change if the company was to survive as an independent player in the insurance sector. Before we examine the restructuring process in depth it is useful to identify the features of the key actors involved.

The Management

Insco is a proprietary company, a company that has shareholders, unlike mutuals, which are owned by their policy-holders. It has deep roots in the UK as a composite insurer. Up to 1994 its management structure and organization tended to match its long 'tradition' as a company. Senior management came from within the insurance sector and usually rose up the ranks of the company. Management organization was based upon divisions that were distinguished by geographical location and product type. Managers had professional qualifications (such as underwriters and actuaries), and promotion was gained with length of service. The stability offered by a traditional, hierarchical management structure was undermined by the company's performance in the period broadly between 1990 and 1994. During this time, for example, the shares of composite UK insurers like Insco 'underperformed the rest of the market by 47 per cent' (*Financial Times*, 2 March 1997). Insco suffered in particular as a result of the imbalance between its general and life or long-term insurance sides. As a consequence, in 1994 management embarked on a programme of change initiated by the recruitment of a new chief executive who had no background in the insurance industry.

The new appointee began a process of change in management organization that had three main features. First, 'professional' executives were recruited with, for example, responsibilities for areas like information technology, finance and human resources. None of these had prior experience in the insurance sector. Second, a programme of management reorganization was initiated through which middle layers were removed. This process occurred division by division over the period 1995–7, commencing with the regulated part of the business, such as pensions and health, and moving on to the general insurance side by 1997. Third, alongside divisional reorganization, the company was restructured into five separate business units: Insco Insurance, Insco Investment Holdings, Corporate Centre, Regional IT and Insco Financial Services. Finally, the separation into five business units was complemented by the introduction of team working. Teams were run by leaders, local managers who took on increased responsibilities for monitoring the performance of those in their charge. There was, in effect, a devolution of management responsibility within a framework in which the senior executive group set down the objectives of each unit, while allowing management at business unit and local level discretion over how policies might be implemented. This programme of management reorganization created widespread redundancies among middle-level management staff and generated a climate of constant flux or 'change'.

The Workforce

Estimates of changes in the workforce size are difficult because job losses were accompanied by acquisitions. A senior union official estimated that Insco lost approximately 2,500 jobs between 1988 and 1997, with numbers falling from just under 9,000 staff to around 6,500. This decline in staff levels was accompanied by the acquisition of companies whose combined staff levels totalled about 1,000. So, by 1997, Insco employed approximately 7,000 staff in its UK companies. Job losses occurred as a mixture of compulsory and voluntary redundancy, as well as through the non-replacement of staff who left the company to work elsewhere.

The workforce was concentrated into regional centres, particularly in East Anglia and the North West, where the company had over 1,000 employees located in each of two sites. Other employees were situated in smaller regional offices which typically employed between 200 and 300 staff. There were six of these smaller regional offices. The remainder of the staff were employed in the company's London offices, at three 'direct sales' workplaces or in offices of those insurers that the company had acquired in the 1990s. The direct sales workplaces, situated in the south of England, were areas of employment growth, while the two main regional centres in East Anglia and the North West had experienced employment decline. Job reductions hit particularly the North West regional centre, where staff levels had fallen from around 2,500 in 1992 to just over 1,000 by 1997.

In summary, the workforce was geographically spread around several locations within the UK, with the largest numbers situated in two main regional centres. The workforce divided evenly between male and female staff, with the former tending to dominant management positions, reflecting the tradition of those with professional qualifications taking up management posts. In the two main regional centres, the company played a significant role in recruiting from the local labour market. This encouraged employees to stay with the company and even in the London offices there was a tradition of long service and a relatively low turnover of staff. In this sense, a feature of Insco's workforce was its traditional expectation of joining the company in anticipation of securing a 'job for life'.

The Union

Insco employees were represented by a staff association until 1979. Staff associations were widespread in the financial service industries in the post-war period. They were company-specific organizations, often set up and supported by management, and they tended to be committed to consultative processes within their respective enterprises. They opposed the use of industrial action to pursue their objectives and provided an employer-sponsored alternative to trade unionism within the financial services sector. Such organizations tended to reflect the belief that trade unionism was for manual workers and not white-collar professional workers. This form of organization has tended to decline over the past two decades as employee relations have shifted from a traditional paternalism to one in which management has adopted more aggressive approaches to employee relations (Waddington, 1995). As this shift has gained momentum, so staff associations have joined trade unions like BIFU and Manufacturing, Science and Finance (MSF). Insco's staff association decided to join BIFU in 1979.

Union organization in Insco took the form of a divisional council which contained representatives drawn from each of the company's main workplaces within the UK. By the early 1990s the divisional council consisted of 24 representatives. These were supported by three seconded representatives, lay union officials with release from the company to conduct union business on a full-time basis. Each of the seconded representatives had responsibilities for a geographical area and carried out negotiating, organizing, recruitment and casework duties. The three officers were joined by a fourth representative, the divisional committee chairperson, who also had secured full-time release for trade union duties. This right, however, had developed as custom and practice and was not written into the union's recognition agreement with Insco, as had been the case with the seconded representatives. These four key lay officials were in turn backed up by a BIFU full-time official with responsibilities for the insurance sector. In addition to the divisional council members, BIFU had approximately 60 other representatives at workplace level in 1994. These divided into active representatives and those who tended to receive and distribute union newsletters and bulletins. The latter were referred to as 'post boxes'. At least one third of the union's lay representatives were considered to be post boxes. The ratio of representatives to members was around 45:1, though this ratio rose to around 80:1 if post box representatives were discounted.

The union had established a membership density within the company as a whole of just over 60 per cent by the early 1990s, about 4,000 out of a little over 6,000 employees. By 1997 this had declined as a result of the acquisition, rationalization and restructuring programmes. Membership was unevenly spread across workplaces. Areas of employment growth, like direct sales, expanded in the mid-1990s to employ approximately 600 staff. These were mainly permanent, part-time employees. None, however, was a union member. During the course of the rationalization and restructuring programme it became increasingly evident that areas of employment growth within the company were those in which there was no effective union presence, while areas in which employment levels were in relative decline were traditional centres of union organization.

By the mid-1990s union organization in Insco experienced a number of significant pressures. First, its traditional role in negotiating with the enterprise at company level was undermined by the establishment of separate business units and the devolution of management responsibilities. Second, the union's representative structure was thin on the ground and increasingly reliant upon an active few. Third, the company used the restructuring programme to launch a review of union recognition rights, with the implied threat that the facility time for seconded representatives would be curtailed. Finally, union membership density was under pressure as a result of the company's acquisition policies and management's apparent determination to establish non-unionized areas within the company. The process of restructuring presented serious challenges to union organization and recognition rights within Insco, and there was increasing evidence, according to union activists, of management pursuing policies designed to achieve union exclusion.

Restructuring in Insco

There is a considerable literature on strategic management. Usually, in the business literature, it is associated with the identification and application of rational approaches to the operation of the enterprise in relation to its market context and domestic or internal forms of organization. The changing market context interacts with the domestic environment, generating shifts in management organization. In recent times, the increasingly competitive demands of the market have, according to several writers, given rise to important changes in the forms of domestic management organization (Treacy and Wiersema, 1995: 41). Often these are perceived as changes which have caused a shift away from traditional hierarchical forms to more agile, devolved or decentralized approaches to the management of the enterprise. This approach was a central theme in the restructuring programme adopted by Insco. The programme may be explained in relation to the development of the company's business strategy, the reform of management organization, the introduction of new technical systems and changes in work organization and, finally, changes in management–workforce relations.

The business strategy

Insco's business strategy emerged through its attempt to cope with changes in 'external' market conditions and to tackle its 'internal' weaknesses in management approach and organization. These external and internal weaknesses were revealed by the company's disastrous purchase of large shareholdings in three Italian insurance companies in 1989, its use of untrained and inadequately supervised staff in the areas of life insurance and pensions, which eventually led to it receiving a large fine from the industry's regulator in 1994, and its unwise use of life funds to invest in its own subsidiary company in 1994. This latter action was widely considered to be 'unethical' by City actuaries and the wider financial community. These failings were reflected in the poor financial performance of the company in the early 1990s, and generated immense pressures upon the company to undertake significant change in order to restore its fortunes.

An indicator of soundness of the financial base of a company is its solvency ratio. In the case of insurance companies this is calculated as the percentage of net assets (shareholders' funds) to written general insurance premiums. The lower the ratio, the weaker is the company's financial position. Insco experienced a severe weakening in its financial position between 1990 and 1993, and only began to achieve a significant recovery as its restructuring strategy took effect, as Table 5.1 suggests.

Insco made tentative steps in the direction of restructuring in the wake of its poor financial performance in 1990–1. The company refocused on its core products within the UK and reverted to its traditional policy of acquiring small niche market companies in the United States. It acquired a foothold in the expanding UK health care sector in 1993 through the purchase of a company that also traded in household and motor insurance and, in 1993,

Table 5.1 *Insco solvency ratios 1989–96*

	1989	1990	1991	1992	1993	1994	1995	1996
Non-life business written premiums (£ million)	2004	2038	2201	2183	2542	2851	2898	2914
Net assets (£ million)	1642	926	947	1132	1681	1542	2228	2306
Solvency ratio (%)	82	45	43	52	66	54	77	79

Source: Insco company accounts 1989–97

announced a new departure, the establishment of Insco Direct, which was to become operational in 1994.

The decisive shift in the restructuring process took place, however, in 1994, with the appointment of a new chief executive who was committed to combining the development of a new product strategy with the process of extensive domestic organizational reform. For the first time, the company was to address both its external and internal weaknesses via extensive organizational reform. The business strategy involved engagement in areas where the company could both influence market operations and achieve a strong profit potential. This was to be achieved through a combination of the expansion of the UK group via the acquisition of smaller companies and the insurance operations of non-financial services organizations and the expansion of the company's overseas activities through acquisitions and partnerships. Between 1994 and 1997, for example, the company entered into partnerships with a motoring organization and a building society in order to provide a range of insurance services to their respective customer bases. Insco also purchased the commercial insurance division of a rival insurance company and developed significantly its Insco Direct general insurance business. The UK direct sales customer base grew from a little under 150,000 in 1995 to nearly 700,000 by 1997. Insco's domestic business strategy was driven by the company's concern to remain an independent enterprise that was capable of expansion in areas in which it had market strength, particularly in the non-life area, while also developing its operations as a 'service' company providing corporate and personal customers with a range of financial services and advice and support.

Insco's domestic reforms were complemented by an expansion in its overseas operations. Through the early 1990s, overseas earnings tended increasingly to compensate for the company's sluggish domestic performance. By 1997, approximately 60 per cent of its total general premium income was derived from its overseas activities, which were located in, for example, the USA, Southeast Asia, South Africa and Northern Europe. In brief, Insco's business strategy was driven by the necessity to restore its financial base through repositioning itself within the UK market via a programme of 'rightsizing', while also expanding its overseas activities in established and emerging markets.

The reform of management organization

Along with these developments Insco undertook a programme of rapid reform in its UK management organization. This commenced with the financial services side of the business – corporate and personal protection in areas like pensions and health care – in 1994–6. The general insurance area – household, motor – followed, with extensive reforms introduced in 1996–7. This area was particularly affected by the growth in the direct sales side of the business. At the same time that these mainstays of the business were reorganized, Insco fostered the growth of its services company, which provided advice on risk management and other financial matters for corporate clients. Management reorganization was designed to cut operating costs, improve methods for measuring product and work performance and facilitate the development of a sales orientation. These were to be achieved via the reduction of middle management layers, branch closures, the introduction of five new business units, the devolution of management responsibilities and the establishment of team working arrangements across the enterprise.

Together these developments constituted a radical change from past management practice within Insco, though they were implemented on a step-by-step basis across each of the main areas of the company's activities. While the overall objectives of management reform may be clear, the method of implementation was piecemeal, with the company making new pronouncements at regular intervals about specific areas of activity. In some cases relatively large numbers of jobs were involved – up to 250–300 – and in others smaller numbers of staff were affected. In virtually all redundancy/restructuring situations a similar pattern of change took place. Management numbers were cut, staff levels reduced, traditional management skills displaced and new work teams established. This process may be illustrated by reference to a union newsletter published in September 1996:

Account Management – Life and Individual Pensions
18 (40%) Jobs to Go

Today, Management announced a major change in the role of Life and Individual Pensions (LIP) consultants. . . . The existing Sales Manager role within the Individual Channel is to be replaced with a new position, National Accounts Manager. This will see a reduction in positions from 9 to 3.

Following on from the account management project, the company no longer see a role for LIP consultants. Therefore, all existing LIP consultants have been told that their jobs are redundant. This is 36 positions. Replacing the LIP consultants will be a new role, Business Development Manager. There will be 24 new positions, a reduction of 12. Management see this role as demanding significantly different skills to the present role. All affected LIP consultants have been given a copy of the new role profile, and all LIPs will be invited to apply for the new role. . . . All LIP consultants will be given time to think about this announcement. . . . They will be given the option to apply for the new position of Business Development Manager, take redundancy or go for redeployment within the Company. Selection for Business Development Manager positions will take place over two days in October. As the role is significantly different from the present role, existing trial periods will apply. For those LIP consultants and Sales Managers who are made redundant, full support services will be provided. this will include joint counselling with a BIFU official and a member of Human Resources (HR). BIFU will also be pressing Management for redeployment of members and retraining for other available jobs. (BIFU Newsletter, September 1996)

Management reorganization involved the displacement of 'traditional' skills – underwriting, risk assessment – with more generic management capabilities in marketing, sales and team-building. This shift, in turn, facilitated the recruitment of new managers with relatively little experience of working in the insurance industry.

At the centre of management reorganization, however, was a process that encompassed both devolution and integration. In 1995 management announced its intention to establish five separate business units in its UK operations, covering general insurance, investment holdings, corporate centre, regional IT and financial services. The separate business units were designed to operate as individual profit/cost centres with budgetary responsibilities set at unit level and cascaded down to the workplace. The rationale for such devolution was based upon management's acknowledgement of the different work systems and labour markets that operated in each of these areas.

There were three main features of the devolution process. First, local managers were required to work within tightly defined policy and financial frameworks that were passed down from above. Second, local discretion was primarily exercised in relation to the implementation of these policies, particularly in the area of work organization. Third, devolution was accompanied by enhanced responsibility for the performance of work teams (through the introduction of performance appraisal in which local managers played a central role). A year later, however, in 1996, management announced its intention to reintegrate several of these separate entities into a single enterprise 'under the direction of one executive management team' (Insco, 1997: 5). The reintegration of the separate businesses was designed primarily to provide greater opportunities for cross-marketing, as well as facilitating the introduction of common capital structures and the development of more integrated IT systems.

The drive towards devolution arose from management's desire to achieve greater flexibility in employment conditions, work organization and employment policies, while the push towards integration arose primarily from the necessity to respond to developments in product markets in which corporate and private customers were increasingly demanding an integrated menu of financial services to be provided on a 'one-stop' basis. While the introduction of separate business units facilitated tighter management control over costs and performance and enabled the adoption of more flexible approaches to the employment and utilization of labour, the market-driven demand for the compilation of complete financial packages was pulling the company in another direction. Assertion of greater management control over the labour process encouraged organizational fragmentation, while the demands of the product market simultaneously promoted organizational integration. In short, there was a contradiction between the projected trajectory for management's organization of labour and the company's own product development and marketing strategy. The attempted reconciliation of these conflicting trends, accompanied by changing legal and political conditions, prompted the company, in mid-1997, to initiate a new review of its human resources policies. The conflicting pressures towards integration and devolution illustrate the conditional character of management strategy and its subjection to the competitive pressures of the market-place.

Work Organization and Technical Change

Four main trends emerged as a result of the changes in work organization that were initiated within Insco between 1994 and 1997. First, management devolution provided the opportunity for significant variations in work practices to emerge between work teams, depending upon their relationship to the customer interface and the work style and culture created by the team leader. Second, the creation of business units, the expansion of direct sales and the erosion of traditional professions and skills, via the introduction of new technical systems, fostered the emergence of assembly line working in the direct line workplaces and the growth of multifunctional team working in other workplaces, particularly in Insco Financial Services (pensions, life and health insurance). Third, Insco employed a leading international firm of management consultants to review work practices and initiate the re-engineering of work processes. Finally, staff across the whole of Insco experienced the introduction of performance measurement and new performance targets which contributed to a rise in the intensity of labour.

The traditional pattern of work within Insco during the boom years of the 1980s allowed for considerable discretion to be exercised by many staff over working hours and the organization of work. This was particularly the case in the Financial Services division, where the specialists in, for example, corporate and personal pensions provision operated flexitime working on the basis of trust. There was 'slack' within the system and an assumption that the customer would remain a 'passive component of the work process' (Interview with corporate executive director, 1997). By the mid-1990s this situation had significantly changed, even in Financial Services. As one employee explained:

> The main change over recent years is that there is a lot less slack than there used to be. In the boom time of the 1980s you could ease your way through work, now the vast majority of staff are working harder. This is for two main reasons. First, there's fewer staff doing the same or more work and, second, everyone has to learn a wider range of skills, moving away from their specialisms and being required to move around tasks and jobs more frequently. (Interview with independent financial adviser, North West Regional Centre, 1997)

The shift towards a 'customer-oriented' service company created within Insco a new work culture and a new set of expectations against which the performance of work teams could be measured. Where work teams had direct dealings with customers, team leaders were required to establish tight targets for, for example, queries handling, the processing of claims and the initiation of new policies. Working time arrangements were organized around fixed rotas in order to maintain phone-based customer links. By contrast, in those work teams where there was no direct customer link, flexible working arrangements operated within a more relaxed style. In these areas, however, the approach of the team leader was important in terms of generating expectations about performance. For example, in the newly created marketing department of Insco's corporate pensions business a new recruit commented that 'I enjoy the job and the use of my own initiative. I have created my own job on the promotions side. You work your own hours and though it is not made explicit by the team leader, you are encouraged or expected to work more than the regular 9 to 5' (Interview with marketing manager, 1997).

In areas where specific professional skills previously applied, such as among underwriters, significant changes took place. As with marketing, the team leader was expected to establish the work culture in the absence of direct association with the customer. In the East Anglia regional centre, for example, the role of underwriters had changed. A few specialists continued to deal with the more complex claims, while standard claims were largely processed by a dedicated software program which merely required staff to input the necessary data. Those underwriters displaced by the software packages were switched to tasks associated with market research into the development and evaluation of existing and new products. The success of such teams was measured by the profitability of the product lines. As the role of traditional professional skills diminished, so they were replaced by broader, generic skills in the areas of marketing, product research and sales. The tendency within Insco was for professional employees to develop these multifunctional skills within teams that were required to work flexibly across a range of tasks and activities.

By contrast, in the customer-facing areas of employment, particularly in the direct line or telesales side of the business, employment conditions and work patterns were very different. Here Insco achieved a significant growth in its customer base between 1994 and 1997, which facilitated the expansion of staff levels in Insco Direct to over 600 staff by 1997. The vast majority of these were new to the company and were employed on different contracts from other Insco employees. Staff divided into established (permanent) and temporary employees. There were four job levels. The first level was that of a team member, the second team leader, the third process leader/implementation manager and the fourth was designated manager. This flatter structure facilitated close supervision of the work process. According to union representatives who had undertaken unsuccessful recruitment campaigns within Insco Direct workplaces, staff performance was automatically monitored via the computer software and staff were subject to disciplinary procedures if attendance was poor or performance fell below what managers considered to be acceptable standards. Salaries were reviewed, normally annually, on an individual basis and, again, according to union representatives staff turnover in the direct line workplaces was far higher than in other workplaces within the company. This view of the factory-like conditions reported by union representatives was supported by a senior executive of the company, who indicated that Insco Direct was certainly a location in which the principles of Fordist production applied (Interview with senior executive director, 1997).

In brief, the transformation of work practices within Insco encompassed two main trends: the establishment of relatively low skilled and low valued employment for mainly women employees in the direct line workplaces; and the setting-up of multifunctional work groups in those areas in which professional skills such as underwriting had previously applied. The multifunctional work teams tended to sacrifice their 'specialist' knowledge in such areas as life, pensions and health insurance for a broader, less specialized understanding across all these areas. Finally, a group that was a clear beneficiary from the changes in work organization outlined above was made up of those IT specialists who were engaged in the replacement of the old branch-based technical support systems with the new local area networks which underpinned the database technologies that ran the dedicated software. This success was reflected in the pay awards achieved by IT staff.

The drive to reduce costs, introduce significant technical change and implement changes in work organization was sustained within Insco through the extensive use of a leading international firm of management consultants. The consultants worked in small teams with staff drawn from the company. They tended to focus on specific work processes, in accord with the tenets of business process re-engineering. According to one senior regional manager, the use of consultants was more effective in those projects geared primarily towards downsizing and cost reduction than it was in facilitating the introduction of new work processes. Two examples illustrate this point. Over a period of eight months in 1993–4, in the regional centre concerned with the corporate pensions business, consultants were employed in a downsizing exercise. The office employed 330 staff at the beginning of the exercise. Using activity-based cost analysis, the management consultant team involved a large cross-section of staff in workshops and seminars aimed at generating new ideas for organizing work. The workshops were organized and run by a steering committee consisting of managers, staff and consultants, and it was the steering committee that was given the job of shaping the proposals presented at the workshops into a planned approach to change. The exercise resulted in a report which, when implemented, realised a 25 per cent reduction in staffing levels, the cutting of five out of ten management posts and the reduction of middle management layers.

By contrast, a follow-up exercise in the same office, involving the same firm of consultants, was far less successful from management's perspective. This exercise involved staff establishing, again through workshops and seminars, their visions of the future. The project excluded managers (with the exception of one who participated in a project team which included two staff members and two consultants) and was referred to as an exercise in business process improvement. Despite running for several months, the exercise produced proposals for change, according to a senior manager and union representatives, that lacked realism and were considerably more costly to implement than local budgets allowed, and as a consequence nothing came from the exercise. Within months of the project failing, the manager on the project team resigned from Insco.

It was estimated by lay union officials that about 12 projects had been run by management consultants for Insco over the period 1994–7 and that the main benefit for management lay in their role as external 'legitimators' of an extensive process of downsizing. The consultants successfully involved staff in downsizing projects and encouraged local managers to implement redundancies on a scale they might otherwise have sought to avoid (Interview with BIFU full-time official, 1996). Finally, the projects involving management consultants tended to provide a useful means by which work organization was removed from the sphere of collective bargaining, with the union role relegated to one concerned only with consequences of implementation.

A final strand in the transformation of work organization was the development of new management approaches to the measurement of performance. This was achieved in three main ways: via devolved budgets and the setting of financial targets for work teams; through the introduction of a variety of measures aimed at setting performance targets for work undertaken; and through the introduction of employee appraisal schemes aimed at linking pay to individual performance. Budgetary targets served to enhance local management's responsibility for financial performance and tended to encourage local teams to find ways of containing operating costs. According to two managers in regional centres, devolved budgets enhanced local management responsibility for the financial performance of those teams for which they were responsible, making the job more interesting and challenging, while, at the same time, sharpening the level of accountability of managers in terms of their relationship with those above them.

A range of new performance measures were introduced across each of Insco's business units between 1995 and 1997. At the heart of these indicators was the shift within the enterprise towards a customer service orientation. In practice, in many areas of work organization this shift was reflected in a move away from the assessment of performance based upon the volume of work completed and towards a system through which the standard of service was the primary measure of performance. An example from a work team concerned with processing life assurance claims illustrates this point.

In early 1997 the life insurance claims section, located at the North West Regional Centre, was subjected to an operational effectiveness review (OER). As a result of the review staff levels were cut by four, from 22 to 18, and the staff who remained were divided into two teams, each with a leader, and required to develop the skills to carry out all the tasks undertaken within the section. Retraining was organized by a training co-ordinator, an experienced member of staff drawn from one of the two teams. While this reorganization took place, two members of staff left on maternity leave but were not replaced by the team leaders, who argued that it was possible to manage without them. Along with this reorganization of work and the introduction of multifunctional working, a new system of performance measurement was introduced. The old system required individual members of staff to keep a daily record of work done. Each daily record would then be added together to record a weekly total, a weekly 'counting-up'. The new system required staff to shift away from the measurement of work volume towards a method through which claims were evaluated in relation to 'turnaround times'. Team leaders accorded each claim that entered the office a 24-hour, 48-hour or five-day turnaround time. Staff performance was evaluated on the basis of the percentage of claims successfully processed within the target turnaround times. The new system gave team leaders a large measure of control over the organization and allocation of work and created a situation in which, according to the local union representative, staff felt more 'pressurized'.

While the development of team working and multifunctional approaches was common across workplaces, pressures upon staff tended to vary depending upon the type of work carried out. For example, in a team concerned with 'discontinuance', the closing of personal insurance accounts, there was less pressure to perform to specific target times. In fact, targets were only set when a customer asked for one (Interview with discontinuance team member, 1997). Overall, however, the introduction of new performance measures created an uneven process of raising labour intensity, took place alongside the development of team working and tended to facilitate the strengthening of the role of team leaders in allocating work and determining the pace at which it would be done.

The introduction of performance measures was complemented by the development of employee appraisal schemes introduced across the five business units between 1996 and 1997. The appraisal schemes were brought in as part of a package of measures which also saw the reform of grading structures and the introduction of a new system for determining pay rises. Appraisal centred on an annual review of individual performance. The review was conducted by the team leader or local manager with each member of her or his team on an individual basis. The interviews reviewed performance against a set of published criteria and the level of an individual's pay increase was determined by the outcome of the manager's assessment.

The implementation of the new scheme, with variations across business units reflecting the different grading structures and job types, did not proceed smoothly in each business unit. In Insco Insurance – the general side of the business – the initial 'performance management' scheme was rejected following a ballot of staff. The scheme was designed to determine the total amount of the pay increase through reference to external 'market' rates (determined by outside consultants whose report was confidential to senior management), while individual appraisals determined how the amount would be divided between staff. The new scheme effectively took pay outside of the bargaining framework and left many staff feeling disgruntled.

Similar problems were raised by the proposed schemes for regional IT staff and for those employed in financial services. The outcome was the renegotiation of these schemes by BIFU. This process occurred throughout 1997 and led to improvements in areas like job descriptions, pay rates for specific grades and the systems for appeals and the review of the operation of schemes. Arguably, management had attempted to achieve too many objectives through the introduction of performance management – the removal of traditional pay bargaining, the widespread redefinition of job families and titles, the reduction in grades as well as the introduction of a new system of appraisal and staff development. While the union won concessions in these areas, the underlying goal of linking performance and reward was achieved. While management made a mess of implementation, the new appraisal schemes underlined the role of local management in setting work targets and evaluating performance, and facilitated the creation of a climate in which the intensification of labour could be effectively pursued.

Work intensification took a variety of forms. The most obvious evidence was provided by the introduction of new performance measures. These took place alongside cuts in staffing levels within departments and work teams, leaving those who remained in employment working harder to achieve their performance targets. A further strand of intensification was evident as a result of the introduction of more flexible forms of working – multifunctional teams – and the implicit requirement placed upon many staff to work hours in excess of those that were contractually required. These incremental steps in intensifying labour were complemented by changes in technical systems and facilitated the shift towards new methods of working which served to undermine specialist skills and employee discretion over the pace of work.

Workplace relations: towards union exclusion?

Industrial relations within Insco followed a similar pattern to those in several other financial services companies in the 1980s and early 1990s. The staff association merger with BIFU in 1979 was achieved following a ballot of members. The merger was supported by the staff association representatives and members on the grounds that the union offered access to greater resources and negotiating expertise, while facilitating a high level of autonomy for the staff association within BIFU.

The traditional pattern of industrial relations was characterized by management and union as highly 'institutionalized', reflecting a 'stable' industrial relations climate. In practice, during the period between 1979 and 1994, the union's relationship with members changed little from the time when staff had been represented by a staff association. There was no incidence of industrial action and the relationship of members to the union was largely passive, with members' views being expressed via an annual ballot on wage claims. Balloting was the main vehicle through which members' views were evaluated. There was no regular pattern of workplace meetings. The annual divisional conference provided the opportunity for members to exert influence over the overall policies pursued by representatives. In turn, representatives pursued collective bargaining objectives through negotiations at company level. This traditional system was rapidly dismantled in the period between 1994 and 1997.

The transformation of workplace relations within Insco had four main features. First, management introduced modifications to the institutions that regulated management–union relations. Second, management took control of the negotiating/consultative agenda, with the union being cast into an entirely reactive mode. Third, the weaknesses underlying the union's relationship with members, which had been inherited from its days as a staff association, were rapidly revealed under the pressures imposed by the company's downsizing and restructuring programme. Fourth, senior management adopted an approach to its relations with BIFU which facilitated marginalization and, potentially, the adoption of a strategy aimed at union exclusion.

At the heart of the institutional changes in management–union relations was the announcement in February 1995 that the company was to review its 'remuneration policies and practices with a view to recognising the needs and constraints of the separate companies in their different market places' (BIFU Newsletter, 4 August 1995). In practice, this meant that the company was to establish five separate business units and bring to an end collective bargaining at company level. To reinforce the strength of this message the company also announced that it would not be possible to raise salaries for executives, managers or staff at the annual review time in July 1995. In practice, the company was placing a freeze on salary increases while putting into place a devolved system of consultation/bargaining at business unit level.

The union response, agreed at the April divisional conference, was to resist the salary freeze and oppose the break-up of collective bargaining arrangements. Following this decision, the union undertook a consultative ballot of all its members, inviting them to accept or reject the company's proposals for the setting-up of separate collective bargaining units. The union recommended rejection of the company's proposal and the consultative ballot supported this position: 1,524 members voted to reject the company's proposal and 898 voted to accept on a turnout of around 70 per cent. The result of this consultative ballot was communicated to the company and the union asked at a meeting with senior management in July 1995 for the company to reconsider its proposals to decentralize bargaining. The company refused, pointing out that only 44 per cent of staff actively opposed the company's proposals, with 26 per cent voting for and nearly 30 per cent not voting at all. The union moved to gain support from its members for industrial action over the issue. A ballot on industrial action followed in August 1995, resulting in staff rejecting action, 1,228 voting against and 663 voting for, in a turnout of just under 50 per cent. The ballot result effectively put an end to the union's ability to oppose the establishment of separate bargaining units and, more importantly, openly revealed the weaknesses in the union's relationship with its own members. The tradition of balloting took place in a context in which members tended still to perceive their relationship to BIFU as with an 'association' rather than a union. There was no link between the outcome of ballots and the expectation that members might be involved in a form of collective action. The ballot represented an exercise in giving opinions rather than a means of legitimating collective action. The union was revealed as a hollow institution when it attempted to pursue collective action.

The separation into five business units provided the catalyst for management to marginalize the union and expose its weaknesses in several ways. First, the union lost its regular contact with management at the executive level, where employee relations policies were decided. Second, union representation was spread unevenly across the five bargaining units, with the consequence that two of the weaker areas of representation – corporate centre and investment holdings – were effectively removed from the collective bargaining arena. Third, the union's divisional council found considerable difficulty in developing a collective bargaining strategy that could be applied across each of the bargaining units. Fourth, the loss of a central focus for negotiations fostered a new climate at workplace level, where, over the period 1995–7, local consultation/negotiation took on an increasing sporadic character. By mid-1997 only one regional office continued to hold regular joint local committee meetings. Rather than acting as a stimulus to local negotiations, devolution facilitated its demise in all but one regional centre.

The process of institutional change, coupled with the continuous announcements of redundancy and work reorganization, effectively undermined union morale and organization. The union representative structure weakened between 1995 and 1997, with the number of delegates on the divisional council falling from 22 to 15. At workplace level, the number of activists declined relative to the size of membership. Between 1995 and 1997 the company moved to clarify the areas in which the union had an active presence. It effectively ensured that the union was excluded from direct line workplaces and was not provided with facilities to recruit staff in newly acquired companies. These union 'no-go' areas were complemented by other areas in which union membership density was in severe decline, particularly in the company's London-based offices.

While the union maintained its opposition to compulsory redundancies, in practice its role was confined to ensuring that staff received effective counselling concerning the options facing them when their posts were lost. In this gruelling task union representatives were very effective. Undertaking joint counselling also ensured that the union was informed of all redundancy situations and was, therefore, able to modify management plans even though they could not substantially alter or challenge them. Through such activity, and via the efficient conduct of individual casework and grievance handling, the union sustained a presence within Insco throughout the implementation of the restructuring process. In practice, however, the union's role was reduced to one in which it charted each twist and turn in company policy and procedures and used its communication systems with members – particularly newsletters and e-mail – to inform members and expose management. In effect, the union controlled communications with staff, much to the annoyance of senior management (Interview with human resource manager, East Anglia Regional Centre, 1997). Despite this spirited though limited opposition, it was recognized by union representatives that the union's position within the company was weak and its future under threat.

The union's weakness was not only revealed by the failure to stop the devolution of collective bargaining to the five business units. Following their establishment, management initiated proposals to introduce 'core' benefits that applied to all staff across each of the new business units. The core benefits package was presented by management as providing a substantial improvement to staff terms and conditions. In practice, however, according to union representatives, the package saw the worsening of conditions for particular categories of staff, like new starters. The core benefits changed the basis of calculating, for example, pensions and holiday entitlements and housing loans, while also providing the 'carrot' of private health insurance for all staff. The proposals were put to the union on 8 November 1995. Following consultations, the union balloted members on the proposals, recommending their rejection. The ballot produced a 2:1 majority (on a 65 per cent turnout) for rejecting the company's proposals. Despite this, management unilaterally introduced the core benefits package, informing all staff in a circular, on 10 February 1996, that the core benefits package would be applied as from 1 January 1996. The core benefits issue illustrated the extent to which the company was prepared to impose change, irrespective of the views of the union and the majority of its members.

By 1997 the cumulative evidence drawn from such issues as core benefits, devolved bargaining and employee appraisal schemes demonstrated the marginalization of the union's influence over workplace affairs. When management initiated its review of human resource policies in that year, union representatives and the full-time official began openly to accuse the company of adopting a deliberate policy designed to achieve, in effect, the derecognition of the union (Interview with full time officer, 1997). In turn, the company accused the union of living in the past and being incapable of grasping the new circumstances in which the company found itself (Interview with human resource manager, East Anglia Region, 1997). By July 1997, the future of the union was in the balance. The company announced its intention to redefine recognition arrangements, taking into account areas of union membership strength and weakness. It also indicated its intention to move all staff within each of the five business units into a new single service company that would be free of many of the constraints imposed by the industry regulators on those employed in an insurance enterprise. These steps tended to suggest that the company was shifting towards a policy of union exclusion, in so far as exclusion may be defined as removing the union's right to represent the collective interests of staff via formal systems of consultation and negotiation.

For the union an opportunity to resist this shift arose from the company's plans to implement the provisions of the European Social Charter that required Insco to establish a works council consultative arrangement. The company initiated its discussions for establishing a European Works Council through its company located in Ireland. These discussions were lent an added impetus with the election of a Labour government, committed to the implementation of the Social Charter, in May 1997. Soon after the election the company announced, without reference to the union, its intention to set up a European advisory group, involving representatives directly elected by staff. The company pursued a policy of excluding direct BIFU representation. The union, assessing that it was unable to reject the proposal since this would contribute further to its marginalization, was faced with a challenge to ensure that its nominees were elected to the committee. It was possible, in the view of the union's divisional council, for the union to use this institutional innovation as a lever to begin to return it from the margins of workplace affairs. Paradoxically, a company strategy aimed at pressing the union further to the margins of company affairs provided an opportunity for BIFU to commence a process designed to achieve its renewal. Of the four seats on the European advisory group allocated to representatives of the company's UK staff, union candidates won two.

The events surrounding the ballot for staff representation on the European advisory group provided an important catalyst for the union's divisional council to review its role within the company, its approach to collective bargaining at company and business unit levels and its relationship with members. By the end of 1997, the union leadership within Insco was designing a strategy that focused on the rebuilding of union organization from below. The renewal strategy that began to emerge focused on rebuilding workplace organization through the establishment of effective local lay representatives (using educational workshops and seminars for initial training), establishing a wide range of methods for canvassing members' opinions and views and developing a new initiative to press management into negotiating at company level. Arguably, the attempt at renewal was at the 'eleventh hour', since Insco management had achieved considerable success in its attempts to marginalize the union's influence over workplace affairs and minimize the union's ability to moderate the worst affects of the restructuring process.

Union activists demonstrated a considerable degree of resilence, despite the numerous setbacks arising from the process of company restructuring.

Evaluation

Restructuring within Insco was initiated by a new management team, established in office in 1994. The restructuring process unfolded rapidly between 1994 and 1997. The process attempted to address both the external pressures placed upon the company as a result of changing market conditions and the internal weaknesses that these had sharply revealed. An important catalyst of change was the decision to establish five separate business units that were required to operate within a policy framework driven by Insco's executive management team. This policy focused on devolution rather than decentralization. Decentralization implies a considerable level of local management autonomy over the strategic development of business lines, cost and profit targets and the methods used to achieve them. By contrast, within Insco devolution took the form of lower levels of management taking on enhanced responsibilities, while continuing to work within a tightly defined, centralized management decision-making structure. Cost and operating targets were defined by the centre, with management at business unit, department and workplace levels working within the parameters cascaded down the organization. Autonomy was exercised in relation to methods of implementation and was particularly evident in the latitude given to local managers in changing systems of work organization. Here, however, this local discretion was tempered by the extensive involvement of management consultants, who lent an external legitimacy to an often painful process of downsizing and delayering. The company was apparently successful in this process. By 1997 it was possible for Insco to claim that it had reduced its cost base by nearly 50 per cent in a little over five years; its solvency ratio was restored to a healthy position and it had made steps to improve its long-term product portfolio, while steadily improving its overseas performance (Insco Annual Report, 1997).

The price of restructuring fell overwhelmingly upon staff. Around 2,500 jobs were lost through a combination of work restructuring and branch closures. Work reorganization took the form of the development of multi-functional teams in areas previously dominated by 'specialists', and the rapid expansion of direct line workplaces which contained many of the characteristics of the white-collar factory. In both these areas new technical systems facilitated the transformation of work organization through the introduction of dedicated software systems and databases. A piecemeal process of labour intensification took place, driven either by the work system (as within tele-sales) or by the internalization of the expectations created through the new work culture generated within work teams.

The restructuring programme not only addressed the weaknesses of the company and management organization but also exposed the weaknesses of a form of union organization that relied heavily upon its institutional role rather than its members' willingness to express their collective aspirations and interests. The break-up of the traditional institutional forms of regulating labour–management relations served to underline the union's tenuous links with its members. The union was revealed as a relatively hollow institution unable to challenge effectively the company's strategy of marginalization. None the less, the process through which the company pursued the marginal-ization of the union also revealed contradictions between a devolved form of management organization and the market pressures for the reintegration of product lines. At the same time, changes within the wider legal and political setting provided opportunities for union renewal, albeit from a relatively weak organizational base. Insco reveals the conditional character of manage-ment strategies buffeted by the demands of the external market and by the unpredictable capacity of labour to begin to reassert itself even in the midst of the most inhospitable conditions.

PART 3

HEALTH SERVICES

RESTRUCTURING IN THE NHS

The National Health Service (NHS) is the largest employer in the UK, with over one million staff. Established by a Labour government in 1948, it has been at the centre of the state's attempts to create social consensus and stability in post-war Britain. The NHS was established to provide maximum access to health care without imposing charges on the user, and was organized as a centralized national institution. The basis for this form of organization was established during the Second World War, when the Emergency Medical Service received considerable state investment and proved relatively successful in meeting the nation's needs. This centralized system was vastly superior to the patchwork provision offered by local authorities, voluntary bodies and the private sector in the decades preceding 1939.The newly formed NHS received wide support within society, though the details concerning its day-to-day operation provoked considerable controversy.

From the outset, the management of the NHS was a messy compromise between the desire of medical professionals to maintain their autonomy and the attempts by administrators to manage the service. Several different forms of management coexisted for the service's first thirty years. General practitioners (GPs) managed their own local surgeries as, in effect, small businesses; community and public health services were organized by district or county authorities in conjunction with a chief medical officer appointed by the Ministry of Health; and in the hospitals management was shared between doctors, nurses and administrators. Finally, the leading teaching hospitals (mainly located in London) achieved considerable financial and organizational autonomy within the service. This system was criticized for its in-built inefficiencies from the outset but was maintained until the early 1970s, when the first real crises in public spending prompted renewed efforts to review the funding and efficiency of the NHS. Since then NHS reform has been a high priority for successive governments.

The reforms of the early 1970s attempted to coordinate community health and social services provision but in practice left their delivery in the separate hands of the county and district local authorities and area health authorities (Moon and Kendall, 1993: 177). The critical response to the 1974 changes ensured that the reform of the NHS continued to be a high priority into the 1980s (Moon and Kendall, 1993: 176–7). The impact of the economic crisis of the early 1980s on the UK economy strengthened the call for reform. Under successive Conservative governments, the public debate on the role and future of the NHS took a decisive shift. While in the 1970s many of the problems facing the NHS were considered to be caused primarily by a funding crisis, by the mid-1980s government and influential commentators had shifted the terms of the debate (Mohan, 1995: 25–43). They argued that the crisis within the NHS was less a matter of under-funding and more a question of organizational inefficiency. Despite the fact that Britain was spending a declining proportion of its national wealth on health, discussion focused primarily upon the NHS's operational inefficiencies.

Letwin and Redwood (1988), for example, referred to the NHS as a 'bureaucratic monster' that could not be controlled. The NHS neglected the interests of patients, treated people as cases, desperately overstretched some doctors and nurses, diffused responsibility and redistributed funds in incomprehensible ways (Letwin and Redwood, 1988). Other commentators, while recognizing the relative decline in funding, argued that increased financial support was not a solution to the NHS's problems, primarily because advances in science and technology made it technically possible to improve health care provision continuously but also meant that costs would continue to spiral. The key to breaking such a spiral was an open debate on what was affordable within the framework of existing funding (Teeling-Smith, 1986). As the debate on the NHS's inefficiency gained momentum, so government and commentators publicly discussed a number of options for NHS reform. These included the introduction of charges for particular kinds of treatment, the extension of competitive tendering for clinical as well as support services and even the full privatization of the service. The political task was to promote patient choice and increased local accountability, alongside maintaining access and the efficient allocation of resources.

The American health care system offered a useful point of comparison. By the early 1980s, the privatized system of health care in the USA had created an increase in costs that reached, according to some business analysts, an unacceptably high proportion of GDP (Coddington et al., 1985: 129). Health insurance schemes encouraged those who were in them to make maximum use of the services provided, while the providers of services charged high costs in the knowledge that the insurance companies would pay. Most of these health care schemes were funded by employers, and the government provided tax incentives to support the employer contribution. The rising costs of health care provision directly impacted upon the profitability of US employers and contributed to a growing government budget deficit. In response to these problems, the USA introduced a system of 'managed competition' through the establishment of health maintenance organizations (HMOs). HMOs provided both the insurance and the health care. A per capita fee was paid by employers to the HMOs to cover a group of employees and the HMO contracted hospitals to provide health care for the employee group. The contractual relation between the HMO and the hospital acted to exert market pressures on the latter to keep costs down and efficiency high in order to keep the contract. This innovation contributed to a major reorganization of US health care provision. Its originator, Alain Enthoven, indicated that such a system could benefit the health service in Britain, with district health authorities (DHAs) acting as the UK equivalent of HMOs (Enthoven, 1985; see also Chapter 2, note 1).

Enthoven identified a series of problems facing the NHS in the mid-1980s. First, he argued that the power of the vested interests within the service – the autonomy of its GPs, the long-term contracts of its consultants, the highly unionized workforce – produced 'gridlock' when it came to discussing proposals for change. This gridlock meant 'it is more difficult to close an unneeded NHS hospital than an unneeded American military base' (Enthoven, 1991: 62). Second, he indicated that there were no incentives within the service to improve efficiency. Third, he argued that there existed 'perverse incentives' which tended to penalize the efficient hospital and reward the inefficient. Fourth, he identified overcentralization as producing waste and inflexibility. Fifth, he suggested that the system was provider dominated, with no body responsible for assessing patient needs. Sixth, he indicated that accountability was based upon 'inputs' (operating within budget limits) rather than outputs or the quality of service provided. Seventh, he argued that there was no flexibility at local level to trade off capital and operational spending, leaving hospitals, for example, unable to sell valuable real estate that might no longer be needed. Eighth, he observed that there was no systematic development of management information systems. For Enthoven the introduction of an internal market, via a purchaser/provider split, could act as a catalyst for significant improvements to be made in each of these areas of fundamental weakness. Enthoven's key proposal to introduce a new purchaser role for DHAs was coupled with another that suggested that GPs could play a central role in determining the local demand for resources by themselves becoming fundholders. In practice, the government, as a result of a prime ministerial review undertaken in 1988, decided to adopt a combination of the two proposals or models. These provided the basis for the White Paper *Working for*

Patients in 1989 and subsequently the 1990 National Health Service and Community Care Act.

The 1980s debate on funding and health care provision was inevitably linked to discussions concerning the reform of NHS management. The principles underlying the reform of management organization were clearly set down during the Conservatives' 1979–83 administration. The assumption underpinning reform was that a superior system of private sector management should be introduced into the public sector (Moon and Kendall, 1993: 179). An NHS management inquiry team published a report in October 1983, which subsequently became known as the Griffiths Report, after its chair Roy Griffiths, a managing director of Sainsbury's. The report indicated the necessity for a clearly defined management function at all levels of the service. The tradition of shared responsibility for management between clinicians, administrators and managers should end. A new professional management function was recommended for introduction at all levels within the NHS – district, regional and national levels – and at national level a general management board should run the whole service. The implementation of these proposals led to the rapid introduction of a new managerial ethos in which the traditional powers exercised by clinical professionals soon began to be challenged. The new managerialism also saw the widespread introduction of performance measures for monitoring and evaluating the quality of service provision.

The reform of management organization in itself did not create conditions for significant restructuring to take place. Only when coupled with the legal reforms contained in the 1990 Act did it create the potential for a fundamental reform of the NHS. At the centre of the 1990 legislation was the introduction of the internal market and the decentralization of the service. This was to be achieved through the establishment of self-governing trusts, each with its own trust board run by a chief executive. It was these trusts that would provide the services to be purchased by the newly established GP fundholders. Secondary and primary care relationships would be bound together by an internal market where local fundholders in the primary care sector (GPs) would purchase services from hospitals that were organized into provider trusts. The provider units would compete with each other on the basis of price and the quality of service offered (Moore, 1993: 1270). The reform of management organization was integrated into a new structure for service delivery. These developments created a potential for a significant reordering of NHS workplace relations.

Throughout the 1980s, despite the introduction of the 'best practices' from the private sector, management–workforce relations remained relatively untouched, with a centralized system of pay review bodies (covering the pay of doctors and dentists; nurses and midwives and professions allied to medicine) being coupled with the operation of a system of national collective bargaining. While some ancillary staff experienced the rigours of competitive tendering (provoking occasional strikes), relatively few changes occurred to a highly institutionalized relationship between management and a large number of trade unions, professional and staff associations. The NHS remained throughout the 1980s an industry in which trade union membership density was high, with a little over 70 per cent of staff being members. The 1990 reforms created the potential for a considerable reshaping of work organization and the transformation of workplace relations based upon the entry of new forms of market relations which overlaid the traditional relationships between workforce and employer. The process of change took place over the first half of the 1990s in an incremental fashion. The move to trust status, for example, occurred in four phases. The first saw 57 trusts established in England and Wales in April 1991. By the fourth phase in April 1994, over 90 per cent of NHS units had acquired trust status and these accounted for over 95 per cent of NHS expenditure (Bryson *et al.*, 1995: 120). A similar process took place in relation to GP fundholding, with some GPs quickly becoming budget-holders, while others refused to do so (Bain, 1993: 1185).

Throughout the early 1990s considerable debate took place about questions concerning the impact of reforms on the quality of health care provision and the necessity for its rationing, but relatively few studies explored the impact of restructuring on workplace relations. To what extent were they transformed from the highly institutionalized structures that existed in the 1980s and to what extent did the introduction of the market help create a new customer-oriented form of provision? In short, to what degree did the NHS begin to assume the features of the service sector restructuring model outlined in Chapter 2? The features of the model had their origins in the reform programmes introduced by management in the US services industries. Equally, the NHS reforms were partly inspired by those who had a strong influence on the new direction taken by the US health care system in the 1980s. There appears, therefore, some justification in suggesting that the restructuring of the NHS amounted to a shift towards its 'Americanization'.

The next two chapters address these issues by drawing upon evidence from a community health care (CHC) trust, established in the fourth wave, and a metropolitan ambulance service. CHC Trust is located in a large metropolitan area of southern England. The ambulance service is also situated in a large metropolitan area and services the needs of a consortium of purchasing authorities. The case studies address some specific themes arising from the complex process of NHS reform. They identify the changing character of trust management organization and, in particular, explore the extent to which management assumed a decentralized character. Second, the two case studies identify the main changes in service provision and their impact upon forms of work organization, exploring the relationship between the introduction of market mechanisms and developments in work organization and employee relations. Third, the case studies examine the process of labour intensification at workplace level. Finally, they focus upon the theme of continuity and change in workplace relations, assessing the extent to which relations were 'transformed'.

6 CHC TRUST: HEALTH CARE IN THE MARKET-PLACE

The Origins of CHC Trust

CHC Trust is located in North Metropolitan Health Authority. North Metropolitan was created through the merger, in 1994, of two health authorities. The new authority covered a densely populated urban area in the north of a major city located in southern England. North Metropolitan Health Authority had five hospital trusts under its jurisdiction from its inception in 1994. The trusts included three providers of acute (accident and emergency) care and two providers of community health care, one of which was CHC, serving two metropolitan boroughs whose populations were ethnically diverse. When established as a trust on 1 April 1994, CHC employed 1,400 staff and had an annual income of £40 million. The bulk of this income (93 per cent), and the basis of the viability of the trust, rested upon a single contract with North Metropolitan Health Authority.

CHC's main base was located at St Jude's Hospital. It also provided community health services from 17 other premises located in the two boroughs. St Jude's offered two main kinds of community care: for the elderly (192 beds in 1994) and for the mentally ill (202 beds in 1994). In addition to these two key activities, the trust provided a variety of specialist care and treatment services for its local population. This included treatment for people with sickle cell and thalassaemia and specialist support for those with eating disorders and drug users (CHC Annual Report, 1994–5: 1). CHC had been a beneficiary of the closure of two large mental health institutions located in neighbouring health authorities. The progressive closure of these institutions provided the basis for the expansion of mental health provision at the St Jude's site. St Jude's took those mental health patients who could not be cared for within the community. In addition, St Jude's continued to expand as a provider of care for the elderly. These two activities provided a stable base for the financial operation of the 'fourth wave' trust.

In brief, CHC was a relatively small trust with most of its staff and activities located on one site. From the outset, CHC was a beneficiary of the reorganization of the mental health service provision within the North Metropolitan area. While it was largely dependent upon a single contract with the local district health authority, it was not subject to the volatility in demand often experienced by trusts with accident and emergency provision. In consequence, CHC's position within the NHS's internal market was a relatively stable one, though it potentially competed with the other community trust within North Metropolitan Health Authority in bidding for, and developing, community care provision.

CHC Management Organization

On its establishment as a trust, CHC set up a board of directors. The board consisted of the chair, five executive directors, including the chief executive, and five non-executive directors. The chair of the board was an ex-deputy director of the Confederation of British Industry (CBI), a consultant in strategic management and an author of publications on NHS reform. His four non-executive associates were local business persons drawn from the public and private sector. The five executive directors were trust senior managers and were responsible for its day-to-day operation. These were led by the chief executive, who in turn was supported by executive directors responsible for medical provision, human resource management, nursing and quality and finance. Consistent with the legal requirements pertaining to the establishment of trusts, the chair's appointment was established as a period of five years. According to local union representatives, the chair was a Thatcherite, an enthusiast for NHS reform and keen to develop policies within CHC that were consistent with the objectives of market reform. The trust board was aware of its location within an ethnically mixed community. When, for example, in its first year of operation two non-executive members resigned due to external work commitments, the board decided to advertise in the local ethnic minority press for two replacements. Applications were received from 90 people and a shortlist was drawn up by the trust board. From the shortlist the chair of the regional health authority chose one and the secretary of state's office selected the other successful candidate. The new appointments were from the local ethnic minority community, one a local businessperson and the other a local councillor.

Beneath board level, management organization within the trust consisted of a senior manager responsible for each of its main areas of activity: mental health, care of the elderly, specialist, therapeutic and clinical services and child and adult community health services. Each of these specialities functioned within a departmental structure. From the outset, management provided 'core briefings' for key staff within the trust and established teams at workplace level who were led by team leaders. This system of team work was largely operational within the departmental structure. The tendency to embrace new management approaches to the operation of the trust was tempered by the style of the director of human resources, who had been a trade union member and representative. According to both management and union sources, the director was willing to maintain an established tradition of consultation and negotiation within the trust. This was reflected in the role of the deputy director of human resources, who was considered to be a person whom the union side could trust and reach agreement with (Interview with UNISON branch secretary, 1997). From its inception, therefore, the trust embraced a combination of new and traditional management approaches to workplace relations. Trust status facilitated a significant level of decentralization of management functions. The trust board, while working within a framework of regulations provided by the 1990 Act, was responsible for negotiating contractual relations and determining its own approach to the development of community services and industrial relations. On the other hand, this independence was tempered by the relatively high level of dependence upon the regional health authority for a single contract that determined the viability of the trust. The discipline established by this internal market relation in turn affected the latitude available to local management in its development of service provision and in the style it adopted for the management of its workforce.

More widely within the NHS, where market conditions imposed tight financial constraints on trust management, this tended to produce a more confrontational, 'crisis management' approach to restructuring and workplace relations (Mohan, 1995: 150–1). Where market conditions created a measure of financial stability, it was open to trust management to develop a less confrontational style. The discipline imposed by the internal market was not, however, the only factor in determining local management approaches to workplace relations. Decentralization lent management a real degree of discretion over the style adopted. In practice, this discretion could be 'contested' within management, as the CHC case study reveals. From its inauguration in 1994, the trust had a chair who demonstrated a willingness to pursue those new management techniques often associated with a 'Thatcherite' outlook (market testing, contracting out, benchmarking and performance measurement), while at the same time its senior human relations management team maintained a more 'traditional' management style informed by a belief that change within the NHS could be achieved through consensus and compromise. Within CHC these contrasting styles were reflected in a series of issues and, as illustrated below, provided opportunities that the trust's unions could use to their advantage.

The CHC Workforce

Of the 1,400 staff employed by CHC Trust, 70 per cent were women. The majority of staff were nurses or nursing care assistants. Nursing, or nurse-related posts, accounted for a little under two-thirds of the total staff. In addition there were around 150 medical professionals – consultants, doctors and dentists – employed by or contracted to the trust, and the remaining staff were administrative, managerial and clerical grades or craft and ancillary workers. On the creation of the trust, a programme of voluntary redundancy realized a reduction of approximately 40 posts. In the following two years, with the progressive closure of nearby mental health institutions, over 200 staff were transferred to St Jude's to take responsibility for running the mental health wards that were set up to take those patients who, following the closure of the institutions, were moved to the hospital. From the outset there were inadequate facilities to cope with the demand for mental health provision. While the majority of staff were located at St Jude's, small numbers were also employed in the community clinics spread round the trust's area of geographical responsibility. These clinics included health centres and community-based centres for the elderly. In 1997 the trust reported that 72 per cent of staff provided front-line medical services, while 28 per cent were support staff.

The transfer to CHC Trust of those previously employed in the nearby mental health institutions created the necessity for the new trust to blend together staff from different working environments and traditions. Those from the mental health institutions had different employment and working conditions from those who had worked in St Jude's in its pre-trust days. For example, the mental health staff were accustomed to working considerable amounts of overtime to compensate in part for staff shortages. Conversely, staff at St Jude's traditionally worked less overtime and management drew upon agency and bank nursing staff to fill in when shortages in staffing occurred. The bank system consisted of a list of qualified nursing staff who could be asked to undertake 'casual' shifts at relatively short notice. Often these staff would be drawn from those employed part- or full-time in neighbouring health authorities.

The system of union organization also reflected the bringing together of staff from different institutions. The staff who worked in St Jude's prior to the achievement of trust status were mainly National Union of Public Employees (NUPE) members, whilst those who transferred to the hospital from the mental institutions were members of the Confederation of Health Service Employees (COHSE). The Royal College of Nursing (RCN) had approximately 200 nursing staff, around one-quarter of the total of unionized nurses, and there was about 50 Manufacturing, Science and Finance (MSF) union members working as laboratory technicians. NUPE also organized the majority of the staff in the works department, despite the fact that most of these had skilled or craft backgrounds. Professional medical staff were members of their respective professional associations, such as the British Medical Association (BMA) and the British Dental Association (BDA), and a small proportion of the administrative staff were National Association of Local Government Officers (NALGO) members.

This range of unions and professional staff associations was common to most areas of the NHS. The professional staff associations, like the RCN, typically excluded the use of industrial action to progress the interests of their members and focused on influencing policy-makers in government and the Department of Health (DoH) in pursuing improvements in employment conditions, training and career development opportunities. Trade unions, like NUPE, COHSE, MSF and NALGO, mainly represented ancillary and nursing staff (NUPE and COHSE), technicians (MSF) and clerical staff and administrators (NALGO). In addition to these main NHS unions, in most NHS workplaces, the relatively small numbers of craft and maintenance workers were members of the Electrical, Electronic, Telecommunications and Plumbing Union (EETPU), the Amalgamated Engineering Union (AEU) or the General, Municipal, Boilermakers' and Allied Trades Union (GMBATU). Historically, the large number of trade unions and professional associations within the NHS spawned considerable rivalry between them, both in relation to recruitment and in terms of their respective capacities to proclaim themselves as representative voices of the workforce. The complex mix of trade union representation at CHC Trust was reduced when NUPE, COHSE and NALGO merged to form UNISON in 1993. NUPE, and subsequently UNISON, was by far the majority union at CHC.

The predominance of UNISON within the trust was reflected in the location of the union's own office in a well appointed spot at the heart of the sprawling St Jude's 'campus'. The union office provided a 'drop-in' point for union members. The office had a part-time administrator and was served by a branch secretary who had full facility time to undertake her trade union responsibilities. The union also had eleven shop stewards, seven of whom worked on the St Jude's site. The remaining three stewards were located in community clinics. In addition to the stewards or 'activist' representatives, the union also had twelve other members who acted as 'post-boxes' on behalf of the union. These would transmit union information to members but were not engaged in other ways in union affairs. In short, the form of union organization within CHC Trust had many of the characteristics of the public sector workplace of the 1970s. Located within a metropolitan area, with a large proportion of its members drawn from ethnic minorities, the culture of trade unionism had persisted despite the harshness of the wider social and political climate of the 1980s.

Work Organization at CHC

In the first two years of its functioning as a trust, CHC worked within its financial targets and achieved the efficiency gains required by the DoH. In 1994–5, for example, the trust achieved its financial target and made an operating surplus of £99,000. Overall, however, in 1994–5 the trust made a notional loss of £619,000 as a result of the downward indexation of fixed assets. This downward indexation, required by the DoH, was arrived at using the indices provided by the district valuer for all the trusts located within the metropolitan area. In 1995–6 the trust achieved its agreed financial target and managed an operating surplus of £178,000. This money was made available for additional capital expenditure in 1996–7. The trust was not allowed by the regional health authority 'to spend this surplus on other things' (Management Core Briefing Document, May 1996: 2). The relatively stable financial position of the trust was also reflected in its capacity over the first two years of operation to achieve its targets for financial performance and efficiency gains (CHC Trust Annual Report, 1994–5, 1995–6). Despite its relative financial security, trust management undertook changes in work organization and workplace relations that threatened the stability of workplace relations and illustrated how NHS restructuring affected even those who found themselves in relatively favourable market positions. This may be illustrated with reference to three examples: the development of mental health provision; the pursuit by the trust board, particularly its chief executive, of new management policies towards, for example, contracting out, market testing and benchmarking; and the goal of achieving greater labour flexibility.

From the outset, CHC Trust was required to expand its mental health provision within a financial framework in which the demand for acute beds for mental health patients could not meet their supply. Each year the trust renegotiated its main contract with North Metropolitan Health Authority. The contract set down quality standards and activity levels and required the trust to achieve efficiency savings. In turn, the efficiency savings, some 3 per cent of the value of the total contract, were returned by the purchasing authority to the trust and made available for capital investment projects. In this way the contract provided a means by which the savings squeezed from operating costs provided the seed corn of subsequent expenditure on capital projects, including the expansion of mental health facilities. In short, the contractual relation within the internal market supported a system by which the trust provided from its own improved efficiency the basis for the expansion of service provision. This system imposed immense pressures on those working within the trust. This was particularly evident in the area of mental health provision.

The closure of the two mental health institutions saw CHC make provision for some patients to be cared for within the community. Others were transferred to wards established at the St Jude's site, where the trust established a new acute ward and an intensive care ward during 1995–6, as well as introducing an emergency reception centre for those who required urgent psychiatric assessments. The process of developing mental health provision between 1994 and 1997 took place within a context in which demand for mental health provision continued to rise not only in the CHC's geographical area of responsibility but throughout the metropolitan area as a whole. While there was widespread support among professionals for the closure of the great Victorian institutions that ringed the metropolitan area, in practice these were replaced by a combination of underfunded community care places and the emergence of smaller institutions like CHC. Within the metropolitan area as a whole the pressures on these smaller institutions and community care facilities were considerable in the first half of the 1990s. The closure of the Victorian 'bins' saw a reduction by more than half of the psychiatric beds available within the metropolitan area during the period 1982–96: from a little under 17,000 beds to fewer than 7,500. There was, in particular, a decline in the provision of long-term stay beds (UNISON, 1997: 8). This programme of closures led to their reprovision in the smaller trusts like CHC.

While there were undoubted improvements in the organization of provision and in the meeting of patients' needs, the reorganization of services placed considerable pressures upon staff at trusts, like CHC, that were the beneficiaries of reprovision. The pressures arising from reprovision were felt acutely at the St Jude's site. They were reflected in several ways. First, management sought to reorganize shift working arrangements in 1996, moving away from permanent day/night shifts to a new system involving shift rotation. Night shift staff were particularly opposed to this proposal, since it removed their right to additional payments for night working. The night shift additional payment was perceived as a key compensation by staff for working in a stressful and demanding working environment. UNISON was called upon to introduce a ballot on strike action. The threat to do this was sufficient to cause management to climb down, withdraw the rotating shift proposals and reopen negotiations which aimed at achieving more modest changes in shift patterns. A second illustration of the pressures arising within mental health provision at St Jude's arose over the tradition by which staff worked overtime to cover staff shortages and absenteeism, rather than relying on the bank nursing system. The use of nurses drawn from the 'bank' system and nursing staff agencies provided management with the flexibility to ensure that budget-holders could operate within their staff cost targets (Interview with deputy director of human resources, 1997). Overtime working tended to be more costly and often involved some staff working extremely long hours, in some cases over 60 hours per week. This issue potentially caused divided interests to emerge within UNISON, with ex-COHSE representatives favouring the continuation of overtime working and those from the old NUPE branch at St Jude's preferring to reduce levels of overtime and grudgingly accept the use of bank and agency nursing staff. Under these circumstances, union and management reached a compromise in which overtime continued to be worked, but with a limit being placed upon the discretion left to ward managers on the number of overtime hours that staff might be allowed to undertake. Finally, and most significantly within the context of mental health provision, the expanded provision at St Jude's failed to keep pace with the growth in demand for beds. Throughout the period 1994–7, bed occupancy rates tended to exceed the number of beds available. This resulted in massive overcrowding in the wards. By early 1997, for example, the total number of beds in admissions wards at St Jude's stood at 110. Between January and March 1997 the actual number of occupants varied from a low of 166 to a high of 176. This overcrowding created a situation in which the number of violent incidents on wards increased and the number of serious incidents, including suicides, tended to rise. Such conditions created considerable stress among staff, and union officials found themselves in situations where they were regularly raising with management the need to provide additional support for staff affected by these incidents (Interview with UNISON branch secretary, 1997). It was the persistence of these working conditions that caused management to back down from attempts at cost-saving changes to overtime and shift working arrangements, but these successes for staff and union alike were tempered by the knowledge that holding on to traditional work practices did little to alleviate the underlying problems associated with working in the area of mental health provision.

Management took more decisive action in other areas of work organization. It was among groups like ancillary staff that the chief executive could implement changes that were consistent with the policies underlying the new managerialism. Towards the end of 1995 management announced its intention to introduce competitive tendering in the areas of domestic and catering work. Specifications were drawn up and domestic and catering contracts, mainly affecting staff working at St Jude's, were put out to tender. UNISON local representatives were reluctant to participate in the competitive tendering process, though an in-house bid was prepared. The union concentrated primarily upon ensuring that the private companies that tendered for the work would accept the requirement that staff transferred to the successful bidder would be safeguarded by the Transfer of Undertakings (Protection of Employment) (TUPE) regulations. These TUPE rights, which applied to most cases of contracting out in the public sector, ensured that the contractor took over the existing workforce on the same rates of pay and conditions of service. The contractor was required to provide a comparable pension scheme to the one enjoyed by staff during the period of their employment by the NHS. The contractor also had to provide rights of union recognition and consultation. The successful bid for the domestic and catering contract with CHC Trust came from Pall Mall. The contract commenced on 1 April 1996 and was to last for five years.

From the moment Pall Mall took over the contract, the UNISON branch secretary was engaged in regular informal negotiations over transfer arrangements, including working hours and staffing levels. Pall Mall was prepared to negotiate with the union. Throughout the first months of the contract protracted discussions took place over the interpretation by the contractor and the union of what amounted to 'broadly comparable' conditions of employment (Interview with UNISON deputy branch chairperson, 1997). After a few months of the contract's operation, Pall Mall experienced increasing difficulties in carrying it out effectively and within the cost framework agreed with the trust. By early 1997, the company sought to change working hours and conditions. It proposed the loss of between 600/900 hours, while maintaining its verbal commitment to maintaining service standards. The union responded with regular 'petitions' to the trust board. The petitions provided details of all the instances in which the contractor was unable to fulfil its contractual obligations. In its campaign against the contractor the union's representatives boycotted the 1996 staff Christmas party as a gesture of opposition to the chief executive's implementation of competitive tendering policy within the trust. By March 1997 there was growing evidence of cleaning and catering standards declining. The chief executive's ideological commitment to competitive tendering was not supported by an effective management of the contract by Pall Mall, nor was it supported by the trust's own senior management staff. After only one year of the five-year contract, on 1 April 1997, it was brought to an end.

According to union representatives, three main reasons were given for the early termination of the contract. First, arrangements for the transfer of pension rights had developed into a protracted and complex affair. Second, Pall Mall had failed to deliver services to the standard required. Third, the company had attempted to maintain service provision while cutting staff hours, which resulted in enormous pressures being placed upon the catering and domestic staff, who simply could not complete the work assigned to them in the time available. In the last few weeks before the termination of the contract, some members of the trust management team were actively but informally encouraging the union to submit as much information as possible to the trust board about the failures of the contractor. This information helped to tip the balance within the board towards the decision to terminate the contract. The union's campaign against contracting out had succeeded despite the chief executive's ideological commitment to the contracting out process. On the termination of the contract, the chief executive asked the union 'not to be triumphalist' about its success (Interview with UNISON branch secretary, 1997). The 150 jobs were transferred back to in-house provision. There were no redundancies but there was a protracted period during which CHC management and the union negotiated over the introduction of the most effective ways of restoring domestic and catering provision to acceptable levels of service performance.

The contracting out episode ended in a considerable success for the union. The union had launched a sophisticated campaign based around the petitioning of the trust board and stuck to its task of maintaining regular negotiations and consultations with Pall Mall management. The union sought to safeguard members' working conditions by using the requirement for transferred staff to continue working under broadly similar terms and conditions of employment. This demand created significant problems for Pall Mall in its attempt to vary working hours and workloads. While the domestic and catering staff were all union members, they had no union representatives drawn from their ranks. Support came primarily from the union's branch secretary. The union's high profile presence on the St Jude's site made it difficult for Pall Mall to ignore it, despite the fact that catering and domestic staff were not themselves well organized. Moreover, as the failings of the contract operation became increasingly clear, so some sections of the CHC management came to support informally the union's position. In this respect, the chief executive's hawkish adherence to the pursuit of a contracting out policy was moderated by opposition from within his own management team. The union's undoubted success was, however, tempered by the acceptance that its representatives had to find ways of working with local management to ensure that the staff who returned in-house to provide catering and domestic services did so within a framework that closely adhered to the Pall Mall contract. This led to a period of lengthy negotiations during which the union side found itself assisting management to find ways of meeting the exacting contractual conditions.

During the same period from April 1996 to April 1997, management launched several other initiatives in attempts to improve the efficiency and productivity of the directly employed staff. Underlying management's activities was the attempt to improve labour flexibility at the same time as reducing direct labour costs. This policy was pursued in a variety of ways. In the nursing area, for example, management pursued a medium-term policy of changing the skills mix of nursing staff. Broadly, this amounted to replacing qualified staff who left by employing less qualified staff as health care assistants and increasing the trust's reliance upon the use of bank and agency staff. In the mental health area, for example, an increasing proportion of trust staff shifted from overtime working to participating in the bank nursing system. Nursing staff employed within this framework were not entitled to overtime payments but worked additional hours at the basic rate of pay. Several staff undertook an additional two bank shifts per week over and above their contractual 37 hours. This meant a significant proportion of mental health nursing staff working 55 hours per week.

In non-nursing areas management attempted to introduce market testing: comparing the costs of in-house provision with those incurred by staff undertaking similar work in other institutions. Attempts were made to introduce market testing in areas like telephony and the works department (maintenance staff). These initiatives were successfully rebuffed by UNISON, but at the price of agreeing to renegotiate work practices and work organization. In telephony, staff agreed to the introduction of a new three-shift system in return for a lump sum payment not consolidated into basic earnings. According to union sources, this resulted in a satisfactory deal for staff, particularly as the threat of market testing was dropped for an agreed period of two years.

In the works department, a more protracted period of negotiations took place over the introduction of a common grading structure and work reorganization. At the centre of these discussions lay the conflict between management's desire to increase job rotation and flexibility and the maintenance staff's wish to maintain pay differentials and hold on to traditional skills. Management sought to introduce new methods of working, referred to as the introduction of 'first line response'. This amounted to a system of prioritizing maintenance and repair work, with urgent jobs being completed, wherever possible, within a day of their reporting and others being undertaken in accordance with a specified time schedule. The union recognized that improving the performance of the works department might help to safeguard it against the threat of contracting out, and there was evidence of inefficiency in the conduct of repair work (Interview with UNISON branch secretary, 1997). In this respect there was common ground between management and union, though for the latter striking the balance between increased flexibility and the maintenance of differentials (in accordance with the wishes of some maintenance staff union members) was a difficult task. Negotiations took place for several months in the first half of 1997. Management attempted to introduce a new grade of maintenance care assistants, who worked alongside qualified staff. It also wished to introduce job rotation across broadly similar areas of skilled work. While some groups, like the electricians, agreed to increased flexibility in return for improvements in basic hourly rates, others, like the fitters, did not. A piecemeal process of negotiation took place, at the end of which all groups adopted greater flexibility in work practices, while some protection was maintained on differentials between the new grade of maintenance care assistant and fully qualified maintenance staff.

The period from 1994 to 1997 saw a protracted process of negotiation and consultation over changes in work practices and conditions within CHC Trust. The process revealed a number of significant features about work organization and workplace relations within the context of a decentralized system of management organization. First, the relatively favourable market position of the trust, its relatively secure financial status, provided some latitude for the trust board and senior management to develop its own style and approach to workplace relations, rather than being driven by the imperatives of crisis management. In CHC Trust this style was 'contested' within management. The chief executive pushed policies that contained many of the features of those techniques associated with the new managerialism – contracting out, market testing and increased labour flexibility – while his own senior management team, particularly in human resources, tended to adopt a more pragmatic approach that included a willingness to maintain the tradition of consultation and negotiation with the recognized trade unions. In relation to the contracting out of domestic and catering services, the chief executive's approach suffered a severe setback with the early departure of the contractor, Pall Mall, which was only one year into its five-year contract. In this successful campaign, the union received informal support from sections of the senior management team. Conversely, in the negotiations over increasing labour flexibility, particularly in the works department, union representatives found common ground with management in attempting to improve the efficiency of the maintenance and repair operations. The union was prepared to deliver increased flexibility at a 'fair price' as an insurance policy against the threat of contracting out. In this sense, the union had to overcome its own members' anxieties over the dilution of skills and differentials. The contest within management between the new managerialism and the tradition of negotiation and compromise enabled the union to achieve some real successes in protecting jobs and conditions. Equally, however, the union conceded ground on the demand for enhanced labour flexibility, acknowledging that efficiency could be improved, and, arguably, strengthened the position of the 'traditionalists' within the senior management team.

A second feature of work reorganization was the fact that despite the union's efforts to modify the pressures towards the worsening of working conditions, the underlying trend was towards an increased intensity of work. This was implicit to the functioning of the internal market and the requirement to achieve efficiency gains, and the financial effects of these contractual arrangements worked through in a variety of ways. Over the period 1994–7, for example, management achieved a gradual change in skills mix, with, in each area of operation, less skilled and experienced staff being taken on to replace those skilled staff who left the trust. The change imposed greater responsibilities on the skilled staff who remained, and who were required to take on roles as budget-holders and team leaders. Management also pursued a policy of containing staff costs via the increased use of bank and agency staff, particularly in the nursing area. Even in the provision of mental health services, the tradition of overtime working was gradually eroded, replaced by a bank system which left many continuing to work long hours but without the same level of pay that they would have secured through operating the overtime arrangement. This containment of staff costs and staff levels saw increased pressures being placed upon nursing staff, particularly in a context in which there were increasingly crowded wards and more incidents of patient violence towards staff. Finally, in non-clinical areas, like telephony and repair and maintenance, staff accepted changes in shift patterns and work arrangements as a means of reducing the likelihood of being subjected to the greater evil of market testing and contracting out. In short, while the union succeeded in moderating the consequences of changes in work organization, trust management achieved incremental increases in labour intensity across the majority of work areas.

Workplace Relations and the Internal Market

CHC Trust was a modest beneficiary of the internal market operating within North Metropolitan Health Authority. Its financial performance was sound in its first three years of operation and it was a beneficiary of the reprovision of mental health provision within a densely populated area. Given this financial context, management had room to exercise discretion over the style it adopted towards workplace relations. The management style was a contested arena within CHC Trust, with, arguably, the traditional approach of consultation and negotiation winning out over the more aggressive Thatcherite approach of the trust's chief executive. The contested style was fully exploited by an active union organization led mainly by UNISON.

Workplace relations followed a rather different pattern in other trusts operating in North Metropolitan Health Authority. An interesting point of comparison is with the other community trust located within the region. Within a year of its establishment, Farm Trust was required by the regional health authority to cut its budget by 3 per cent over and above the efficiency savings that all trusts were required to achieve. Farm Trust was a community trust with its main operation on a single hospital site. It had 2,000 staff. The trust board at Farm adopted contracting out policies, with domestic and catering given over to private contractors in 1995. In the same year staff were 'invited' by local management to shift from NHS contracts to local trust contracts. Management offered the 'carrot' of the immediate payment of the 3 per cent annual pay rise that had been recommended by the nurses' pay review body.

Union organization at Farm Trust was divided more evenly across a number of trade unions and professional associations than was the case at CHC Trust. Overall, union membership density was lower than at CHC Trust. While CHC had a membership level of around 70 per cent, Farm Trust had a little over 30 per cent of staff in unions. Farm Trust had indicated its intention to stop check-off arrangements for trade union members in 1995. (A subsequent 'sign-up' campaign carried out by the TUC-affiliated unions had ended in the loss of nearly 50 per cent of its membership.) The unions organized a campaign against the acceptance of the local trust contract on the grounds that signing it would lead to local management increasing its control over staff's conditions of employment. The opposition was relatively successful, with only 25 per cent of staff signing the local trust contracts. Nevertheless, this shift towards strong local management control was reflected in management's continued pursuit of contracting out and market testing. During 1996–7 management successfully extended contracting out to a wide range of support staff and introduced a voluntary redundancy scheme.

The negotiating structure at Farm Trust was based upon an interim recognition agreement reached in 1992. The structure consisted of separate joint negotiating and consultative committees on which representatives of the six main unions and senior management were represented. There was a high level of full-time officer involvement in the committees, reflecting a situation in which falling membership levels had led to a decline in the number of union activists within the trust. It was this level of full-time officer support that maintained the union presence within the trust. It was, however, a situation in which, as a full-time officer commented, the 'culture of trade unionism' was being lost within the trust. Undoubtedly the adverse market position of this provider trust contributed to its management's commitment to a form of workplace relations that sought to marginalize trade unions.

While, in 1991, Farm and CHC Trusts had broadly comparable levels of membership density, within six years union organization at Farm Trust was in danger of collapse, while that at CHC Trust had been maintained. The process of decentralization provided opportunities for management to adopt different approaches to the conduct of workplace relations. The adverse market position of Farm Trust encouraged management to pursue policies aimed at marginalization and, potentially, union exclusion. By contrast, at CHC Trust management style was contested, with a less adversarial style appearing to win out by mid-1997. According to the deputy director of human resources at CHC Trust, the market had begun to 'bite' at Farm Trust by the mid-1990s, whereas, by contrast, at CHC, a smaller sized trust, the demand for its services had increased, it had not inherited large historic costs (unlike the large teaching hospitals in other parts of the Metropolitan area) and it had successfully bid for contracts within the health authority for the provision of mental health and other smaller speciality community services. These factors contributed to a climate in which there was a continuous 'dialogue' between management and union (Interview with deputy director of human resources, 1997). Decentralization within the North Metropolitan Health Authority facilitated a process by which trade union organization tended to polarize between trusts that remained relatively well organized and trusts in which trade union organization was in danger of extinction.

Evaluation

CHC Trust illustrates a number of issues relating to the restructuring of the public services in the UK. First, the development of the internal market created within the provider trusts (at least temporary) distinctions between winners and losers. CHC Trust was a winner, while Farm Trust was a loser. CHC Trust's relatively sound market position was reflected in its financial performance and its ability to win contracts, particularly for the reprovision of mental health services within the North Metropolitan area. This evaluation of its position as a winner in the market has to be tempered, however, by the acknowledgement that the renegotiation of contracts, often on an annual basis, and the provider dependence on one or two major contracts, created a precarious situation in which the 'purchaser' was able to impose demands for efficiency gains and service standards that might become increasingly difficult to achieve. This market relationship overlays the traditional relationship between management and workforce within trusts. The push from management for improvements in efficiency, service standards and labour flexibility may be attributed to a combination of market demands and the style adopted by management at local level. While management style is not simply contingent upon market position, it is arguably more likely that a winner trust has more latitude to adopt a less aggressive approach to the conduct of workplace relations than a trust faced with a deteriorating market position.

In CHC Trust, management style was a contested arena in which the chief executive was associated with the 'new managerialism', while his senior human resources managers tended towards a more pragmatic approach to industrial relations. In this context, decentralization within the NHS contributed to the strengthening of management independence at trust level in relation to the conduct of workplace relations. In addition, the operation of the internal market enabled the state to pass downwards the responsibility for the financial management of the service. Financial problems could be associated with the operation of contractual relations between providers and purchasers, rather than being attributable to a hierarchical relationship between the local tier of the service and its central management. In this sense the organizational reforms were consistent with the transformation of the debate on the future of the NHS. The development of the internal market served to place the focus on questions of efficiency and organization, rather than on the overall funding of the service.

Whether staff were located within winner or loser trusts, the internal market began to bite by the mid-1990s. Changes in work organization followed discernible patterns across trusts. Skills mix changed, new methods of working and shift patterns were introduced, labour was required to become more flexible and policies of privatization of specific services, along with market testing, placed increased pressures on staff to improve their performance. Trusts increasingly relied upon bank and casual staff, particularly in metropolitan areas, where there were shortages of skilled nursing staff within the local labour market (NUPE, 1993; Mohan, 1995). The combination of these policies, driven in large part by marketization, facilitated the development of workplace practices in which the introduction of new working methods and performance measures enabled local management to raise labour intensity by emulating the methods of production industries. At CHC Trust, for example, this was reflected in measurable terms by rising levels of bed occupancy over and above the number available in mental health, and a consequent rise in the proportion of patients to staff. Even the relatively successful CHC Trust experienced significant changes in the 1990s as a result of the introduction of the internal market and the decentralization of the service. These developments contributed to a significant restructuring of work organization and were justified by management as arising from the operation of the purchaser/provider relation. In this sense, the demands of the purchaser provided an external legitimation for CHC management to make demands for significant concessions in employment contracts and working conditions.

CHC Trust does, however, suggest a further important conclusion. Restructuring within the NHS has created an uneven process of change in workplace relations at workplace level. The market position of the trust and the contest over management style provided, within CHC, for example, an opportunity for well organized local union representatives to exercise considerable influence over the conduct of workplace affairs, as illustrated by the successful rebuff of Pall Mall. However, within the wider context of the metropolitan trust area as a whole, the development of internal market relations encouraged other provider trusts to adopt policies more directly aimed at diminishing union influence and potentially securing their exclusion at workplace level. Decentralization facilitated significant change in some trusts, while allowing elements of continuity to persist in others. Elements of continuity, expressed by the continued willingness of management to consult and negotiate change at CHC Trust, were sustained where there was commitment from key senior management and support from a well organized shopfloor. There were, however, ambiguities in the achievements of the union at CHC Trust. Their success at avoiding marginalization was achieved at a price of reaching agreements which, at best, moderated the adverse affects on members' employment conditions and, at worst, contributed to the smooth implementation of changes that achieved a rise in labour intensity. Finally, in the wider political context, the combination of decentralization and the development of market relations represented an important shift in the debate about the reform of the NHS. The terms of debate in the early 1990s shifted in focus towards concerns over the efficient operation of the internal market rather than being primarily driven by public concern about state underfunding.

7 METROPOLITAN AMBULANCE SERVICE TRUST: CRISIS AND REFORM IN AN EMERGENCY SERVICE

Issues like the impact of competitive tendering and privatization in the NHS were the subject of numerous reports and articles in the late 1980s and early 1990s (Cousins, 1988; Bach, 1989; UNISON, 1994). Authors also drew attention to the consequences for management and unions of the shift away from centralized bargaining, the Whitley system, and the development of local negotiations over pay and performance (Beaumont, 1990; Bailey, 1994). To date, however, relatively few have examined the introduction of trust organization, the expansion of the internal market and the effects of these on work organization and workplace relations (Lloyd and Seifert, 1993; Lloyd, 1997). This chapter explores these themes through an analysis of an emergency service located within a large metropolitan city in southern England.

The focus on a metropolitan ambulance service is particularly useful in helping to explore these themes. The service studied here operates across a number of NHS trust units and its contractual relations with several purchasers provide insights into the complex transactions of the internal market system. In market terms, the ambulance service transports the consumers of NHS services across the boundaries of primary and secondary care and is often the first contact point of the patient or 'consumer' with the NHS. It therefore offers insights into the changing pattern of demand for emergency and acute provision. As an emergency service, it is also the safety net if all other forms of service provision 'fail' or are not available. In this respect it provides a highly visible and public measure of the strengths and weaknesses of local NHS provision. Finally, ambulance services have experienced significant changes in workplace relations over recent years as technological and organizational innovations have been introduced in an effort to modernize the accident and emergency service. Ambulance service management, at trust level, has pursued a variety of strategies aimed at the reform of employee relations, including, in a few cases, union derecognition (Bryson *et al.*, 1995). The emergency service offers, therefore, a rich source of insights into the relationships between the development of the NHS internal market and changes in work organization and workplace relations. Before we look at the main features of management, workforce and unions in the emergency service, it is necessary to explain the crisis-ridden context in which they worked.

The Background: Crisis in the Metropolitan Ambulance Service

The Metropolitan Ambulance Service (MAS) achieved trust status in April 1996. The service operates across a large metropolitan area in the south of England, covering a geographical span of over 600 square miles. It was established as a metropolitan ambulance service in 1930 when it took over responsibility for the management and operation of the service from the Metropolitan Asylums Board. In 1965 its geographical area was enlarged to its present size and, in 1974, in common with other ambulance services, it was transferred into the newly reorganized NHS. The service covers a resident population of nearly seven million people but has a daytime population, especially in its central area, that is much larger. It is the largest unified ambulance service in the world. The service broadly divides between an accident and emergence service (A&E) and a non-emergency patient transport service (PTS). By the early 1990s, the MAS was carrying over 5,000 patients, and receiving over 1,500 emergency calls and over 1,000 other calls, per day.

The MAS was one of the last ambulance services in the UK to be accorded trust status. The reasons for the delay reflected the problems it had experienced for a number of years. It suffered from a history of chronic underfunding throughout the 1980s and early 1990s. During this time, the demand for A&E services (measured by the number of calls received) within the metropolitan area remained stable for most of the 1980s but rose by approximately 10 per cent per annum in the early 1990s. In other areas of the UK, the demand for these services remained broadly stable or modestly increased over the same period of time. While demand had risen and resources were more stretched, the service was also operating within a context of extensive NHS reorganization within the metropolitan area. Throughout the 1980s and early 1990s the area experienced considerable pressures to have its resource allocation reduced so that a transfer of health resources could take place, away from the south east and towards the north of England. The demand for such changes came from politicians, researchers and health specialists who were concerned by the tendency of the specialist teaching hospitals located in the metropolitan area to suck in health service resources at a level that the local pattern of health demand did not warrant. By the early 1990s it appeared that the operation of the internal market had led to purchasers withdrawing funds from central metropolitan hospitals. Throughout this period there was a programme of hospital closures and a reduction in the total beds available in the metropolitan area (Mohan, 1995: 73–101). One consequence of these developments for the ambulance service was that ambulance station location was no longer related to proximity to hospitals or the patient demand profile.

Problems came to a head between 1990–2. During this time, the MAS received considerable publicity about its failure to meet Ambulance Performance Standards set down by the Department of Health. These standards required ambulance services to achieve the activation of crews within three minutes in 95 per cent of emergency calls, be at the scene of the emergency within eight minutes in 50 per cent of cases and within 14 minutes in 95 per cent of cases and, in cases where doctors classified patients as 'urgent', the ambulance service was required to deliver them to hospital within 15 minutes of the arrival time specified by the doctor (DoH Steering Group, 1995). The MAS consistently failed to achieve these standards throughout the 1980s and early 1990s. This failure was compounded by the inability of the service to improve its technological capabilities, particularly in central ambulance control, to facilitate a significant improvement in service efficiency. Two costly computerization programmes had failed in 1990 and, most spectacularly, in November 1992. The latter failure provoked considerable public concern. It proved to be 'the last straw'. A public inquiry took place into the failure and the report, published in February 1993, initiated a period of extensive restructuring of the service.

This chapter examines the factors that gave rise to this restructuring process and explores the ways in which it took place within the context of the development of the internal market and, paradoxically, increased state intervention into the workplace affairs of the NHS. The implications of the development of internal market mechanisms and service restructuring for work organization and workplace relations is also analysed. In particular, the case study reveals how the adoption of a less confrontational management style has been accompanied by an intensification of work, accomplished through the introduction of more efficient work methods and technical change. The chapter reveals the persistence into the 1990s of a form of workplace trade unionism that has much in common with those characteristics attributed to unions in the mid-1970s. It concludes, however, with the view that this type of workplace unionism is unlikely to withstand the pressures for reform arising from the extensive restructuring of the ambulance service in the period between 1993 and 1998.

'The Last Straw': Computerization in the Metropolitan Ambulance Service

The MAS began to consider the use of a computerized command and control system in the 1980s, around the same time as many other emergency services, such as the fire and police services. The computerization programme was aimed at improving the efficiency of the system through which emergency and urgent calls were received and from which ambulances were activated or despatched to the scene of the call. The manual system operated along the following lines. On receipt of a 999 or urgent call, the control assistant in Central Ambulance Control (CAC) took down the details of the call on a printed form. The incident location was identified from a map book and the precise coordinates of the incident location were recorded. On completion of the form, a conveyor belt was used to transport the information to a central collection point within the CAC. At this point another staff member decided which resource allocator should deal with the call. This person was chosen on the basis of the geographical location of the incident point. The metropolitan area was divided into four divisions: central, south, north east and north west. The resource allocator identified, at this stage, if there were any duplicate calls within the system before working with a radio operator to determine which resource should be mobilized. The resource would then be chosen and information about it recorded on forms in an 'activation box'. The resource identified would then be recorded on a further form before being passed to a despatcher. The despatcher telephoned the relevant ambulance station and passed the mobilization instructions to a radio operator if the ambulance chosen to undertake the activation was already mobile. According to the performance standards, referred to as the ORCON standards, this manual process should have taken three minutes.

The deficiencies of the manual system included problems associated with: identifying the precise location of the incident; the difficulties of deciding whether the incident was a special priority, requiring the activation of a rapid response unit; the physical movement of the paper around the control room; the maintenance of up-to-date information about the location of ambulances (voice communication with ambulance staff was time-consuming and, at peak times, created mobilization queues); and the identification of duplicate calls, requiring human judgements that relied on memory. The introduction of a computerized system was intended to rectify many of these weaknesses through the installation of a computer gazetteer, the elimination of the movement of paper, the automatic identification of duplicate calls and the facilitation of the direct mobilization of ambulance crews. The automation of the system was estimated to improve the mobilization time by reducing it from three minutes to one (Inquiry Report, 1993).

Between 1987 and 1990, the MAS made its first attempt to introduce a computerized despatching system. It spent around £7.5 million. Its abandonment was decided upon when trials revealed that the system was unlikely to be capable of dealing with the level of demand placed upon it. This first computerization attempt ended in acrimonious rows between the service management and the contractors, with the latter claiming that the ambulance service management had regularly changed specifications while the project's development was being undertaken. The second attempt at computerization quickly followed from the abandonment of the first. This time it took place under the direction of a new senior management group, appointed in the wake of the failures of the service in the 1980s. A project team was set up, and included the director of support services, the systems manager, a contract analyst and a control room services manager (Inquiry Report, 1993: 19). While union representatives were invited to participate in the development project, they refused because industrial disputes over working conditions and staffing had created a poor industrial relations climate within the service at that time.

The new system was designed to provide a 'state of the art' automated despatching service. It was also decided to move from a manual to a fully automated system in one leap. Systems already in operation in other emergency services were considered and rejected for a variety of reasons, including cost and appropriateness (one system considered, for example, was used in a fire service, and the company that had designed it was unwilling to adapt it for ambulance service use). As other systems were considered and rejected, the small management team drew up very detailed systems requirement specifications. These were completed in early 1991 and were mainly the work of the contract analyst and the systems manager. While the new system envisaged by the specifications documentation would significantly change the working practices of crews, no attempt was made to consult over the proposed new system of working (Inquiry Report, 1993: 20).

The new system incorporated three elements: computer-aided despatch, a computer map display and an automatic vehicle location system. It was intended for these three elements to interact with mobile data terminals that had been installed as part of the earlier, abandoned system. The new system was ambitious: 'in an ideal world it would be difficult to fault the concept of the design. . . . if it could be achieved there is little doubt that major efficiency gains could be made. However, its success would depend on the near 100% accuracy of the technology in its totality' (Inquiry Report, 1993: 21). In compliance with the DoH's regional health authority standing financial instructions, the specification was put out to tender and the lowest tender had to be accepted unless there were strong reasons to the contrary. The lowest tender was accepted, despite the fact that the contracting company had no previous experience of implementing systems in a similar emergency service environment. The contractor was chosen from a field of 35 companies. During the contract negotiations, the successful bidder had indicated some concerns at the timescale for development and implementation that the ambulance service required. The whole project was to be completed by January 1992, providing less than a year for development and implementation. This timescale was adopted by the ambulance service management team despite recommendations provided by external consultants, reporting on the earlier computerization failure, which considered that a timescale of 19 months would be appropriate if a suitable package solution could be found. In the absence of an 'off-the-shelf' solution, the timescale of less than 12 months was, to say the least, extremely ambitious.

The successful bidders were a consortium of three companies, led by an established computer firm. Their bid for the supply of the whole system was a little over £900,000, some £700,000 cheaper than the next nearest bidder. The consortium's bid was hardware-led, reflecting the orientation of the lead company within the consortium, while the software costs were considerably lower than those of competitors. The software was to be provided by a second company from within the consortium, and a third was contracted to install the electronic equipment. Those mainly responsible for accepting the bid were the systems manager, a career ambulance service employee with no specific IT expertise, and a contract analyst who had five years' experience of working with the MAS but who knew that he was to be made redundant in the near future. As the Inquiry Report into the failure of the system noted, two unsuitable staff were: 'put in charge of the procurement of an extremely complex and high risk computer system with no additional computer expertise available to them. This added to the high risk nature of the procurement' (Inquiry Report, 1993: 25).

Early meetings between the contractors and the MAS project managers revealed concerns about the methodology by which the project would be managed, the fact that no senior ambulance manager was devoted full-time to the project and the timescale for implementation not allowing for review or revision. The tight timescale imposed considerable pressures upon the software designers. Throughout the project, software was delivered late and none of the tests conducted took place when all the software was in place. Elements of the system were tested, but the fully integrated system was never effectively tested prior to the launch. The deadline of January 1992 passed for the full implementation of the system. A decision was taken to implement a partial solution in which 'call taking routines would be implemented and incident reports printed out for manual allocation and voice dispatch' (Inquiry Report, 1993: 31). The gazetteer was also brought into operation. Over the period January to October 1992 the system was implemented on a piecemeal basis. Throughout that time the system continued to experience failure and instability and the timescale between initial staff training and the implementation of what they had learned grew longer. When, on 26 October, the computer aided despatch (CAD) system was fully implemented for the first time it quickly became apparent that to function properly it required complete and accurate data. There was, for example, on that day late reporting of vehicle locations. These inadequacies contributed to an increase in the number of 'exceptions messages', messages requiring the rechecking of locations, and these, in turn, produced a high rate of 'call backs' from the public checking the estimated time of arrival of the ambulance crew.

The build-up of calls and the inaccuracy of the data fed into the CAD system provoked its breakdown on 27 October. Since a decision had been taken to rely exclusively on the computer-based allocation system, no manual back-up system was in operation. The system failed, not primarily for technical reasons but because of the inaccuracies of the data entered, the development of a radio and telephone communications bottleneck and the lack of accuracy concerning vehicle locations. The system finally 'fell over' (Inquiry Report, 1993: 50). After this failure the service returned to a semi-manual system, involving calls being taken by the CAD system, using the gazetteer, incident details being printed out in the CAC and the mobilization of the vehicle via CAD to the station printer. This system operated successfully until 4 November when:

> shortly after 2am . . . the system slowed significantly and, shortly after this, locked-up altogether. Attempts were made to re-boot . . . this re-booting failed to overcome the problem with the result that calls in the system could not be printed out and mobilisations via CAD from incident summaries could not take place. . . . CAC management and staff, having taken advice from senior management reverted to a fully manual, paper based system with voice or telephone mobilisation. (Inquiry Report ,1993: 5)

The system failure was traced to a minor programming error. During work on the system a few weeks earlier, a programmer had left within the system a piece of program code that caused a small amount of memory in the file server to be used up and not released each time a vehicle mobilization was initiated by the system. Over a three-week period the available memory was gradually used up and, finally, the system failed.

The Inquiry Report into this failure presented strong criticisms of the NHS's financial and procedural instructions, which required purchasers to consider the tendering process primarily in terms of financial criteria rather than other factors particularly relevant in the case of IT procurement, such as the experience and expertise of those who submitted tenders in systems development and delivery. The report was also highly critical of the process of implementation: the failure of ambulance service management to place appropriate staff in charge of the project, the unrealizable timescale, the failure to ensure that adequate time was allocated for testing and developing the system, the inadequacies in training provision and the piecemeal method of introduction which served to undermine staff confidence in the system. The report, however, reserved its most significant criticisms for, and presented its most sweeping recommendations on, the questions of management organization and management–workforce relations. In short, management was criticized for seeking a 'technical fix' to what were primarily, from the management perspective, social and organizational problems.

The restructuring of the NHS in 1991, involving the establishment of the first wave of trusts, the devolution of financial management and the widespread introduction of performance measures, imposed significant pressures on service managers. MAS management was no exception. In fact, the highly visible frontline service that it delivered provoked widespread comment from the media and politicians. The inquiry team, in acknowledging these pressures, also pointed to the primary motives underpinning the NHS reforms. While arguing for time to be given to MAS management to 'put its house in order', it also stressed that 'the NHS reforms necessitate a change in relationships. The MAS and the Regional Health Authority (to which it was responsible) have to secure agreements on the level, quality and scope of A & E services that purchasing RHAs will purchase and fund' (Inquiry Report, 1993: 7). To achieve this it was necessary, for example, 'to develop quickly a partnership between executive management and trade unions' (Inquiry Report, 1993: 7). The partnership was to be fostered by the reform of management organization, the introduction of single table bargaining and an urgent review of policies on manpower planning, training, consultations and other terms and conditions issues. The Inquiry Report provided a 'blueprint' for the reform of workplace relations as a necessary complement to the development of the service's capacity to participate fully in the NHS internal market. Implementation of the blueprint incurred many problems. Nevertheless, later than many other areas of the NHS, the MAS was pressed into embracing new management approaches to work organization and technical change, which, in turn, had significant implications for trade union organization and workplace relations.

MAS Management: Managing the 'Battleground'

A report published in 1995 by the regional health authority with responsibility for the MAS referred to the service as a 'battleground' for much of the 1980s and early 1990s. The 1980s had seen the service suffer under a relatively weak and ineffectual management that had a poorly organized relationship to the regional health authority. Throughout the decade, the service experienced deterioration and neglect. Ambulance stations were run down, the ambulance fleet was aged and disputes constantly occurred between management and workforce over operational issues (Regional Health Authority Report, 1995). Management was organized along divisional lines. Four divisions covered the metropolitan geographical area: north east, north west, central and southern. Divisional commanders were responsible for managing their specific areas and were supported by industrial relations managers and administrative staff located at the divisional level. The divisions were small 'fiefdoms' from which managers had an often uneasy relationship with their counterparts at the centre.

In preparation for the implementation of NHS reorganization, a new chair and general manager was appointed to the regional health authority in 1989. He gave priority to implementing a programme of reform within the MAS. The introduction of reforms was, however, delayed by the national ambulance pay dispute, which lasted from the autumn of 1989 to the spring of 1990. The national dispute exacerbated the already poor labour relations that existed within the MAS. On its completion the regional health authority (RHA) was faced with introducing a fundamental restructuring of NHS provision, including making significant changes to its relationship with the MAS. The reforms required RHAs to remove themselves from having direct responsibility for running such operations as ambulance services. Following consultations with the NHS Management Executive, the RHA decided to set up a MAS board that would have its own chair and non-executive members who would be accountable to the RHA but would operate at 'arms length' from it (Regional Health Authority Report, 1995: 2).

In the summer of 1990 a chief executive was appointed to the new MAS board. He was given a brief to implement a fundamental programme of change designed to improve service efficiency. Between 1990 and 1992 a new more combative management style was adopted, alongside a commitment to achieve the successful implementation of the computerization programme. Both of these failed. The more aggressive approach to workplace relations merely resulted in a further deterioration in management–workforce relations, particularly between central management staff and union representatives. The staff unions rejected proposals for changes to work rosters, seen by management as a necessary complement to the programme of computerization. In turn, some senior managers, parts of the media and some politicians accused staff of engaging in sabotage to ensure the failure of the new computer system. While no real evidence of sabotage was discovered in subsequent inquiries, the levelling of the accusations was a testimony to the degree to which workplace relations had deteriorated. The failure of the dash for change between 1990 and 1992, and in particular the events surrounding the crash of the CAD system, prompted the chief executive's resignation just two years after he had taken up the post. The RHA's deputy regional general manager was appointed acting chief executive officer of the MAS, under the direct supervision of the RHA. He was given the task of implementing the blueprint for change that had emerged from the inquiry into the 'last straw' – the second failure of the computerization programme.

Implementing the blueprint

Within a month of the inquiry team's report being published, in February 1993, a new management strategy and structure was introduced within the MAS. It began the process by which a 'new managerialism' was to emerge within the framework of the restructured NHS. A team of new senior managers was appointed, including technology and finance directors. Additional funding (£14.8 million) was secured to support investment into increased staff levels, replacement vehicles and new technologies. The RHA's role changed from working jointly with the MAS to monitoring its progress. A team of external management consultants, with extensive experience of working with ambulance services in the UK, was brought in to provide a detailed analysis of the pattern of demand for A&E services and provide recommendations on resource deployment and rostering options. Their report was published in March 1994 (Consultants' Report, 1994: 2). Negotiations on new rosters commenced early in 1995 and were implemented in May of that year. The new management team produced a business plan that outlined a programme of change to be implemented over a period of the five years between 1993 and 1998. By 1995 the MAS indicated to the Secretary of State for Health that it was ready to make the necessary preparations for a move towards the achievement of trust status. In 1995 a shadow trust board was established and, finally, trust status was conferred in April 1996. This significant change in its fortunes was not achieved without continuing difficulties. In mid-1994 the death of a patient who had waited 50 minutes for an ambulance triggered widespread public condemnation and prompted a further independent review of the service's performance.

This review was followed by an inquiry in 1995 by a House of Commons Select Committee, which was highly critical of the service and particularly damning about the slow rate of change it had achieved over the previous two years. Despite these setbacks, sufficient change took place between 1993 and 1996 to facilitate the MAS's integration into the NHS's internal market. During this period, management reforms and the service's entry into the internal market had significant implications for work organization and the conduct of workplace relations.

The Workforce

Between 1985 and 1990, MAS staffing had fallen by around 5 per cent to a figure of just over 2,500 (whole time equivalents). This drop was consistent with the national pattern, where staff levels had declined by just under 7 per cent between 1987 and 1992. Nationally, this amounted to a loss of around 1,330 jobs, with most losses occurring among ambulance officers and control assistants (UNISON, 1993: 3). While staffing levels fell in the MAS, the demand for A&E services rose, particularly in the early 1990s, at a rate of around 10 per cent per annum. A poorly managed service using outdated vehicles was required to meet a steadily increasing demand across a highly densely populated region. The vacuum left by inadequate management was, in effect, filled by staff at station level. Despite the emergency nature of the service and the required adherence to procedures, there was discretion over the conduct of operational matters. The 1980s saw ambulance staff, through their union representatives, exercise considerable influence over the day-to-day operations of the service. Work organization was contested between local management and work groups. Effective 'shopfloor' organization, during this time, in many respects compensated for weak management and ensured that an emergency service was maintained despite the persistence of adverse conditions (Interview with UNISON full-time official, 1996). The 1989–90 ambulance dispute and the period between 1990 and 1992, during which senior management attempted to reassert its control, only served to strengthen the strong sense of collectivism at shopfloor level. This collectivism was reinforced by the demanding nature of the work of ambulance crews and the high public profile that the service experienced. Close public scrutiny of the service, particularly from Westminster, reinforced the collective outlook of ambulance staff who were constantly pressed through their unions to articulate their cause and concern. As a consequence of these special factors, a strong union identity persisted at local level throughout the 1980s and early 1990s, despite the adverse political conditions in the UK that trade unionism experienced during that time.

Trade union organization in the MAS

A complex set of historical factors shaped union organization within the MAS. Prior to the merger that created UNISON in 1994, there were six main unions within the service. The Amalgamated Engineering Union (AEU) organized repair and maintenance staff, the Transport and General Workers Union (TGWU) and General, Municipal and Boilermakers (GMB) had a relatively small membership of around 200 staff and the vast majority of staff were in the Confederation of Health Service Employees (COHSE), the National Union of Public Employees (NUPE) and the National Association of Local Government Officers (NALGO). When the latter three unions came together to form UNISON, the new union became, by far, the main union within the ambulance service, representing around 60 per cent of those employed within the service. Senior management officers had their own organizations, which represented the higher grades of management staff. The service was, therefore, traditionally highly organized.

The base for union organization was the ambulance station. Union members within a station elected their 'station rep'. The election of this representative took place among all union members, irrespective of their specific union membership. It was, therefore, possible for a member of a relatively small union, the GMB, to represent, for example, staff who were UNISON members. This situation was based upon an 'open shop' principle in which local workplace democracy prevailed over the representative structures of each specific union. The system tended to produce strong local leaders and a collectivism at workplace level which did not necessarily coincide with a corresponding loyalty felt towards the union of which the representative was a member. The system of trade union organization at workplace level placed an emphasis on the individual's capacity to be an effective representative and provided opportunities for unions with relatively small memberships to play a significant part in industrial relations affairs. Equally, the arrangements for union recruitment tended to support this 'open shop' principle. New staff were recruited to the union at training school. The union that new recruits joined was determined by where they were to be located. They joined the union that had a majority membership at the station to which they were to be attached. This facilitated the maintenance of union membership levels for the smaller unions at station level. The mix of union membership occurred at this level because staff who were transferred from one station to another would remain within the union they had initially joined.

The 'station rep' structure also ensured that a strong activist:membership ratio was maintained. In the early 1990s, for example, there was one union representative for every 15 union members. In brief, this system of union recruitment and representation encouraged a strong shopfloor collectivism at the same time as ensuring that the relationship with the unions outside the workplace was less strong. Full-time union officers were perceived by many local representatives as 'outsiders' (Interview with UNISON full-time officer, 1996). The sense of collectivism among the staff was further reinforced by the jargon-ridden complexities of the operational procedures that existed within the uniformed service and by the demanding nature of the service provided. It was these special conditions, coupled with the intense public scrutiny of the service, that created a 'siege mentality', and reinforced the strong collective identity felt by many staff, particularly those who were ambulance crews, or operational staff, who worked in the field. In many respects this form of union organization, which persisted into the 1990s in the MAS, had similarities to that which existed in Fleet Street in the 1970s (Martin, 1981). Paradoxically, this model of trade unionism flourished under the adverse conditions of the 1980s and early 1990s, but came under increasing pressures to change as a result of the management reforms introduced in the period between 1993 and 1998.

The Reform of Work Organization

While the domestic catalyst for reform had been the failure of the second attempt to computerize the MAS, the underlying pressures for change arose from the commercialization of the NHS, a process that had accelerated with the introduction of the internal market in 1990 and 1991. Ambulance services throughout the UK were under considerable pressure to improve service standards at the same time as achieving 'efficiency savings'. The mechanism for raising efficiency was the purchaser/provider contracts that were at the heart of the new relationships struck between ambulance services and their respective local health trusts. As ambulance services achieved trust status, they adopted many of the attributes of the commercial concern. Trust status was accompanied by a new emphasis on financial performance in four main areas. First, ambulance services were required to explore ways of increasing their income through selling their specific skills and expertise. Second, they were required to demonstrate a capacity to exercise financial control over their own activities. Third, services were made responsible for developing their own investment plan. Fourth, they were required to demonstrate 'value for money'. Like other trust units, ambulance services were set target rates of return, an income 'surplus' over operating costs, for each financial year of their operation. These developments created significant pressures for the internal reform of work organization and management–workforce relations. A minority of ambulance trusts established in the 'first wave' between 1991 and 1993 quickly moved to reorganize service provision by, for example, contracting out non-emergency patient transport services, and some made radical changes to industrial relations arrangements. The Northumbria Ambulance Service, for example, on the conferment of trust status, shifted to a single union agreement with the non-TUC affiliated Association of Professional Ambulance Personnel (APAP) and derecognized the other unions that had previously represented the majority of ambulance staff (Gall and McKay, 1994; Fitzgerald and Stirling, 1995).

Progress towards the establishment of devolved financial responsibility and the implementation of new market arrangements was slower in the MAS than in other ambulance services within the UK. Despite the fact that NHS authorities were required to operate within their cash limits, the MAS had revenue overspends between 1991 and 1993. The RHA responsible for the MAS, and senior MAS officers, negotiated service agreements with the other RHAs within the metropolitan area. These agreements covered four RHAs and included over 80 hospitals and many community units. These contracts were relatively 'open ended' and were only loosely related to the volume of A&E services actually provided. This contract system did not facilitate effective evaluation of costs; nor did it provide an effective means of measuring 'value for money'. It also failed to take into consideration the rise in demand for A&E services that was experienced in the early 1990s. As part of the attempt to restructure the service, following the report into its failings in 1993, the reform of the contracting structure was pursued alongside an investment programme and extensive changes in work organization. The implementation of this 'package' of change began in earnest in 1994.

In 1994 the MAS presented its specifications for an outside consultancy to examine demands made on the A&E service in relation to the resources available and the service standards achieved. The consultancy that successfully bid for the tender had considerable experience of research into ambulance services in the UK. It used its own modelling package for evaluating resource deployment and staff rostering options. In practice, the consultancy undertook a work study exercise that:

> took account of achievable travel times and the geographical distribution of incidents and allowed the optimal distribution of demand to be met by each division's crews that were identified. Separate optimal databases covering calls only within the target demand set for each division were then prepared and used as a basis for modelling resource deployment options for each division. (Consultants' Report, 1994: 5)

The review of the work process took place over a representative 25-day sample period in September 1994. It revealed that crew utilization rates were relatively high compared to those of other ambulance and emergency services. This rate refers to the actual time that a crew is engaged in active service. The ambulance crews in the MAS were on active duty for over 50 per cent of their duty time, significantly higher than, for example, fire service crews in the metropolitan area, who were active for around 11 per cent of their duty time. The review also confirmed that station configuration was poor in relation to the demand profile, and that while performance standards had improved in 1994, demand had increased and staff rostering arrangements did not fully match the hourly demand levels. The main recommendations of the Consultants' Report included a number of proposals that, when implemented, were to have a significant impact on work organization. The proposals were introduced under the title of the Resource Deployment Project.

The key recommendations included the introduction of standby points and the development of a system of dynamic cover. Standby points were locations away from the ambulance station where crews would be situated in their vehicles, ready to be 'activated' at a moment's notice. Dynamic cover arrangements would enable crews to be moved by controllers to 'strategic positions on standby, or in backing up another station area temporarily without cover' (Consultants' Report, 1994: 12). The effect of these recommendations was, according to the consultants, an improvement in the range of cover offered by ambulance crews, thereby mitigating the effects of the poor configuration of ambulance stations within the metropolitan area. The implementation of the recommendations required changes to rostering arrangements, shift patterns and staffing levels. Negotiations between central management and unions took place in the first half of 1995, resulting in an agreement in May. The union side secured one-off payments (£500 for each member of staff required to change shift patterns and a further £250 for those required to transfer to another station) for the introduction of new rostering arrangements, while the principle of standby points was accepted, with detailed arrangements being decided upon through divisional negotiations. The agreement resulted in improved performance levels but also brought with it significant concerns, especially within the busiest, central division, about the deterioration in working conditions experienced by crews. They were required to remain within their vehicles for long periods without amenities and at locations that made them vulnerable to attacks and vandalism (Interviews with UNISON full-time officer and senior industrial relations manager, 1996). Disputes arose, therefore, over standby point locations and the operation of this system during the 'dead' nighttime hours. In spring 1996, in the central division, disputes broke out between local management and crews which resulted in the reorganizing of standby locations and the rejigging of some shift arrangements. From management's perspective the rejigging did not work. In early 1997 management sought further, more extensive alterations to shift patterns.

The traditional shift pattern involved staff working one of three shifts: early (7 a.m. to 3 p.m.); late shift (3 p.m. to 11 p.m.) or night shift (11 p.m. to 7 a.m.). The revised shift rotas, initially recommended in the Consultants' Report, were aimed at matching shift patterns with the peaks and troughs in demand for A&E provision. A system of staggered shifts were introduced that varied between divisions, according to local patterns of demand. Staff could be employed on shifts of varying duration (six, eight or ten hours), with a variety of start and finish times. Staff could complete their shifts in the early hours of the morning (at 1, 2 or 3 a.m.) and be required to work a different pattern of hours the next day. Rotas were drawn up by station managers, with local stations having no fixed 'hand-over' times between crews. According to an ambulance crew member, the new shift arrangements were 'designed to get as much out of you as possible' (Interview with central division ambulance crew member, 1997). The new shift rotas were complemented by the use of the standby points. The combination of these changes created considerable tension among staff in the busiest central division. The tension culminated in industrial action in the summer of 1997, when crews simply refused to go to their standby points and took it upon themselves to return to their ambulance station base following the completion of a call-out. Management was forced to concede changes in standby arrangements, with the unions involved in rene-gotiating standby locations and the times during which such arrangements would be applied. While the new pattern of working was contested, the new shift patterns and modified standby arrangements contributed to a significant rise in the proportion of staff time spent 'on the road'. A service that was already operating at higher efficiency levels than other A&E services increased the proportion of operational time from an average of 55 per cent of available work time to about 65 per cent per shift worked (Interview with union branch officer, central division, 1997).

The changes in work organization were complemented by investment in new technologies and vehicles, increased staffing and new training pro-grammes for managerial, administrative and operational staff. A technology director was appointed to oversee the introduction of a new control room for the location of the CAC system. A new telephone service was introduced and controllers were reallocated to seven geographical sectors to take advantage of the new standby point arrangements. A new system was tested and imple-mented to enable the computerisation of call-taking. This was linked to a gazetteer system which facilitated the automation of the despatching system on a trial basis in spring 1996. These changes in work methods were intro-duced alongside the recruitment of over 200 new staff to the operational side, with a growing proportion of these receiving paramedic training. The para-medic workforce increased from 360 staff at the beginning of 1994 to 680 by the end of April 1996 and, over the period 1996 and 1997, agreement was reached with a local university to provide a certificate in paramedic science, a first stage in the introduction of a full diploma and degree award scheme for ambulance staff. This move towards the professionalization of the service was perceived to be a key development in ensuring the future stability in staffing and workplace relations (Interview with senior industrial relations officer, 1996). The unions, particularly UNISON, supported the shift towards the pro-fessionalization of the A&E workforce. UNISON was also aware, however, of the potential difficulties that such a shift could create among members. The polarization between the higher and lesser skilled sections of the ambulance staff adversely affected solidarity. The contracting out of some PTS contracts in 1996 and 1997 met with little union opposition, primarily because the PTS work had less status or significance attached to it by key front-line staff (Inter-view with UNISON full-time officer, 1997).

The Market and Workplace Relations

The investment in infrastructure and staffing levels within the MAS were linked to the service's integration into the internal market in two main ways. First, the management reforms implemented between 1994 and 1996 took place within the context of preparing the MAS to become a separate NHS trust unit. Second, the implementation of trust status was accompanied by the reform of the contractual relationship between the service and the purchasing authorities. A 'shadow' trust board was established in 1995, taking on the responsibilities of devolved financial management, and a trust prospectus was published. The inauguration of trust status occurred on 1 April 1996. Most significantly, the new form of contractual relations between the ambulance service and the purchaser health authorities began in 1995. The purchasers came together in a consortium of 16 health authorities, with four of these acting as 'lead' authorities within the contractual negotiations. The consortium negotiated annual contracts with the MAS for A&E services. Over 80 per cent of MAS income came from these emergency service agreements in 1995 and 1996.

The 1995 and 1996 agreement had four pricing elements: a block price (which included the cost of recruiting an additional 240 staff in 1994); a price to meet the cost of additional staffing to fulfil the higher projected workload for 1995 and 1996; and recurrent and non-recurrent costs arising from the improvements implemented by the MAS as a result of the 1994 Inquiry Report. The funding for the implementation of the recommendations was 'subject to the achievement of operational performance targets' (MAS Business Plan, 1995–6: Appendix 3). In this way, additional funding to improve efficiency was linked to the potential imposition of financial penalties if performance targets were not achieved. The purchaser/provider contract offered the mechanism through which performance could be jointly monitored and financial penalties introduced if standards fell below those agreed between the parties. Monthly performance figures were to be sent to the consortium members and quarterly meetings were scheduled to review overall progress. This contractual relationship provided external pressure on the MAS to ensure that internal efficiencies were achieved. In this way, the disciplines associated with the NHS market mechanism increased the pressures for greater efficiencies in work organization and the increased intensity of labour.

The purchaser/provider contracts had another effect on the organization of the domestic labour market within the MAS. The shift to a cycle of annually negotiated contracts with the consortium led to many new employees in non-operational areas being recruited on one-year rather than permanent contracts. This casualization of the employment of non-operational staff stood in sharp contrast to the professionalization of the role of 'core' operational staff, whose career development was guaranteed via the introduction of the paramedic service. Professionalization of the A&E provision also created a sharper divide between it and the PTS. It was the latter that felt the brunt of the competitive tendering process. In 1995 and 1996 the PTS contract held by the MAS with the consortium was trimmed from £13 million to a little over £11 million as a result of the failure of in-house bids. Staff in the PTS area were redeployed, but it was recognized in spring 1996 that this process of redeployment could not continue. It was likely that staff would be encouraged to take voluntary redundancy in future years (Interview with senior industrial relations officer, 1996).

A third feature of the purchaser/provider contracts which had implications for employment within the MAS, and the health service within the wider metropolitan area, was the way in which market relations facilitated modest increases in staffing and resources in one service to 'compensate' for much greater losses elsewhere. The MAS's main contracts with the purchasing consortium excluded provision for additional resources that might be needed as a result of the closure of a major A&E unit within a specific health authority. To cover for such a loss, and to ensure that the service could continue to meet the performance standard required to respond to emergency and urgent calls, the MAS undertook 'side negotiations' with individual health authorities. These resulted in the MAS receiving additional income for increasing A&E cover in the health authority affected by the closure. The 'side deal' lasted for the duration of the year in which the facility was closed. Following this, the new level of resourcing would be incorporated into the annual round of contractual negotiations between the purchaser consortium and the MAS. The beneficiary of the side deal was the MAS, and indirectly its staff. However, within the overall context of budget limited health service provision, the modest success achieved in increasing A&E resources arguably hardly compensated for the significant loss of resources that occurred within the purchaser health authority in which the A&E unit closure occurred.

The devolution of financial management and the introduction of trust status had implications for the conduct of industrial relations within the MAS. The institutions through which collective bargaining took place remained relatively stable throughout the period of restructuring. These were based upon a constitution drawn up by the service when it became a part of the NHS in 1974. Under this structure representatives of different employee groups – craft, clerical and administrative and operational staff – held separate negotiations at the centre and divisional levels. In 1994 this changed with the introduction of single table bargaining. A central staff council was formed to deal with industrial relations issues of a service-wide nature, while divisional committees consisting of representatives from all occupational groups met to discuss local operational issues. In practice, these negotiating forums, and their predecessors, had all been dominated by 'day-to-day' operational 'crises' (Interview with UNISON full-time officer, 1996). While collective bargaining arrangements were reformed, the union role was sustained. There was no attempt to marginalize the role of the trade unions. In practice, the reforms were designed to encourage union representatives to participate more in discussion of the strategic issues facing the service. This development was consistent with attempts by management to build partnership. The partnership approach to collective bargaining relationships was developed, however, within a new market-oriented setting.

The emergence of the internal market and the introduction of purchaser/provider contracts determined the resources available for such matters as additional staffing and training as well as setting the service's projected workload and performance targets. All of these decisions were taken in forums that were outside of the influence of the trade unions within the MAS. The parameters within which collective bargaining could take place were structured by the contracts agreed between the MAS and the purchaser consortium. Trust status and its associated set of market relations placed significant limits on 'local' collective bargaining, creating the potential for a new pattern of workplace relations to emerge. The operation of the internal market severely limited the scope for trade union influence to be exercised over workplace affairs, while at the same time fostering a climate of partnership between management and union representatives to ensure that performance standards continuously improved, so that the service remained efficient and 'commercially viable'.

Marketization created a new climate for the conduct of workplace relations and facilitated the development of a culture of partnership which was aimed at burying differences and encouraging cooperation in implementing the changes required to comply with the performance levels demanded by the contractual relation with the purchasers.

New Managerialism, the Market and Labour Intensification

The new managerialism that emerged in the MAS between 1993 and 1998 reflected similar trends taking place elsewhere in the public services (Fairbrother, 1994, 1996). The new management approach had its origins in the commercialization of the NHS, and, in particular, was shaped by the 1991 reforms which saw the widespread introduction of trust organization, the development of GP fundholding and the emergence of the purchaser/provider contractual relation. A little later than other services, the MAS developed many of the attributes of the new management model. Senior management posts were professionalized through the appointment of staff with specific responsibilities for such areas as technology and finance. Responsibility for financial management shifted from the RHA to the service, and, subsequently, trust level, and a more clearly defined division between clinical and general management roles was established.

While these developments shared common characteristics with the new managerialism established elsewhere in the public services, there were also significant differences. The new management approach adopted within the MAS was moderated by the specific set of social relations in which it was applied. A strong shopfloor collectivism modified and contained the more strident attempts made by management to reassert authority and control. This was particularly evident between 1990 and 1992, when a more aggressive management style was adopted and subsequently abandoned following the failure of attempts to computerize the service and implement new work practices. The strength of workplace unionism also moderated management style in other ways. First, there was little evidence of management adopting many of the new HRM techniques associated with the fashionable models applied elsewhere within the public and private service industries. Management documents, for example, were devoid of the terms and phrases associated with the HRM model. There was no attempt to establish new forms of employee communications that by-passed union representatives and no evidence of attempts to individualize employment relations through the introduction of performance appraisal schemes. The absence of these attributes of the new managerialism, as applied to the conduct of workplace relations, provides a sharp contrast to developments elsewhere in the ambulance service (Fitzgerald and Stirling, 1995) and many other areas of the NHS. In short, the MAS example provides strong evidence to support the case that public service managers, despite experiencing the common pressures associated with the commercialization of the public sector, may follow very different approaches to the restructuring of service provision (Fairbrother, 1996: 123). In this case, the emergence of a more professional management structure between 1993 and 1996 coincided with the development of a more cooperative 'deal making' approach to the trade unions. An important corollary of this conclusion is an evaluation of its implications for ambulance workers and their employment conditions. Paradoxically, the evidence suggests that the cooperative deal making approach, adopted from 1993 onwards, achieved more for management than the strident anti-union approaches often associated with the new managerialism. This conclusion is supported by the evidence in three main ways.

First, between 1993 and 1996 management successfully introduced significant changes in the pattern of work organization. At the heart of the changes were the introduction of standby points and dynamic cover arrangements. These initiatives, in turn, gave rise to the transfer of staff between stations and the reform of work rosters and shift arrangements. By spring 1996, MAS management could report significant improvements. In ambulance response times, for example, the percentage of emergency calls that obtained an ambulance arrival at scene within 14 minutes rose steadily from a baseline of 64 per cent, achieved in September 1993, to a level of 78 per cent in January 1996. This was despite a 16 per cent increase in the volume of calls received during that period. For the month of March 1996, the MAS 'responded to 42,386 emergency calls within the Patients Charter Standard of 14 minutes – a record in the history of the ambulance service and over 200 patients per day more than a year before' (MAS Business Plan, 1996–7). While these improvements were partly facilitated by investment in new vehicles and communications technologies and an increase in operational, or front-line, staffing levels, from 1,480 to 2,000 between 1993 and 1996, they were also accompanied by improvements in the patterns of staff utilization and deployment.

Second, in the context of a continued rise in the demand for A&E provision, new investment in capital and labour was accompanied by an increased intensity of work, particularly through the introduction of standby points, new shift rotas and dynamic cover arrangements. These reduced the time required for the mobilization of ambulance crews and increased the proportion of working time in which crews were actively engaged in A&E duties. Prior to the introduction of standby points MAS crews spent over 50 per cent of their working time on active duties. Following the reform of working arrangements and the introduction of standby points, the proportion of working time on active duty rose to an average of approximately 65 per cent per shift worked.

Finally, with the integration of the MAS into a new system of purchaser/provider relations, funding increases to pay for additional staffing and new technologies were directly linked to improvements in performance standards. The market mechanism provided the external discipline through which MAS management would be required to demonstrate continuous improvements in internal service standards. It also provided the framework through which many of the issues affecting workplace relations would be shaped by the purchaser/provider contracts rather than through the development of a system of local bargaining at trust level. This market-led innovation helped managers to represent the requirement for changes in work practices as an externally imposed necessity and not one arising primarily from their own initiative. As a result, local bargaining, and the strength of the workplace or station unionism that underpinned it, was weakened by the intervention of the new pattern of market relations.

Evaluation

Without overtly challenging the workplace unionism that had its roots in the special conditions prevailing within the MAS, the programme of reform that commenced in 1993 helped management to achieve significant change in work organization and work practices. The reform of the service was facilitated by internal changes in management personnel and was catalysed by external pressures arising from government and the media. The decentralization of the NHS was accompanied by a renewed vigour in the regulation of service standards by the DoH (through the performance standards demanded by purchaser/provider contracts) and direct interventions by government where front-line services were seen to have failed. The reforms, mainly recommended by outside management consultants, undoubtedly produced improvements in service provision and performance, particularly through the successful third attempt at computerization and the increase in A&E staff numbers. Management also developed a new approach to the A&E staff by expanding the proportion of paramedics and introducing new approaches to their training. This, in turn, generated a shift towards the professionalization of ambulance work and distinguished it from the services provided by the PTS. The shift towards professionalization of ambulance work facilitated the emergence of a skills divide between the paramedic and other ambulance staff, whose jobs were increasingly susceptible to the process of competitive tendering and contracting out.

The NHS internal market provided a new framework for these reforms to take place. The funding of reform was linked to improved performance, and performance measures became the currency around which contracts were agreed. In short, the purchaser/provider split intervened or cut across the traditional relationship between management and workforce. Management could identify the source of the pressure for changes in work organization and practices as arising from the demands of the purchasing consortium, and sought to replace the traditional 'us and them' approach to industrial relations by a new social dynamic in which both sides were united as 'service providers'.

The MAS also revealed the tenacity of a 'traditional' form of workplace unionism that persisted into the 1990s, although, arguably, the shift in management approach, associated with the implementation of the reform strategy, began to reveal the limits of a collectivism that focused primarily upon the workplace rather than on the market-place in which the ambulance service had become an integral part. Marketization was coupled with the development of a new management style that, while not openly embracing the language of HRM, achieved a significant increase in labour intensity through the rejection of confrontation and the adoption of an approach that aspired to the formation of a partnership in raising performance and improving service provision. While such an approach experienced setbacks, and even provoked industrial action, the underlying trend was towards a partnership between management and unions based upon a common identity as 'service providers'.

PART 4

CONCLUSIONS

8 Restructuring Services

This book commenced with the proposition that our understanding of the transformation of work in the late twentieth century was largely based upon debates about the changing character of production industries. New theories arose from attempts to analyse Japanese resurgence, the challenge to US economic supremacy and the demands facing enterprises in an increasingly competitive international economy. Several authors argued that these developments provided the conditions for the emergence of new production approaches and techniques. Innovation in work organization was associated with broader social, cultural and political change. The proclaimed demise of the assembly line became a metaphor for the end of industrial society, the rise of services and the birth of post-industrialism. There were, however, relatively few analyses of work organization in those industries considered to be the beneficiaries of change. While some authors discussed shifts in employment patterns and helped to establish an expanding literature on service work, mainly based upon case study approaches, few attempted to theorize the process of change in the service sector. This book has addressed this analytical gap.

The analysis in Part 1 commenced from a recognition that the very industries that many claimed provided the foundation of the post-industrial economy in the early 1980s were themselves in deep trouble by the end of that decade. Any analysis of service work had to address the messy dynamics of its own restructuring. In the examination of this process, it was argued that the demise of industrialism was much exaggerated. The growth of service industries was intimately linked to the fortunes of productive industries and in the latter there was a tendency towards a spatial separation of the process of production and a capacity, fuelled by technical change, for constant to displace variable capital. Production industries provided the infrastructure that underpinned the expansion of the service sector. In turn, while service industries might be located in forms of production, circulation or unproductive work, the underlying trend within each was towards the 'industrialization of intelligence', the subjection of knowledge and information-based skills and activities to a process of routinization. This trend was, in turn, facilitated by developments in information technologies and the introduction of new forms of management organization and control. Paradoxically, while many authors proclaimed the end of an industrial society based upon the assembly line and mass production in manufacturing industries, new assembly lines were appearing within service industries via the construction of white-collar factories employing staff engaged in the processing of paper and electronic data. Rather than experiencing the demise of industrial society, the late twentieth century witnessed a process of industrial restructuring in service industries which enabled the tentacles of industrial capitalism and industrial forms of work organization to spread wider across a more complex technical and social division of labour.

In the 1980s the service sector appeared to offer solutions to the economic problems arising from the protracted restructuring of production industries. In the 1990s several service industries, like finance and health, became an integral part of the problem. Understanding the interaction between service and production industries was a prerequisite for explaining the changing character of services in the 1990s. This interaction was best understood in terms of developments in the social division of labour. Understood from this perspective, it was possible to explain why several tasks essential to the process of production, but often physically remote from it, were wrongly characterized as services. It was also possible to see why service work and unproductive work are not the same thing. The downturn in the fortunes of service industries was first experienced by those economies in which the changes in the social division of labour were more advanced and where the impact of the early 1980s' recession on manufacturing employment bit hardest. The USA took the lead in the restructuring of services and several UK enterprises and industries learnt lessons from the American 'model'.

The process of emulation created a watershed in service sector workplace relations in the UK. Traditional forms of management–workforce relations were undermined and a new pattern of workplace relations emerged in the first half of the 1990s. This chapter draws upon the evidence provided by the case studies to outline some of the features of this dynamic process of change. Inevitably, the case studies provide an incomplete picture. The attempt here is to identify some trends in service sector restructuring that might inform further comparative case study analysis of a wider range of service industries. The chapter commences with a discussion of the role of the state in promoting the restructuring of service industries. Second, it examines the nature of management reform and explores the extent to which this has been influenced by processes involving decentralization or devolution. The analysis then shifts to enterprise and workplace level to outline the specific character of changes in skills and work organization and labour intensity. Finally, drawing upon the evidence of change in management organization and the utilization of labour, the chapter concludes with a discussion of the extent to which the restructuring of services has been informed by an American model.

The State and Restructuring Services

The state has played a significant role in the restructuring of work and employment relations in the service industries, though the precise character of state intervention has varied across the advanced industrial nations. The types of intervention have been structured by specific political and social conditions relating to, for example, the federal or centralized forms of government, the historical role of financial institutions and the different political struggles and traditions that have influenced the shaping of welfare provision. Despite these national variations, recent patterns of state intervention in several advanced nations have moved towards the opening up of service sector markets to competition, the replacement of direct state ownership by new forms of legal and self-regulation and the reordering of employment relations, often to the disadvantage of organized labour (Clarke, 1997: 205–33).

In Britain, the state's role in facilitating the restructuring of service industries has been considerable. This has been achieved in a number of ways. First, legal reform has directly impacted upon the structure and organization of industries and established new ways of regulating their activities. These reforms have been prompted by a combination of European-wide and domestic legislation. Second, successive Conservative administrations introduced employment legislation aimed at creating a more flexible labour market and curbing the activities of trade unions. Third, the state 'as employer' took the lead in implementing these policies, and the new management techniques associated with them, in the public services.

In the public sector, privatization, compulsory competitive tendering for the provision of local and national public services, initiatives directed towards the private financing of public sector projects and the introduction of new forms of internal market relations have changed the boundaries between the public and private sectors of the economy. In private service industries, such as the financial services, direct legal intervention has broken down traditional distinctions between insurance companies, banks and building societies, and been accompanied by requirements for the development of new forms of industry-wide regulation. A broadly similar approach to regulation has been adopted within the recently privatized utilities, with quasi-independent watchdogs being created to oversee the operations, pricing policies and associated activities of the utility companies. These changes have had important implications for developments in product markets and the reform of management organization, as the case studies have revealed.

Insco, the composite insurer, fell foul of the life insurance and unit trust regulator (LAUTRO) over its selling of pensions and life insurance business in the period 1988–90, eventually receiving a substantial fine in 1994, and subsequently being pressed by government in the following years to tackle more effectively a considerable backlog of compensation cases. This experience encouraged the company to reorganize into separate business units that distinguished the regulated and unregulated areas of activity. The company also decided to transfer all employees into an umbrella services company within the UK so that it could create a more flexible movement of staff between the regulated and unregulated areas of business. In Credit UK, government concern over the operation of the credit card industry prompted investigations by the Monopoly and Mergers Commission and encouraged the company to develop a greater distance from its founding institutions.

Within the National Health Service, the establishment of the internal market determined the structure of the purchaser/provider split and spelt out the system of decentralized management that took control at trust level. Within the metropolitan emergency service, government involvement took a more direct course through the establishment of an inquiry into the performance of the service following a series of failures to improve efficiency and a number of adverse press reports. A significant reorganization of the ambulance service was a prerequisite for its eventual inauguration as a trust in 1996. While CHC Trust was also a late entrant to the internal market, being a fourth wave trust, it was a 'beneficiary' of government policies aimed at the expansion of care in the community, particularly in the area of mental health provision. Here, rapid closure of many larger-scale mental institutions led to impossible pressures falling on community services and the subsequent reprovision of mental health services in many smaller institutions, of which CHC was one. In short, rather than 'rolling back' the tentacles of state intervention through the creation of an 'enterprise culture', successive Conservative governments between 1979 and 1997 made significant changes to the traditional patterns of intervention and, arguably, increased their influence over the forms of enterprise and management organization and the shape of product and labour markets: generating expanded markets for private health care and pensions provision, creating an internal market system in the NHS and, through these policies, establishing a direct influence over the conduct of workplace affairs. As Fairbrother (1996) has argued, in relation to public services, state policies were designed to simultaneously enhance management authority and responsibility at local level while, at the same time, achieving an 'insidious and comprehensive reaffirmation of central control' (Fairbrother, 1996: 116). Arguably, the insidious form of this control was exercised via the operation of the invisible hand of the internal market in industries like the NHS. What is also evident from a view that looks across other service industries, like the financial services, is that state policies played a significant part in reshaping product markets and indirectly influenced the restructuring of enterprise organization via the reform of the systems of industry regulation.

From the evidence provided by the case studies, the nation state is a central agency of change in industrial affairs. Such a conclusion runs counter to arguments presented by those for whom the demise of industrialism was associated with a corresponding decline in the influence and role of the nation state. Pakulski and Waters (1996), for example, claimed that the 'multiple crisis' of the state was leading to a 'destatization' or state weakening, and a corresponding opening for political globalization. The state was pulling out from key areas of welfare provision, reducing military expenditure and giving over to technocrats and administrators areas of policy-making that were previously within the ambit of national politicians. Such developments contributed to the nation state progressively becoming an irrelevance (Pakulski and Waters, 1996: 108). Such conclusions fly in the face of the empirical evidence provided at industry and enterprise levels and, arguably, ignore the underlying ideological reasons for the state's apparent reticence to play a leading role in the conduct of key areas of a country's economic affairs.

As Bonefeld and Burnham (1996) have explained in the particular case of Britain's entry to the Exchange Rate Mechanism (ERM) (an argument that could be extended to Labour's decision in May 1997 to give over responsibility to the Bank of England for setting interest rates), the government's approach amounted to an attempt to depoliticize discussion of economic policy and thereby reduce the potential for social conflict that might arise from its implementation (Bonefeld and Burnham, 1996: 32–3). Depoliticization, from the perspective of state managers, arises from the adoption of policies which 'marketise aspects of state activity and publicly shift responsibility for management onto external regimes and independent organisations' (Burnham, 1996: 8).

Burnham's argument concerning policies towards the ERM may be applied to a broader analysis of the government's reform of the state sector in the 1980s and 1990s. Privatization of the utilities, the introduction of the internal market and the accompanying decentralization of management responsibilities shifted the terms of debate on welfare and infrastructure provision away from problems of state underfunding and towards an emphasis on organizational reform or, as in the case of the utilities, the behaviour of the 'fatcats' who ran them. This ideological distancing of the state from its traditional responsibilities within the corporatist welfare model was well served by the implementation of organizational and regulatory reform. Even in the financial services, which experienced a considerable shift towards a global system in the late 1980s and early 1990s, the UK state moved away from allowing financial markets to regulate themselves informally and towards a system of regulation undertaken by quasi-independent bodies. This shift, in turn, influenced managers' approach to the structural reform of their enterprises and the range of products they sold. In short, the state, rather than giving way to the hidden hand of the global market-place, redefined its role in relation to key areas of welfare provision (like pensions), redrew the line between public and private sectors and re-regulated the financial markets in a manner that increased its 'insidious' and 'depoliticized' influence over workplace and industrial affairs.

Management Reform

Management reform was a central feature of the transformation of service industries in advanced industrial nations like the USA and UK. The process of reform gathered pace in the USA in the early 1980s and in the UK in the early 1990s. But what were the key components of reform? The argument developed here is that the process involved a decisive shift in management values, strategy and structure. By contrast with management in production industries, service sector management had few guiding principles that had been codified into an effective 'scientific' practice in the first half of the twentieth century. The downturn in their economic circumstances in the latter part of the twentieth century prompted, for the first time in their history, attempts to develop and subsequently codify new management practices that addressed problems of high costs, low productivity and inefficient work practices. The main strands of the model that emerged were identified in Chapter 2. To what extent were these strands illustrated by the case study evidence?

Structural reform

The underlying principle of structural reform was the disaggregation of previously highly integrated companies and industries. Integration was a feature of national institutions such as the NHS. It was also a characteristic of leading financial institutions in the retail banking and insurance sectors, where stable and segmented markets traditionally prevailed. The combination of legal and political reform and changes in industry boundaries and market structures prompted experimentation with structural change. The underlying feature of structural reform was the shift towards decentralization or devolution. Decentralization encompassed greater autonomy or independence over a wider range of management functions than did the devolution model. Decentralization facilitated independence from the 'centre', with local management taking a key role in business strategy and product development, financial management, the introduction of new patterns of work organization and employee relations. Previously integrated institutions could pursue a diversity based upon closeness to the market and the customer. In principle, decentralization represented a significant step towards the setting up of independent enterprises that acted as autonomous economic units in their specific market sector, or, as in the case of NHS trusts, in their local internal market relationship as either purchaser or provider. By contrast, devolved management was designed to enhance the role of local managers, while requiring them to work within the clearly defined policies and financial frameworks established by the 'centre'. Management discretion was confined effectively to specific aspects of implementation.

In practice, the case studies illustrate the constraints upon decentralization as a management strategy. Decentralization was most likely to succeed in those enterprises where separate and distinctive product markets were identifiable and where management benefited from separating regulated and non-regulated activities. Insco's shift towards disaggregation was primarily led by the establishment of five separate business units within its UK operations. At senior executive level within the company there was a strong commitment to increase local management autonomy, particularly in relation to employee relations. There remained, however, a tight central control over policy direction and financial management. Local management autonomy amounted to enhanced discretion over the detailed implementation of policy. Even the establishment of separate business units ran into difficulties in the face of changing product markets. As the configuration of product markets changed to reflect a growth in the provision of 'integrated' financial packages for private and corporate customers, so the company found that this pattern of product development tended to conflict with the relative autonomy of the business units. The most successful element of devolved management took place in the sphere of employee relations. Here it was possible for Insco to establish different employment conditions and work practices in areas like Insco Direct, where unions were excluded. Areas of employment and business expansion were non-unionized, while those where rationalization and restructuring had taken place were where the unionized workforce was situated.

Credit UK commenced life in the 1970s as the data processing arm of a consortium of UK banks. Its management structure and employment conditions tied it closely to the traditions of the UK retail banking industry, despite its distinctive role within the sector. During the 1980s the company began to distance itself from the enterprises responsible for its creation. This distancing – the transition from cost to profit centre – facilitated a significant shift in management style and strategy that enabled the company to develop as an independent 'third party processor'. This shift in the company's identity reflected a broader pattern of change within the sector in which data processing, fuelled by the expansion of the credit card market, became a separate economic activity, according to some commentators a separate 'industry'. This disaggregation of processing activities enabled management to assume the strategies associated with a high level of decentralization. Management sought to expand the company's role as a third party processor, break into new markets and, most significantly, push its employee relations policies away from those typically associated with the banking industry and towards a more industrial orientation, akin to the employment conditions of a 'white-collar factory'. The take-over of the company by a US multinational, Global Data Corporation (GDC), in the early 1990s accelerated the shift in employee relations policies away from bank industry employment conditions. Management style and strategy, however, tended to shift from decentralization to devolution as the US parent company stamped its mark on all aspects of the UK subsidiary's activities. A more aggressive marketing style was adopted, a programme of redundancies accompanied downsizing and employee relations were transformed by a new approach that combined employee involvement schemes, performance appraisal and the aggressive introduction of a new 'customer orientation'.

In the NHS, the establishment of trusts with their own executive boards and business plans created a significant shift away from a centralized to a decentralized health service. The relative autonomy of trusts was apparently underpinned by the introduction of market relations in which trusts were, in effect, designed to act as independent economic units required to achieve target rates of return on their activities. Even here the move to decentralization was modified by several factors. First, the internal market constituted an artificial creation in which pricing mechanisms and contractual relations between purchasers and providers would always be subject to central controls exercised through the budgetary mechanism. Second, the subjection of local trusts to market forces was moderated by the requirement to meet nationally defined service standards and performance criteria. This created potential conflicts between local trust attempts to balance the books and centrally determined requirements to maintain emergency and acute provision. Third, the budgetary mechanism severely limited the degree of independence exercised by trust management in provider trusts in terms of their relationship with purchasers. Finally, even in the sphere of employee relations, the continued existence of pay review bodies and political sensitivities – for example, concerning pay awards to nurses and doctors – tended to moderate attempts by local managers to exercise greater local variation in conditions of employment.

A significant variable in the equation of trust status with decentralization, particularly in relation to employee relations, was the approach adopted by the trust chair, chief executive and senior management team. A hawkish approach could realize an important break with traditional employment relations (such as in Northumbria Ambulance Trust) and a more conciliatory approach could ensure some continuity with the features of the pre-trust, centralized system of industrial relations. Within CHC Trust, the more strident hawkish values of a Thatcherite chair were moderated by a human relations management team that largely sought compromise and negotiation with local unions. In the Metropolitan Ambulance Service, trust status was not on the agenda until the crisis within the service was resolved. The resolution of the crisis was perceived by management to require the restoration of a conciliatory approach to the ambulance service workforce, particularly those involved in 'front-line' accident and emergency provision. Through the period of its restructuring, management–workforce relations assumed a character that was more typical of the traditional NHS approach, involving the negotiation rather than imposition of change.

Within the NHS, decentralization was intimately linked to the introduction of an internal market that simultaneously unleashed conflicting pressures that sought to impose uniform standards of service provision alongside a system of distribution determined by competition. The push towards decentralization was modified by the political sensitivities concerning service standards, the presence of senior managers in some trusts, who clung to a more traditional consultative management style, and the activities of local union organizations that attempted to contain or limit the erosion of nationally determined pay and conditions.

The case studies reveal a complex pattern of decentralization or devolution. Management organization in each of the case studies was characterized by fluidity. The broad trend was towards a downward push of responsibilities for management functions, but this was accompanied by considerable variation in the degree of independence or discretion exercised at local level. Local discretion tended to be exercised most in the area of the employment contract and employment conditions and in the customization of relations with the consumer of the services offered. On the other hand, responsibility for policy development and financial management tended to assume a devolved form in which local management acted within the clearly defined parameters set by the 'centre'. Indeed, in the case of NHS trusts decentralization was accompanied by the tightening of insidious forms of central control, and in the case of Insco contradictions emerged between a policy aimed at decentralized employee relations and the reintegrative trends evident in the market for insurance products. The analysis of management organization cannot be divorced from the market environment in which it operates, the industrial structure in which it is located and its social relation with the 'collective' labour (Carter, 1997) that it seeks to control. In each of these areas, management was confronted with significant turbulence in the 1980s and in the first half of the 1990s. Its response was to push downwards management responsibilities through devolution and decentralization, with private sector services adopting more of the features of the former, while public sector institutions implemented reforms associated with the latter. Neither of these types of organizational reform could escape, however, the contradictory pressures arising from the social influences that mediate centre–local relations.

Labour and Work Organization

Post-industrial theorists have associated the expansion of service sector employment with a liberation from the mundane and repetitive jobs associated with manual occupations in the production industries. The most strident ideologues among them have linked the emergence of a post-industrial society with the development of a new social stratum, a new knowledge class, whose occupations are centred on the acquisition and analysis of information (Warhurst and Thompson, 1998: 3). This new class, according to the post-industrial theorists, has the attributes of a highly skilled, computer literate group of managers, professionals and technical workers. They work within an open and democratic structure in which information flows are based upon networks, 'flat' organizations, rather than the traditional hierarchical forms associated with an earlier industrial age. Stonier (1983) has gone as far as to suggest that in the post-industrial information society, an era of mass entrance to higher education, everyone becomes 'an aristocrat, everyone a philosopher'. This celebratory approach to the transformation of work in the late twentieth century has also been adopted by influential management consultants and business authors. For them, service companies have become 'learning institutions' in which individual employees have been empowered as a result of the use of new technologies which restructure work processes in a manner that facilitates the fulfilment of individual potential.

By contrast with this optimistic, even utopian, outlook, writers influenced by the work of Braverman (1974) have argued that service work has been subject to the same process of routinization and deskilling as blue-collar work (Barker and Downing, 1985; Ainley, 1993; Ritzer, 1998). Others, arguing broadly in support of Braverman's views, have identified a trend in service industries and occupations towards a polarization between the 'intrinsically satisfying and economically rewarding jobs' undertaken by about 20 per cent of the workforce and the work of the majority who regularly perform routine tasks or are responsible for the 'daily delivery of mundane services' (Beynon, 1997: 27). The difference in perspectives between the enthusiasts of post-industrialism and those influenced by labour process theory is not simply a matter of contrasting ideologies. The difference also arises from the ways in which the protagonists have conceptualized skill. Enthusiasts of post-industrialism have tended to associate 'upskilling' with the level of educational qualifications needed to apply for a specific job, while the 'deskilling' thesis has focused primarily upon the length of vocational training a person may have undertaken at work or in pursuit of a professionally recognized qualification. In acknowledging these differences, Gallie (1997) developed an approach which identified 'multiple indicators' of skill development. These included the frequency and duration of training and on-the-job experience, as well as taking into account people's own perceptions as to whether or not their skills had changed (Gallie, 1997: 135).

Gallie used evidence from a number of surveys conducted in the mid-1980s and early 1990s. These included: the Social Class in Modern Britain survey (Marshall et al., 1988), which was conducted in 1984 with a sample base of

1,770 persons; the Social Change and Economic Life Initiative (SCELI), which was conducted in 1988 and involved a sample of 6,111 people drawn from six localities in different geographical regions of Britain; and a 1992 nationally representative survey – Employment in Britain – that used a sample of 3,477 employees. The comparative analysis of these surveys caused Gallie to reach several important conclusions. First, employers had responded to rapid technological change and changes in market conditions by raising skill levels and undertaking job enrichment programmes. Second, there was 'a significant devolution of responsibilities for more immediate decisions about the work task', with the most popular employer policy being a move towards 'responsible autonomy'. Third, upskilling involved a considerable increase in the intensity of work. Fourth, the extent of upskilling varied significantly by occupational class, with skilled manual and non-manual employees experiencing upskilling, while semi- and non-skilled staff continued to have 'lower chances of skills development'. Thus, there was a 'growing polarisation in skill experiences between lower manual workers, technicians and supervisors and lower professionals and managers'. Finally, the rapid diffusion of computer technologies tended to produce rising skill levels for both men and women workers, though women's experience of opportunities for skill enhancement was more limited than men's and women gained less autonomy than their male counterparts when upskilling occurred (Gallie, 1997: 156–7).

Gallie's use of multiple indicators of skill and extensive survey data tended to produce a more nuanced view of the patterns of contemporary work transformation than those presented by the post-industrial and labour process camps. Gallie was, however, focusing upon skills development across the whole economy, and not simply upon developments in service industries, and he has recognized the problems associated with the construction of analyses based upon data which distinguished occupational classifications in a relatively simplistic, measurable way (Gallie, 1991). In recognizing such weaknesses, Thornley (1996), in her study of skills in nursing, suggested an alternative theoretical perspective on the 'acquisition, recognition and evaluation of skills', which took into account the problem of defining skills in relation to the dynamics of gender segregation, the existence of internal hierarchies and labour market segmentation within capitalist enterprises and the fact that the delineation of skills within a capitalist enterprise was contingent upon 'workers' own struggles'. For Thornley, skills were 'defined and made subject to ownership by the dynamic interaction of employer and labour strategy' (Thornley, 1996: 160). In reviewing the changes in skills and work organization outlined in the case studies in Part 2, it is appropriate to consider these in relation to the 'optimistic' view of the post-industrial theorists, the 'pessimistic' deskilling view of the labour process theorists and the more 'nuanced' view advanced by Gallie. It is also necessary to keep in focus Thornley's contention that the analysis of skills and work organisation cannot be understood outside of the dynamics of the management–labour relationship.

The two financial services case studies covered different industries – data processing and insurance – and different types of companies, one a US multinational and the other a UK company steeped in the traditions of the UK insurance industry. Nevertheless, they provided evidence of common trends in work organization. First, the restructuring of work took place at the same time that significant numbers of jobs were cut. Insco shed 2,500 jobs between 1992 and 1997 and Credit UK lost around 1,200 jobs between 1992 and 1996. These losses represented approximately 20 per cent of the UK workforce in each company. In turn, the job losses contributed to increased workloads for those staff who remained. Second, Insco followed a similar path to Credit UK by establishing the Insco Direct operation and developing a telesales and data processing facility. For Insco this was associated with the closure of local branch networks and their consolidation into regional processing centres. While Credit UK had been one of the pioneers of this form of work organization, which emerged in the late 1960s and early 1970s, other financial services companies adopted this model in the 1980s and 1990s. In Insco this development had significant affects. Work organization within Insco divided between direct services and sales and the more specialist areas of insurance provision, such as health care and pensions provision. This had a significant impact upon skills and work organization and provided strong evidence of a tendency towards a polarization between the mainly manual, processing tasks undertaken by Insco Direct employees on the one hand, and the more specialized services, requiring mental labour, offered in health, life and pensions provision on the other. While employees in Insco Direct took on mainly manual, repetitive processing activities or had their telephone interface with customers highly structured by call centre routines, staff in the more specialized areas were not exempt from changes in work organization arising from their undertaking predominantly 'mental' rather than 'manual' forms of labour.

In the more specialist areas a variety of new patterns of work organization emerged. Traditional skills associated with the insurance profession – underwriting and risk assessment – were practised by a smaller group of staff who dealt with non-standard cases, while the majority were required to develop more generic capabilities in areas like product market research, sales and marketing and team-building. With the emergence of generic skills came the requirement for teams to adopt multifunctional roles. This trend was reinforced by the move towards the provision of insurance packages or modules tailored to meet the needs of the corporate or individual customer. This change in the configuration of product markets caused staff to specialize less in one area of insurance provision and develop a broad grasp across the product range. Technological change and developments in product markets combined to undermine traditional skills and bring forward new patterns of work organization that resembled 'factory-like' conditions on the one hand and promoted multifunctional team working on the other. In the latter, specialist skills tended to be displaced by generic skills as new software programs were devised to mechanize a process of decision-making that had previously required the exercising of individual judgement and discretion. The routinization of knowledge work was tempered by the requirement for some staff to develop a broad appreciation of a new configuration of insurance products or modules. None the less, if mental work was not entirely routinized in these work areas, it was associated with a rise in work intensity as staff came to grips with the development and marketing of a broader portfolio of insurance products. A further feature of the polarization of skills and patterns of work organization arose from working hours arrangements. Insco Direct staff, and those in areas of mental labour that required direct links with customers outside normal office hours, had working time arrangements that were subject to close supervision and control. In Credit UK, for example, several teams were required to clock in and out of work. By contrast, in areas where multifunctional teams operated – for example, in Insco life and pensions areas – there was greater autonomy exercised by individual staff over their patterns of work. Flexitime allowed staff discretion over working hours and there were few checks undertaken to ensure that staff worked the hours they recorded. It was team leaders in both Insco and Credit UK who were expected to be the exemplars of 'good' work practice, establishing a work culture that team members would be expected to follow.

The beneficiaries of rapid changes in technology and markets were the staff concerned with the development and implementation of IT. The replacement of technical systems associated with the old branch systems by new local area networks created a significant demand for well-qualified systems and programming staff. The demand for such staff was evident at both Credit UK and Insco. In the former, the company was so concerned by the shortage of IT staff that existing employees were offered bonuses if they could recommend to the company an available and suitably qualified person. In Insco, the IT function was increasingly focused on the company's workplaces in the South East in the hope that such a geographical location might help to ease the shortage in skilled IT staff. Finally, the changes in skills mix, particularly evident in Insco, had a significant impact upon management organization. The waning in importance of traditional professional skills left many managers vulnerable to the downsizing exercise.

Finally, work organization at Credit UK and Insco had a sharply defined gender dimension. In the early 1970s, Credit UK was situated in a South East coastal town primarily because of the availability within the local labour market of young married women who were likely to be seeking part-time employment. These provided the labour power required to undertake the mainly repetitive manual tasks associated with telephony and the processing of data. Equally, the introduction of Insco Direct in 1994 saw a similar pattern of recruitment taking place, with women constituting, according to union sources, approximately 70 per cent of the workforce. As data processing and direct sales was a highly competitive area of the general insurance markets, the control of costs, particularly labour costs, was an important company objective. There was little evidence of job or task rotation within these areas of employment, leading to the conclusion that both Insco and Credit UK were prepared to utilize mainly female labour on routine, repetitive tasks. This pattern of employment led to relatively high levels of labour turnover and allowed few opportunities for career development. While a small number of women, part- and full-time, who typically had longer service with the company, were engaged in the supervision of work processes, the overwhelming majority of women staff were deployed in routine manual tasks that were structured by the technical systems that shaped the computer–woman interface.

Credit UK and Insco provide evidence that financial services industries have experienced in less than a decade a sharpened polarization between unskilled manual and skilled mental labour. The evidence, however, also suggests that those employed in the latter category of occupations have experienced other important changes. First, traditional professional skills like underwriting have been rapidly diluted by less 'industry specific' skills like product research, marketing and sales. Second, this shift towards a more generic skills base has been accompanied by the flattening of management hierarchies and the development of other broad managerial skills like budget-holding and team-building. Third, the new generation of technical systems has facilitated a change in the skills mix, with the areas of employment growth being in the unskilled and routinized forms of work. Finally, changes in skills mix and the evidence of a growing polarization between unskilled and skilled occupations suggests that Gallie's contention that significant upskilling and job enrichment has occurred as a result of technological change and employer policies is open to question when one considers the financial services sector. Many women employees were confined to unskilled, repetitive tasks despite their extensive use of technologies in their day-to-day work routines. Software packages tended to undermine traditional professional skills, in part confining, therefore, the upskilling elements to those tasks associated with the assumption of greater 'management' responsibilities. In this sense, upskilling was less about the content of the work done and more about the financial, organizational and administrative processes that facilitated its execution. Upskilling was defined, acquired and valued through the complex interplay of management–workforce relations (Thornley, 1996: 176). Put simply, for management, upskilling was a metaphor for encouraging key groups of staff to think and act as if they were 'managers' themselves.

The CHC and Metropolitan Ambulance Service Trusts also illustrated some complex and revealing trends in skills and work organization that are not very different from those arising in the financial service case studies. Three trends were of particular note. First, at trust level, there was evidence of important changes taking place in the skills mix of key groups of staff. At CHC Trust there was a tendency among nursing staff for a minority of nurses to receive educational and training opportunities that enabled their qualifications to be 'elevated' to degree level. On the other hand, this upskilling was tempered by a trend in which the proportion of professional nurses declined relative to those staff engaged as nursing care assistants, who were less well qualified and lower paid. This pattern of change in skills mix was not confined to CHC Trust, but was a policy widely pursued by managers as part of the reform programme initiated by the establishment of the internal market. Changes in skills mix offered opportunities for local trust management to achieve savings in labour costs and gain 'competitive advantage', as a publication by East Thames Health Authority indicated: 'Those providers who reprofile their labour force will enjoy a comparative advantage over those who do not' (quoted in NUPE, 1993: 4).

In the Metropolitan Ambulance Trust, the programme of reforms designed to improve the efficiency of accident and emergency provision saw a significant investment in upgrading the skills of ambulance staff. Prior to the reform programme, between 1985 and 1990 accident and emergency staff levels had fallen by approximately 5 per cent to a figure of just over 2,500 whole-time equivalents. This decline in staffing began to be reversed between 1994 and 1996 with the employment of 200 new operational staff. These new recruits joined existing staff in a programme of paramedic training which realized an increase in the paramedic workforce from 360 at the beginning of 1994 to 680 by the end of April 1996. In 1997 opportunities were provided for paramedics to attend a local university to gain a certificate in paramedic science, the first step towards the establishment of a degree award scheme for paramedics employed by the trust. In a relatively short period, a pattern of decline was reversed. A growing proportion of operational staff were presented with opportunities to secure undergraduate level qualifications. Paramedics found themselves at the forefront of a programme aimed at the professionalization of the accident and emergency service.

At the time that this process of professionalization was taking place, other ambulance staff, working in Patient Transport Services (PTS) were experiencing changes in their conditions of employment that realized a downgrading of their occupational status. PTS provision was subjected to the process of competitive tendering, with the Metropolitan Ambulance Service Trust losing a significant number of contracts to outside providers for whom the service provision was primarily a matter of the transportation of patients. Contracting out created pressures on employment contracts and conditions. By 1997, there was a creeping casualization of PTS jobs and a widening gulf in employment conditions between PTS and those operational staff engaged in accident and emergency provision, particularly those trained as paramedics. From the union perspective, members whose jobs were being 'professionalized' had little empathy with the problems facing PTS members. The process of professionalization created divisions within the workforce that unions found difficult to overcome in their attempts to protect PTS staff from the consequences of privatization (Interview with UNISON branch chairperson, 1997).

The second trend arising from these changes in skills profile was, as illustrated by the 'paramedic/PTS split', a sharpening polarization between professional and manual occupations. This trend towards the separation of 'quality' jobs concerned with health care provision and those 'quantitative' jobs concerned with tasks like bed-making, cleaning, catering and transportation contains echoes of Drucker's contention that within service industries the key to improved efficiency was the separation of routine activities from those that required the exercise of human judgement and the application of tacit knowledge, features traditionally linked to the activities of the professions.

The third trend linked to professionalization and upskilling was the introduction within the two trusts of devolved patterns of management responsibility. Within CHC Trust, for example, the 'lean' senior management team pushed downwards the responsibility for the running of wards to nurses, who were expected to be managers of the wards and services that were under their charge. In this respect, nursing professionals were also required to develop generic management skills that, just as in the financial services sector, caused them to be as concerned with the administration of the service as they were with its direct provision.

The evidence provided by the case studies supports the arguments presented by Beynon (1997) and others that the service sector has seen a sharpened polarization between skilled 'mental' labour and semi-skilled and unskilled manual labour. This polarization has been accompanied by a form of upskilling that has had ambiguous affects on those employed to undertake the more interesting 'mental' or professionalized occupations. Upskilling has occurred at the same time as the push downward of management responsibilities, with a resulting tendency for the new skills to be associated with generic managerial competencies rather than more specific 'job-related' skills. Second, multifunctionalism has facilitated a blurring of traditional boundaries between professions and occupations, leading to a significant reworking of the mental division of labour in banks, insurance companies and the health sector. Third, polarization and multifunctionalism has, in Drucker's terms, reduced the proportion of knowledge workers and increased the proportion of service workers. Finally, these changes in work organization have been accompanied by an increase, as Gallie (1997) and others have argued, in the intensity of both mental and manual labour. It is to this theme that we now turn.

Labour Intensification

The techniques deployed to raise intensity have emulated those adopted in production industries, particularly in the area of management's pursuit of performance measurement. The service sector also witnessed the emergence in the 1990s of a more systematic management approach to what was referred to in Chapter 3 as the 'internalization of intensification', a codification of a range of practices aimed at the absorption by labour of values designed to encourage participation in its own intensification. This codification has been wrapped in the language of marketization in public services and in the 'customer-oriented' ideologies adopted by private service enterprises. Evidence of a rise in labour intensity was provided in each of the case studies in Parts 2 and 3. Here these are explored in terms of three dimensions: performance measurement, working time and management approaches that encouraged the internalization of intensification.

Performance measurement

Concerns about measuring performance in service industries have arisen from the complexity and diversity of service work. This work often involves the intangible (advice, care, conversation), the perishable (the immediate consumption of the service or product) and the emotional (the provider–client or patient relation) (Timo and Littler, 1996: 7). Over the past decade these obstacles to measuring productivity or performance have been tackled as a variety of quantitative performance measures have been introduced. The introduction of such measures has been facilitated by changes in work organization and developments in technical systems which, in many areas, particularly in the financial services, have created opportunities for management to insert control systems into the software programs that run the computer systems. In addition to the criteria aimed at measuring the efficiency of the work process, a plethora of performance criteria have been used to evaluate outputs or service standards. These quantitative approaches have been applied to the measurement of the performance of individuals, teams and business units. Performance measurement has been linked to payment systems and, in the NHS, performance has become an important feature of the structuring of provider–purchaser relations.

In CHC and the Metropolitan Ambulance Service performance measurement was an important ingredient of their contractual relations with purchasers. While accident and emergency performance standards (ORCON standards) were established in the early 1970s, they assumed a new role in the internal market arrangements developed in the NHS in the 1990s. In the case of the Metropolitan Ambulance Service, achieving continuous improvement in performance standards was a prerequisite for the consortium of purchasers to provide additional moneys for improving the service. Performance standards were recorded on a monthly basis and the figures informed discussions between purchasers and provider during the annual contract negotiations over accident and emergency provision. The performance criteria – recording response times to emergency calls, the time taken to arrive at the scene of an accident or emergency, the time at scene and the time taken to take patients to hospital – provided some evidence of the service's efficiency but was in some ways a crude measure. As, for example, more paramedics were involved in the service, they were likely to spend more time at the scene of accidents and emergencies than less qualified staff, a positive benefit to the patient (particularly those who had experienced heart attacks) but a negative one in relation to meeting performance targets. Despite the simplicity of the measure it was a key ingredient in evaluating service standards and a key element that informed contractual negotiations. A similar set of pressures arose for CHC Trust in relation to requirements to achieve efficiency savings. Efficiency savings, 3 per cent of the total contract per annum, if achieved, were returned by the purchasing authority to CHC Trust for capital investment projects. Savings squeezed from operating costs contributed to subsequent capital expenditure but, in turn, created significant pressures on those required to run the trust on a day-to-day basis.

Performance standards were also enshrined in the specification and tendering process relating to contracting out and market testing exercises within both trusts. They offered opportunities to set service standards, while at the same time encouraging providers to drive down their costs of delivery, particularly through job cuts, casualization and the reorganization of working time. These processes placed particular pressures upon manual and ancillary staff in CHC Trust and on the PTS in the Metropolitan Ambulance Service. The linking of performance measurement to the operation of contractual relations within the internal market was a key element in the intensification of manual and ancillary labour in the NHS.

While performance measurement mainly imposed disciplines on groups of employees in the NHS (in general, only senior management staff had their individual performance linked to pay), in the financial services performance measures were imposed in both their collective and individualized forms. In Credit UK and Insco, management established new ways of recording the performance of work teams, as well as introducing links between performance and pay. Broadly, the new schemes had the intention of focusing upon the efficiency of the work process rather than merely measuring the volume of work done, and served to enhance management control over the conduct and allocation of work. In Insco, the reform of management structures was closely linked to the development of effective ways of monitoring performance and efficiency at local level. In areas like Insco Direct and Credit UK, the data processing and telesales functions were closely monitored via the telephone exchange systems introduced by the companies, and individuals were under pressure to achieve acceptable performance levels or were under the threat of disciplinary action.

In both these companies new performance appraisal schemes were introduced between 1992 and 1997. In Insco the scheme was called performance management and in Credit UK it was referred to as Performance Appraisal and Competencies Evaluation (PACE). Both schemes strengthened line managers' responsibility for evaluating individual employee performance and both led to the erosion of annual collective bargaining over pay. In Credit

UK performance appraisal became the sole means of determining pay rises in 1997, and in Insco, also in 1997, management announced its intention to determine the total pay increase by reference to external 'market rates' (determined by outside consultants) and the use of the performance appraisal mechanism to determine how this total would be distributed among staff. While this approach was hotly contested by the union, particularly in relation to issues raised on behalf of IT staff, management achieved the introduction of a new scheme that established a close link between performance and pay. In addition to performance measurement focusing on the efficiency of work processes (such as turn round times for customer enquiries) and subsequently being linked to pay, team performance was evaluated in relation to new financial performance indicators in those areas of work where 'profit centres' were established.

Performance evaluation became a key feature of management practices in service industries in the early 1990s. They were not only concerned with quantifying what was previously 'unmeasured'. Their introduction was intimately linked to a wide range of other changes within each industrial sector. First, they provided a vehicle by which line managers were drawn into taking greater responsibility for the performance of those under their charge. The performance appraisal schemes, in this sense, were less about employee performance and more about putting into place effective local systems of management surveillance and control. Second, individual appraisal was complemented by a wide range of other performance measures relating to the efficiency of the work process, often becoming an integral part of their re-engineering. Finally, they offered a basis for the measurement of service standards, in terms of outputs, which, in turn, provided the basic 'currency' around which internal markets and relations between business units and profit centres could be organized. In this sense, performance measurement became an all-pervading ideology within service industries, an essential tool in the routinization of service work.

Working time

The extent to which the UK has experienced a significant shift away from full-time permanent employment and towards an economy that provides less secure, temporary and more casual forms of employment has been widely debated. Debates have focused upon issues like labour market flexibility (Atkinson, 1984; Pollert, 1991; Beynon, 1997), job insecurity and the tendencies towards the creation of a new division within society, in which the unskilled lower tier finds itself shifting between precarious forms of non-standard employment and no work at all (Hutton, 1996). What most commentators have acknowledged is that a 'proliferation of contractual forms involving a wide variety of working times, benefits and entitlements' (Allen and Henry, 1996: 180) has emerged, particularly in service industries. Standing (1986) characterized this trend as the 'contractualization' of employment, a situation in which employers have been increasingly prepared to take advantage of relaxed legal and regulatory frameworks to experiment with new patterns of working time.

The evidence provided by the case studies supports this view. It also suggests that changes in working time arrangements have created a heightened sense of job insecurity and uncertainty among employees about their futures within enterprises. Changes in working time impact directly upon the balance between work and home, often affecting an individual's perception of his or her own quality of life. Many of the changes in working time arrangements have been presented by employers as enabling staff to achieve a better balance between work and domestic life. This has been particularly the case for part-time women employees who have to juggle with child care responsibilities at the same time as fulfilling their work commitments. Clearly, the expansion of part-time employment and the multitude of contractual relations and shift patterns that have emerged in service industries over recent years have facilitated this juggling act to be undertaken more successfully by some. Overall, however, the new patterns of working time have been primarily driven by concerns other than the welfare and convenience of employees. In fact, it is suggested here that the balance of interests between employer and worker in relation to working time arrangements has significantly shifted towards fulfilling the demands of the former over recent years.

The changes in working time introduced by management in the case studies were catalysed by several factors. First, management was concerned to increase the efficiency of labour utilization. This was driven by a combination of external, customer-led demand for service provision and an internal management objective aimed at the improved utilization or intensity of labour. Second, changes in service provision were facilitated by technological innovation (products and processes), particularly in the financial services sector. Finally, new forms of work organization brought with them opportunities to reshape work in such a way that its routinization could be best delivered by experimenting with a variety of working hours arrangements, rather than by staff working within more traditional forms of shift working or conventional 'office' hours. A range of new contractual forms emerged, including annualized hours, banked hours and more flexible, varied forms of shiftworking.

In the Metropolitan Ambulance Service, for example, a detailed study by external consultants led to a package of changes in work organization and practices. At the centre of these changes were alterations to shift patterns. While these changes were contested, leading to strike action in the central division, they did lead to a closer matching of working time with periods of peak demand and achieved a significant rise in the proportion of ambulance crews' time spent on active duty. In CHC Trust changes in working time were linked to the contracting out of domestic and catering work. While broadly similar employment contracts and conditions were agreed with the external contractor, it soon became clear that the contractor was unable to fulfil its obligations to the contracted out staff. Within months of the privatization of cleaning and catering, the contractor proposed a cut of 600–900 hours, while requiring staff to fulfil the service standards agreed in the original contract. The rows that followed this demand led to the premature ending of the contract. None the less, the return of the service to an in-house provision, while safeguarding jobs, led to difficult negotiations between trust management and the union, with staff, in the end, working shorter hours and harder, while, at least restoring some improvement in job security (Interview with union full-time officer, 1997).

For those staff who remained directly employed, working time arrangements were constantly under review in two ways. Shift hours and rotas were subject to modest changes and the organization of work for different groups of staff was reviewed in order to squeeze more productive activity out of work teams. In addition to these changes, managers, driven by the necessity to remain within budgets, operated a bank system which enabled them to call in a bank of casual nursing staff to meet shortfalls in staffing that often arose as a result of sickness, holidays and other forms of absenteeism.

In the financial services, working time arrangements significantly altered for large numbers of staff at Credit UK and Insco. Those operations involving telesales and direct line contacts with customers were subject to shift working arrangements that facilitated the operation of a 24-service. Shift systems at Credit UK were changed from 12-hour shifts to an eight-hour continental shift system for employees in maintenance and engineering, and for those staff engaged in production areas a complex pattern of shorter shifts (often of four hours' duration) was introduced. In Insco, a similar pattern of shift working was introduced in the customer facing and data processing areas, while staff whose work patterns were not subject to the disciplines imposed by the customer interface were allowed to establish a more flexible pattern of work. Behind flexibility, however, lay an expectation that staff would commit themselves to work patterns that would enable work to be completed. A culture of 'control through commitment' in these areas complemented a system of 'commitment by control' in those workplaces that assumed the character of a white-collar factory.

In summary, the wide ranging changes in working time introduced in the customer-oriented service companies were designed to achieve significant improvements in the efficiency of the labour process. Changes in working time were accompanied by the introduction of performance measures which provided local management with the means to evaluate productivity and performance levels. This linking of performance and productivity, traditionally associated with production industries, achieved a combination of improvements in productivity and intensity – in some cases by introducing a shortened working day and in others by securing the commitment of employees to raise the intensity of their own labour through, for example, working unpaid overtime. In addition, devolved budgets and contracting out arrangements required local managers to increase their control over labour costs by operating systems of 'banked' hours which either involved direct employees giving a proportion of their working year to managers to utilize at the latter's discretion or concerned the use of agency staff who could be called in at times of labour shortage. Such changes were consistent with an overall pattern of changes in working time that increased management control over labour costs and time and generated a feeling of uncertainty among permanent staff about their own job security. Management placed the demands of the market or customer at the centre of the reasoning for new patterns of working time. The needs of the customer were drawn into the management–workforce equation as a compelling reason for the introduction of change. Traditional distinctions between management and worker were removed as both 'sides' assumed the common identity of service providers to their 'customers'.

The internalization of intensification

The internalization of intensification refers to the ways in which employees have adopted management values that have contributed to the intensification of their own labour. This ideological dimension to management–workforce relations has been a central component of management's attempts to create the 'new worker'. Management has pursued this objective in a variety of ways, mixing old and new techniques in an attempt to transform employee relations. At face value, management has succeeded in several ways. In service industries like hotels and tourism and in the rapidly expanding fast food chains, unions have been kept at bay, despite low wages and often coercive working conditions. Management has taken advantage of a climate of hostility to trade unionism, generated by legal and political change, to impose coercive patterns of control on a workforce that is predominantly low paid, low skilled and casualized (Timo and Littler, 1996: 25). Even in industries where trade union membership density has remained at high levels, in financial services and the public sector, workers have acquiesced in redundancy and restructuring programmes with relatively little disturbance to the stability of management–workforce relations. It is here that the internalization of intensification has emerged as an important subjective element in the intensification process.

Restructuring in financial services, involving significant job losses, branch closures and new patterns of work, has been accompanied by the adoption of human relations policies aimed at securing commitment to change via new systems of payment and reward, employee benefits packages and new approaches to the recognition of those who contribute to the company's or service's goals and objectives. Traditional forms of consensus were based upon mainly male employees progressing through a lengthy period of training and development. Loyalty and long service were rewarded by pay structures that reflected pay improvements as individuals progressed through the grading structure and work was typically organized in small branches where the 'them and us' difference between management and workforce was minimized. By contrast, the consolidation of work into large regional centres, the closure of large numbers of branches and the adoption of new performance and appraisal systems broke with tradition and created conditions in which management redefined the work culture. Traditional banking skills and long service were marginalized as attributes of the successful employee. A new glue had to be found to bind management and workforce together, to avoid the possible emergence of a 'them and us' climate.

The glue consisted of a system of individual reward and recognition, underpinned by a new mix of 'soft' paternalism and 'hard' coercion. The 'soft' approach was based upon the provision of employee benefit packages – typically consisting of private health insurance, counselling for stress and other personal or work-related issues and the provision of public recognition for successful employees. The 'hard' approach was reflected in cutting jobs or downsizing, imposing requirements to achieve performance targets or face disciplinary procedures and being required to accept new, more flexible, approaches to work practices. This combination of coercion and paternalism was adopted by Credit UK under its new American owners in the early 1990s and was also introduced in a piecemeal way by Insco in the period between 1995 and 1997. The new approach was not without its contradictions.

Individual appraisal and recognition rested uneasily with the widespread introduction of team working, and the climate of redundancy and rationalization was hardly conducive to staff considering themselves as an essential 'human' resource. Nevertheless, this hard/soft approach worked in so far as cost-driven changes were concerned. Job cuts and work reorganization met with relatively little opposition and those who remained experienced a rise in intensity of their own labour. The degree to which the internalization of intensification extended to the positive embrace of the new human relations techniques, however, was not proven by the case study evidence. In Insco those employees most likely to welcome the new approach were primarily recent recruits who aspired to management status. They were unencumbered by tradition and less likely to aspire to 'a job for life' with the company.

The approach to human resource management evident within financial services was adopted in more muted form in the NHS case studies. Here, the traditional commitment to patients was 'reworked' into a commitment structured by the purchaser–provider relation. While traditional employment relations were swept away by a new commercial, customer-oriented culture in the financial services, in the NHS the traditional commitment to the patient was subordinated to the demands arising from marketization. The demand to achieve higher service standards was imposed by a management that sought to fulfil its commitments to the purchasers of services rather than to the individual patients who were the recipients. A union representative in the Metropolitan Ambulance Service summed up the shift in management approach in the following way:

> We are constantly told that changes in work organization are not demanded by the ambulance service but by the purchasers. For example, they want a paramedic on every vehicle so we have to provide them. We are told that if we don't give them [the purchasers] what they want they will take the contract away. We are constantly being threatened by our own management to go along with changes because of the demands of the purchasers. (Interview with union branch official, central division, 1997)

At CHC Trust, the reprovision of mental health services at St Jude's created circumstances in which the demand for beds always outstripped their supply, leading to an over-occupancy of wards. According to union sources this caused a rise in violent incidents and created immensely stressful working conditions for nursing staff. While work intensified, it was the traditional commitment to patients from key groups of staff that enabled continuity in service provision. While senior management embraced the language of HRM there was little evidence of this approach being translated into the values or outlook of line managers or staff at local level. The insidious effects of marketization caused an internalization of intensification in a rather different way. Staff and their union representatives felt compelled to work, often with senior management, to implement, and soften or modify, the effects of externally imposed policies like market testing and contracting out. The contracting out of cleaning and catering services at St Jude's illustrates this point. Local union representatives opposed the out-sourcing of the service and proved to be correct in their assessment that the external contractor could not fulfil the terms of the contract that was agreed without adversely affecting employment conditions and the standard of services provided. None the less, the early termination of the contract left the local union representatives with the task of sitting down with management to find ways of providing the service in-house, while also complying with the terms of the contract agreed with Pall Mall. The union's successful campaign resulted in representatives taking on a shared responsibility for the resolution of a problem that could only result in the intensification of their own members' labour.

The intensification of labour in service industries in the 1990s has several dimensions. Intensification arose from the 'routinization' of white-collar work – typified by the labour process introduced into the call centre and data processing operations of such companies as Credit UK and Insco. It was facilitated by the adoption of technologies that were designed to structure the computer operator–customer interface and monitor the performance of the operator. It was also implicit to the new work cultures created within work teams that were required to operate across traditional skill boundaries and specialisms. Finally, and most importantly, labour intensification arose from the ideas and practices that informed the marketization of public services and the adoption of the customer-oriented focus of private service provision.

A US Model?

Ritzer (1993, 1998) has argued that a new US model emerged in late twentieth-century service industries. His account of changes in the nature of service work led him to draw the conclusion that service industries in the global economy have adopted a form of work organization that he calls McDonaldization. According to this view, the standardization of service activities has arisen from attempts to achieve greater efficiency, quantification/calculability, predictability and control. As other authors have suggested, Ritzer's work provides a useful starting point for analysing trends in the service sector, but does not provide a sound theoretical basis for the examination of management strategies and practices (Timo and Littler, 1996: 6). In their own study of work organization in retail banking and tourism, Timo and Littler have identified trends toward Taylorization, a management strategy that, combined with the use of numerical flexibility, contributed to the creation of a culture of casualization and routinization. It is suggested here, however, that analysis of recent trends in service work should not be confined to identifying the ways in which the methods of scientific management have infiltrated the service sector. The US model has other dimensions and embraces more than one dominant trend in patterns of work organization.

Organizational innovation at enterprise level, new forms of work organization embracing assembly line working and multifunctionalism, the introduction of new technical systems that absorbed traditional skills and discretion within the software program and the creation of a 'new worker' through employee commitment schemes were all features of this model. A focus upon the 'Taylorization' of work offers only a partial and incomplete picture of the range of management practices introduced in the service sector. Organizational innovation embraced decentralization and devolution in each of the case studies. Taylorism is regarded as a defining feature of the integrated enterprise. In service industries the routinization of work was linked to disintegration: out-sourcing, privatization and the introduction of business units and budget or profit centres.

Work routinization required the separation of knowledge and manual work processes. In the financial services, knowledge workers embraced a mix of new skills (sales, market research) and new managerial competencies that blurred distinctions between their roles as controllers of the labour process and participants within it. This trend was also evident within the health service, where qualified nurses increasingly combined clinical and managerial roles and a growing proportion of nursing staff were employed on lower grades as nurse care assistants. Taylorism is associated with hierarchical management layers, while the new approach in service industries was the product of downsizing and delayering, resulting in the shift towards shorter chains of command and an increase in management responsibilities taken by those on and close to the office or ward 'floor'.

A further feature of the scientific management model was the measurement of performance and the linking of performance to pay. Here again the service sector is at variance with the classic prescriptions of Taylorism in so far as the performance indicators were more varied than merely measuring outputs, and provided within the public sector the essential currency upon which the introduction of internal markets and service-led agreements was based. Here, a mix of 'real' and artificially constructed market mechanisms acted as the imperative around which the efficiency of service provision was gauged. In short, the routinization of service work followed some of the prescriptions of the Taylorist model but assumed other distinctive features that cohered into a new type of managerialism.

This new managerialism was codified and lent coherence by the projects and reports of management consultants. In each of the case studies management consultants played a significant role in developing the prescriptions for change. In Insco, for example, union officials identified 12 major projects introduced between 1994 and 1997 involving consultancy teams. In Metropolitan Ambulance Service Trust, consultants provided the blueprint for change in work organization and practices, and in CHC Trust consultants were employed to review existing work processes and recommend new ones. Arguably, because the transformation of work organization and the implementation of rationalization policies affected management as much as non-managerial staff, it was necessary to employ consultants to overcome the opposition among traditionalists within middle and senior management to the process of change. Lessons from the US experience was provided not only by management consultants who adopted the fashionable theories of their North American counterparts: at sector level in the health service there is evidence of the influence of US experience on policy-makers committed to the introduction of more competitive cost-conscious approaches to welfare reform (Ferlie *et al.*, 1996: 68).

The growth of service industries in the late twentieth century reflected an expansion of industrialism rather than signalling its demise. The marketization of public services, deregulation of state-owned industries and sharpening of competition in private services – expressed by the adoption of a new 'customer orientation' – fuelled a programme of management reform that, within UK management, lent heavily upon the experiences of its US counterparts. This programme of reform had momentous consequences for workplace relations, the final theme to which we now turn.

9 Labour and the Transformation of Service Work

Over recent years authors have become attached to the epithet 'post' to explain the dynamics of social change in the advanced industrial economies. This has led them to identifying a typology of the preceding social order as a precursor to presenting that of the new. As a result, social 'transformations' amount to the counterposing of 'old' and 'new' – the industrial and the post-industrial, the modern and the post-modern. This methodology is thoroughly flawed and owes much, as Rustin (1989), Clarke (1992), Kumar (1996) and others have explained, to the sociologists' predisposition for ideal type models, models that allow the 'sociological imagination to be freed from the boring constraints of empirical reality' (Clarke, 1992: 15). By contrast to this approach, it is suggested here that all periods of social disjuncture contain elements of continuity and change. The real challenge of social analysis is to evaluate their relative weight and importance at specific points in time. The argument presented here is that the dominant trend in UK service sector workplace relations favoured continuity in the 1980s and change in the 1990s.

The pace of change in industries may vary depending upon a variety of factors, including changes in product markets, management strategies, labour responses, technical innovation, government policies and the economic environment in which the industry or sector operates. In this sense, there is no single catalyst of change in workplace relations, but 'a set of inter-dependent factors' that create the necessity or opportunity for management to adopt new approaches to workplace relations (Kochan *et al.*, 1986: 51). These new approaches are often shaped or informed by those 'leaders' who are perceived as being most successful in transforming or restructuring the industry, enterprise or public sector institution. New approaches become codified into management practices that may be articulated and transmitted between enterprises, particularly in the recent period by such vehicles as management consultants.

The key period of change in UK service industries, such as the NHS and financial services, was the first half of the 1990s. It was during this time, for example, that the internal market reforms in the NHS provided opportunities to ally the new professional management style, initiated in the early 1980s, with organizational changes that subjected staff at all levels within the industry to a creeping 'marketization'. While the effects of contracting out were largely confined to manual and ancillary staff in the 1980s, the establishment of trusts and the widespread introduction of the purchaser/provider split in the early 1990s had a far wider impact on staff and management at all levels of the service. In financial services, employment growth continued throughout the 1980s despite investment in new technologies, and traditional banking industry employment conditions continued to prevail. The sharp decline in profitability caused by the 1989–92 recession, combined with the legal reforms of the mid-1980s and the restructuring of front and back office operations, generated a process of change in the early 1990s that impacted upon all levels of management and all groups of staff. While the seeds of change were sown in the 1980s through, for example, deregulation, which blurred the distinctions between industries and types of financial institutions, and the break-up of national bargaining arrangements in 1987, it was the first half of the 1990s that witnessed a decisive break with the past. In this period the NHS and financial services sector faced, in Kochan's terms, a set of interrelated factors which propelled the balance away from continuity and towards change.

The Workplace Relations Agenda

Throughout the 1990s management concerns dominated the agenda of workplace relations in each of the case studies. Where previously industry- or company-wide employment conditions had prevailed, the shift in the 1990s was towards more varied and localized conditions of service. These were followed by an increasing tendency by the mid-1990s, particularly in the financial services sector, towards the unilateral imposition of change. The management agenda in banking and insurance industries focused upon themes like redundancy, performance appraisal, the dilution of collective bargaining over pay, the break-up of traditional work practices and the introduction of new work patterns that gave rise to an uneven process of labour intensification. Each of these changes generated negotiations between management and union representatives, though the focus of negotiation was mainly on the method of implementation rather than, from the union side, on challenging the substance of management strategy.

In Credit UK and Insco management domination of the bargaining agenda was facilitated by three key developments. First, the fragmentation of collective bargaining arrangements served to enhance the role of local management and enabled diversity in employment conditions to emerge at departmental and work team levels. There was, however, some evidence of this development fostering a modest growth in local pockets, or 'informal' networks, of bargaining led by local union representatives. Second, the weakening of collective bargaining created the opportunity or space for management to implement performance appraisal, staff development and 'employee care' packages that tended to reinforce the individualization of the employment relation. Finally, the union role was recast. The fragmentation of collective bargaining saw the emergence of large groups of employees who were no longer represented by their unions through the collective bargaining process. Management imposed its stamp on the scope and coverage of collective bargaining.

In the NHS, the establishment of trusts was designed to enable a greater flexibility to be exercised at local level in the determination of pay and conditions. Decentralization gave managements the opportunity to devise payment structures that might be more sensitive to local labour market conditions, reward those areas where sound performance and efficiency were achieved and determine their own strategies for the control of costs. This discretion was tempered by the continuation of national negotiations and the existence of pay review bodies for the medical professions. National negotiations, though, provided scope for local initiatives. While the continuance of national arrangements acted as a break on management discretion, bargaining agendas still tended to be dominated by management concerns (Poynter, 1997). This domination was established as a structural condition by marketization. The purchaser/provider split increasingly shaped domestic management–workforce negotiations by providing the financial parameters by which trusts functioned. Market relations determined workloads and workflow, as well as setting the parameters within which trust performance would be measured. Local management discretion was influenced by the necessity to meet the cost controls imposed by the annually negotiated trust contracts. These, in turn, ensured that management sought efficiency savings and did as much as possible to alter the skills mix of its workforce so as to push down labour costs. It was in this way that local management tended to exercise control over local workplace relations. Marketization, coupled with the continuation of contracting out and market testing, ensured that unions were pushed on to the back foot, pressed into situations where they largely concentrated, like their private sector counterparts, on negotiating over the terms of the implementation of management strategies rather than challenging their underlying principles.

Industrial Relations Institutions

Brief examination of the framework of collective bargaining in each case study provides some evidence of continuity in the pattern of management–workforce relations. A narrow focus on the institutions designed to mediate workplace relations suggests that the business of management–workforce relations continued to be dealt with via institutions whose origins lay in the 1960s and 1970s. The argument here, however, is that such a focus on industrial relations institutions offers a superficial picture of the underlying dynamic involved in the employer–labour relation. Examination of that dynamic suggests that the 1990s represented an important watershed, a significant break from the past, which was not fully reflected in the institutional arrangements that underpinned the process of collective bargaining.

In each of the case studies collective bargaining arrangements with the trade unions were maintained. On the face of it, there was evidence of continuity. Management introduced reform to the institutional arrangements but there were relatively few occasions when a direct threat to union recognition was presented. The union at Credit UK was concerned about collective bargaining rights in the wake of the take-over by GDC, the US multinational, in 1991, and unions in Insco and the North Metropolitan Health Authority were concerned by the loss of a trade union culture in areas where union membership density was low. Despite these circumstances, union involvement in collective bargaining arrangements was maintained. Management reform of the institutions was accompanied, however, by a process of marginalization. In brief, structures may have been retained but management strategy significantly changed and, in the process, contributed to the marginalization of the trade unions in the financial services case studies and, in a different way, in the NHS.

In Insco, management scrapped the company-wide negotiating arrangements and introduced five separate bargaining committees at business unit level. At the same time, workplace-level bargaining was allowed to wither where local union representatives were unable to convince local management of the necessity for site-level meetings. At Credit UK, collective bargaining took place via the joint negotiating committee (JNC). The JNC continued to operate throughout the extensive period of restructuring and survived the take-over by GDC. There is evidence, however, that GDC adopted a dualistic approach to workplace relations, continuing to negotiate with BIFU, while at the same time setting up more direct forms of communication with employees and using these to impose unilaterally individual employee benefits and employment conditions that were introduced outside of the traditional collective bargaining forums. In these circumstances, the union attempted to use collective bargaining to modify the impact of the changes in work practices and employment conditions that were imposed.

The reform of the institutions designed to mediate workplace relations was, in practice, complex in the financial services. The union role in collective bargaining was not directly attacked but was undermined by management approaches designed to limit or curtail union influence over workplace affairs. In Insco, the decentralization of collective bargaining arrangements was accompanied by the establishment of agreements, on appraisal and pay, for example, that aimed at enabling or facilitating greater local management discretion over a wide range of employment conditions. This approach was complemented by policies that had the effect of ensuring that BIFU was unable to organize in particular business units or work areas such as Insco Direct. Together, these policies amounted to a concerted effort to marginalize the union, without management openly adopting a policy of derecognition. This approach was reflected in the company's attitude to the establishment of European Works Council (EWC) arrangements in 1997. The company unilaterally declared its intention to set up an employee forum as a precursor to the development of an EWC. It invited candidates to put themselves forward for election. The union was not formally consulted, nor was it given the opportunity to have its own designated BIFU seats. The union decided to participate in the election – failure to have done so would have confirmed its marginalization – and gained two of the four UK seats on the forum. In both the financial services enterprises, institutional relations between union and management were retained, but the content of those relations changed significantly. While both enterprises might be regarded as retaining collective bargaining arrangements, union influence was weakened. In short, collective bargaining was no longer regarded by management as the main channel by which employees' interests could be represented.

By way of contrast, in the NHS case studies there was evidence of collective bargaining institutions continuing to reflect a more central role for the unions in the conduct of workplace relations. Despite the establishment of interim collective bargaining arrangements in the immediate period after the conferral of trust status, in both case studies the unions sustained their influence over the conduct of workplace affairs. Management did not seek to open up alternative channels of communication with employees, nor did it unilaterally impose changes in employment conditions. On the surface there was evidence of continuity in the institutional pattern of workplace relations. This was reflected in the way in which the NHS unions at both trusts were able to exercise a restraining influence over reforms in work organization (Metropolitan Ambulance Service) and impose some limitations on the process of contracting out and market testing (CHC Trust). The exercise of union influence was facilitated by a combination of strong pockets of unionism at workplace level, local management's willingness to adhere to, rather than break from, the national framework of pay and conditions and a sometimes grudging recognition that exercising greater management control over work organization was difficult in circumstances in which workers' commitment played an important part in determining the maintenance of standards of service provision.

That the collective bargaining institutions in the NHS retained elements of continuity in the 1990s, reflected in the maintenance of union influence as opposed to its marginalization, is supported by evidence from other studies (Lloyd and Seifert, 1993). Such a conclusion, however, requires qualification. First, by the mid-1990s, there were examples in other NHS trusts of local management adopting approaches aimed at significantly reducing union influence over workplace matters, as the evidence from trusts located in close geographical proximity to CHC Trust revealed. At workplace level, there were increased opportunities for local management to adopt different approaches to industrial relations and, clearly, a minority chose to do so. Second, and most importantly, the development of internal market mechanisms in the NHS, during the course of the 1990s, tended to impose increasingly tighter limits on the scale and scope of local negotiations. The financial structures imposed by the internal market acted as an effective constraint upon local bargaining and, arguably, generated circumstances in which local negotiations took the form of how best management and unions could work within the contractual strait-jacket imposed by the annual round of purchaser/provider negotiations. In effect, while unions might negotiate with their management counterparts within trusts, the key decisions affecting the staffing levels and working conditions of their members were shifting elsewhere to the purchaser/provider negotiations that took place at regional health authority level. In brief, the whittling away of the centralized system of determining pay and conditions and the introduction of the internal market significantly influenced the role and scope of local industrial relations institutions. Marketization may have left the institutions intact, but their role was significantly curtailed. Finally, within CHC Trust and Metropolitan Ambulance Service Trust the effect of contracting out was to reduce the numbers of employees covered by formal collective bargaining arrangements. In CHC Trust, ancillary staff were represented via 'informal' negotiations with the contractor, while in Metropolitan Ambulance Service Trust many staff working in the patient transport service area were effectively excluded from negotiations when their contracts and employment conditions were transferred to external contractors.

While in each workplace case study elements of continuity could be found in the institutions that regulated workplace relations, management reforms (at either industry or enterprise level) amounted to a significant step towards the marginalization of union influence over workplace matters. This was particularly the case in the financial services and was, arguably, less overtly evident in the NHS cases. In the NHS, however, the bedding in of the new internal market mechanisms that took place during the early 1990s created circumstances in which the role of local collective bargaining institutions was increasingly structured by the constraints imposed by the contractual relations between purchaser and provider. Local negotiations between management and unions largely become a matter of how best to modify the adverse and insidious effects of the operation of the internal market mechanism.

Evidence of institutional continuity in workplace relations in each of the cases should not be interpreted as the maintenance of a system of industrial relations which provided for the effective articulation of the interests of both management and labour. The early 1990s saw a significant shift towards management interests dominating this relationship. While the formal institutions that mediate management and workforce relations remained, the role of the trade unions significantly changed. In Credit UK and Insco, management unilaterally imposed changes in work organization, working conditions and employment contracts, and pay bargaining was effectively removed from the negotiating arena. In the NHS, imposition took the form of an externally imposed necessity arising from the internal market mechanism.

In the 1970s and 1980s the orthodox view of industrial relations theorists, following in the footsteps of Flanders (1964), Clegg (1972) and others, argued that the deeper the penetration of the formal institutions of collective bargaining the more likely it was that unions would play an influential and constructive role in the conduct of workplace relations. Unions would contest the agenda of issues arising at work, broaden the scope of collective bargaining and increase the roles and authority of local representatives. In the 1970s this dominant view within the discipline expressed a wider set of social values and reflected the development of real events. By contrast, in the 1990s the set of values implicit to this outlook, and underpinning industrial relations as a discipline, no longer reflected the pattern of real events. Industrial relations institutions could remain untouched or be reformed, with a tendency to shift downwards to the local level, but they no longer provided a significant indication of a real contest between management and union interests (Poynter, 1993). Job cuts, the imposition of change, the removal of negotiations over pay, hours and working conditions (revealed, in particular, in the financial services) and the subjection of local bargaining to the constraints imposed by marketization could occur alongside a continuity in the institutional relationships between management and labour. In this context, the maintenance of institutional depth and continuity thinly disguised a significant shift in the balance of management–workforce relations in favour of the interests of the former.

Union Organization and Representation

In each of the case studies, the influence of workplace trade unionism was severely challenged by a number of factors. First, changes in management organization, and in particular the role of industrial relations managers, disturbed traditional relationships between management and union representatives, leaving the latter uncertain about their negotiating role. This was particularly evident in those enterprises and institutions that fragmented into business units. Second, organizational reform, allied to the fragmentation into business units and contracting out, tended, in turn, to fragment union membership across a number of enterprises, causing problems for representative structures and leaving groups of members no longer covered by collective bargaining arrangements. Finally, local union organization found itself subject to the imposition of change from a variety of sources – management consultant reports and projects, the demands of the market mechanism and their own senior management – which affected members' perceptions of the capacity of union representatives to influence workplace affairs. These adverse conditions had an important impact upon union organization and representation.

Three main trends may be identified in union organization and representation in this hostile climate. First, the case studies revealed across both sectors a shrinking activist base, even among the relatively well organized groups of workers. The activist core could no longer effectively represent members who were increasingly spread across a range of business units and, in the case of the NHS studies, different employers. The case studies illustrated how workplace representatives faced a growing volume of work alongside increased difficulties in securing the time to carry out their union roles. In Insco and Credit UK, union representatives found that an increased workload tended to squeeze the available time for union activity and in all cases, with the exception of the Metropolitan Ambulance Service, there were large groups of members without any local union lay representation. In the Metropolitan Ambulance Service, the tradition of electing local 'station reps' ensured that the representative structure achieved a sound geographical spread, though this form of local democracy, where union members could elect a representative who might be in another union, ensured that the local representation structure did not match up with the branch structures of each individual union. Paradoxically, the system of local workplace democracy served to weaken the role of the union branches and dilute the external influence of the national and regional union organizations. The relatively narrow activist base in all the other case studies tended to create circumstances in which union organization was heavily dependent upon the roles of local lay union representatives, who by custom and practice or written agreements had achieved significant time off from their work duties to conduct their union roles. This dependence made local union organization prone to employer interference. In Insco and Credit UK, for example, management gradually reduced the number of lay representatives with the right to time off for union duties.

The second challenge to local union organization arose from a decline in union membership density and the tendency for areas of employment growth to exist outside the ambit of union organization. This was particularly evident in the financial services sector. In Credit UK, union membership density fell from around 50 per cent of the workforce at its peak in 1989 to a level of around 15 per cent in 1996, and in Insco, Insco Direct operated effectively as a 'no-go area' for union organization. In Metropolitan Ambulance Service Trust, while membership density remained high among the core accident and emergency staff, membership density waned among the patient transport service staff as contracting out took its toll. Only in CHC Trust was union membership density sustained during the 1990s.

The third challenge to local union organization arose from the relative lack of membership involvement in union structures. In the financial services cases, there was no history of local workplace or branch meetings. Traditionally, union membership involvement had been confined to occasional crisis meetings, or members were asked their views through individual postal ballots. This approach in Insco, for example, was a legacy of the days when it operated as a staff association. While members were well informed about developments within the company, the union had not found effective ways of encouraging members to engage actively in debates or discussions. As a consequence, ballots were exercises in the passive presentation of opinion rather than being an active means to motivate members to pursue any form of collective union action. In the NHS cases, union branch meetings involved local lay representatives in branch committee meetings rather than meetings with members, although members were occasionally engaged in local workplace meetings when issues arose of direct concern or interest to them. In this sense, in each of the case studies, there was evidence of a relatively limited engagement of members in union affairs, particularly through the traditional mechanism of the branch meeting.

This relatively bleak picture of local union organization – a thin activist base, falling membership density and a weak relationship between formal union structures and members – was leavened by evidence of a close informal identity between some groups of members and their union representatives. In the Metropolitan Ambulance Service, members willingly engaged in industrial action when reforms in work organization in the central division created intolerable conditions for ambulance crews. Equally, in CHC Trust, union members at St Jude's closely identified with their union representatives and regularly called into the union office for advice, support and discussion. In Insco and Credit UK, the union used imaginative ways of communicating with members and continuously exposed the adverse consequences of company policies and perspectives. In all four workplaces, there was a core of union activists whose commitment and dedication to their union duties was exemplary, and their relations with full-time officers were cooperative and constructive. Overall, however, workplace unionism was in danger of hollowing out, its organizational weaknesses being an expression of a deeper social and political malaise in which the salience of ideas based upon a distinction between 'them and us' had all but disappeared.

In the financial services, union organization was ill-prepared for the shift away from the traditional 'paternal' consensus that had underpinned workplace relations in the 1970s and 1980s. Personnel management during this period had pursued policies that generated largely uniform terms and conditions of employment across the industry. Staff were rewarded on the basis of length of service, and career paths, particularly for men, were designed to enable them to develop occupational expertise and an expectation of a job for life. In turn, union organization rested primarily upon the role of seconded representatives who continued to receive their company wage while working full-time on union matters. The challenge in the early 1990s, which saw the fragmentation of enterprise organization and a rapid differentiation in terms and conditions of employment, also gave rise to a direct challenge to traditional forms of union organization. The new management approach exposed the overreliance of the union on the 'goodwill' of the employer and revealed the weak links between the union and its members, causing union membership density to decline rapidly in Credit UK and the union in Insco to undertake organizational reforms at what might be called the 'eleventh hour'.

The lack of preparedness to meet the challenges posed by management in the 1990s was not only expressed in organizational weakness; more significantly, it demonstrated the limitations of a union outlook whose values were informed by the 'professionalism' associated with 'white-collar' occupations when, in reality, these were rapidly eroding in the face of the routinization of work within the sector. Understandably, the union fought to defend these 'white-collar' conditions in Credit UK in the 1980s, when the company was rapidly expanding as a data processing firm, adopting many of the work practices and employment policies associated with the transformation of work in other financial institutions in the 1990s. Unfortunately, the lessons from such companies as Credit UK were slow to be learnt. As a consequence, the union was unable to respond rapidly to changes in work organization that resulted in the relocation of staff into larger regional centres. Paradoxically, staff were brought together in large white-collar factory environments, which demanded closer and more interdependent forms of working, at a time when their employment contracts were increasingly individualized via staff performance and appraisal schemes. The weakness in labour's collective identity left staff exposed to the individualistic values associated with the new management techniques, values that enabled management to introduce new work practices that encouraged workers to cooperate in the intensification of their own labour.

In the public services, despite the adverse political and legal conditions of the 1980s, the impact of management reforms were largely felt by manual employees. White-collar, professional and clerical staff were largely untouched and were ill-prepared for the management reforms of the 1990s. Decentralization, including the fragmentation into business units, was 'misread' as an opportunity to develop local bargaining when, in practice, it circumscribed local negotiating arrangements and served to expose the weaknesses of local union organization, revealing its incapacity to come to terms with the new demands arising from the operation of the internal market in the NHS. While there was a stronger tradition of workplace unionism in the public services than in the financial services sector, it too was in danger of hollowing out in the 1990s, its rate of decline being slowed only in the case studies by, for example, the resilience a small core of union activists and officers, pockets of membership resistance such as in the central division of the Metropolitan Ambulance Service Trust and the presence in the NHS of management doves who were reluctant to give up the consensus-based model that characterized the public services in their golden age of the 1970s. Despite these influences slowing the process of union decline, the underlying trends were towards the marginalization of union influence over workplace affairs and the hollowing out of trade unions as effective representatives of collective aspirations.

The Prospects for Union Renewal

Assessing the potential for unions to reverse the trends towards marginalization and hollowing out is a complex affair. Trade union membership in the UK is unevenly spread across industrial sectors. Union density as a percentage of total employees in the UK fell from 39 per cent in 1989 to 32 per cent in 1995. Over the same period, density levels in production industries fell from 45 to 33 per cent. In service industries a slower rate of decline occurred, with density levels dropping from 37 to 32 per cent (Labour Force Survey, 1996: 216–17). Union membership density is broadly comparable in production and service industries, with approximately one in three employees in unions in each sector. However, with service sector employment accounting for a much greater proportion of total employment in the UK, arguably the future prospects for trade unionism rest primarily with those organizing in service industries.

The discussion on union renewal has focused on identifying the conditions and appropriate actions that could enable unions to re-establish their influence in the workplace and wider society (Fosh, 1993; Fairbrother, 1994, 1996). In particular, Fairbrother has linked the prospects for renewal to the necessity for building union organization from below, at workplace level. This could be achieved by rebuilding local lay representative structures, rekindling links with members and developing a strong local foundation for membership involvement in union affairs. Effective renewal also required minimizing tendencies towards accommodation with management and resisting the trend towards the philosophy of 'partnership' that has its origins in the business unionism approach developed by the maverick electrician's union (EETPU) in the 1980s (Fairbrother, 1996; Poynter, 1997). Since renewal is intimately linked to the revival of workplace unionism, recent shifts away from centralized and industry-wide bargaining towards the local level provided an important opportunity for commencing the process of renewal (Fairbrother, 1996).

Both the NHS and financial services have experienced the shift away from industry-wide bargaining over recent years. They provide, therefore, a useful indicator of how unions may respond to this opportunity provided for workplace renewal. The evidence provided by the case studies is, at best, mixed. Marketization in the NHS created new problems and impediments to renewal, as local union representatives were drawn into cooperating with management to achieve, for example, the performance targets set by purchaser/provider contracts. In Insco, devolution of collective bargaining to business units tended to underline the existence of union 'no-go' areas. In this sense, fragmentation, involving the downward shift in employee relations responsibilities, created new impediments as much as new opportunities for union renewal. Second, the ideological dimension of management restructuring – the individualization of the employment relation and the focus on the new 'customer-oriented' worker – were important ingredients in the intensification of work which the unions found difficult to challenge. In this sense, management policies were directly and successfully aimed at weakening the collectivist values on which workplace unionism relies. On the other hand, the shift towards decentralization and devolution of employee relations policies exposed the weaknesses in union organization that had previously remained hidden by national and company-wide bargaining arrangements. This was recognized by trade union representatives, particularly in Insco and the NHS trusts, and led them to devising the initial steps towards strategies for renewal. The potential for success is not entirely in their hands. Union renewal relies on the development of local activities – new ways of engaging with members, revitalizing union representation and re-establishing collective organization – linked to changes in the wider social and political environment. This involves, in particular, the necessity for the re-emergence of labour power as an agency of social change. In the absence of this wider social agency, workplace unionism is likely to be sustained only by the tireless efforts of a core of activists for whom a central task will be to organize sporadic challenges to management authority while at the same time seeking to avoid the pitfalls of accommodation or marginalization (Cohen and Moody, 1998).

A narrow analytical focus on the institutions that regulate management–labour relations cannot capture the complex changes that have taken place in management–labour relations in the UK service industries. Unions have retained an institutional role in the workplace, while, at the same time, the new social relations of service work have contributed to a significant reduction in their influence over workplace affairs. The new pattern of social relations in UK service industries has absorbed many of the values, policies and practices associated with the US model. At a time when the US management 'mystique' (Locke, 1996) appeared to be on the wain in the manufacturing enterprise, a new US managerialism was establishing a significant influence over the restructuring process in the services sector.

The Decline and Resurgence of Americanization

In his provocative and clearly argued book on the decline of the US management mystique, Locke indicates that US managerialism lost its role as a hegemonic centre in the 1980s in the face of weak US economic performance and the rise of Japanese management approaches which were better tuned to a post-Fordist world. US managers lost faith in the theory of knowledge that underpinned US managerialism (Locke, 1996: 176). It appeared that the Japanese and German models offered better paths to follow. As a consequence, 'nobody these days . . . talks much about an Americanisation of their management' (Locke, 1996: 208). A decade on, Locke's analysis of the decline of US hegemony looks a little premature, not merely because the Japanese and German economies faltered in the 1990s but also because Locke's focus on a paradigm based upon the manufacturing enterprise led him largely to ignore the transformations taking place in US approaches to the management of service industries. It was here that US managerialism was busily constructing the codes of conduct and the internalization of work values that he claimed US companies, with their top-down rules and sanctions, were incapable of developing (Locke, 1996: 225). While temporarily under strain in relation to its hegemony in the manufacturing sphere, a new US managerialism was rapidly achieving a hegemonic position in services industries.

Rather than witnessing the triumph of mental or intellectual over manual labour, advanced industrial economies, with the USA in the lead, have taken considerable steps over the past decade towards the industrialization of intelligence, the development of new divisions of labour that have begun to undermine the 'professionalism' of white-collar work and those occupations concerned with the delivery of public service provision. In the course of its attempts to subordinate service labour, management has adapted the techniques aimed at the real subordination of labour in production industries and applied them to services. Just as it led the way at the beginning of the twentieth century in production industries, US management took the lead in the restructuring of the service sector at the century's end.

The Americanization of UK Service Industries

The US model had a particular influence in the UK. In the financial services and the NHS, a growing proportion of the workforce was subjected to the stultifying consequences of management reforms that contributed to the stripping away of individual discretion, the dilution of job-specific skills, the routinization of intellectual processes and the erosion of professional autonomy. Supporting this transformation in work organization was the emergence of ideas and values which sought to remove the distinction between management and labour and replace it by a common identity through which everyone became a customer-driven service provider. In this sense, the market-oriented management techniques of the late twentieth century borrowed from the constructs of the vulgar neo-classical economists of the late nineteenth century. The old world of 'buyers and sellers' was reinvented as the new world of 'providers and purchasers'.

In this context, changes at workplace, enterprise and industry levels reflected the broader structural and cultural transformations occurring in society at large. In the post Cold War world, there was no longer perceived to be a serious alternative to the market as the mechanism for organizing society. In turn, this dominant discourse within society infected the relationship between management and labour at workplace level and provided a compelling set of values which informed the restructuring of the labour process itself. This was reflected in a number of ways. Management experimented in adopting a variety of new organizational trajectories aimed at coping with the increasingly competitive environment in which it operated (Castells, 1998). Devolution and decentralization, for example, were designed to encourage the more effective performance of organizations through the achievement of a closer proximity to customers and markets. In turn, organizational reform was accompanied by attempts to change traditional forms of work organization, and to transform the ways in which workers perceived themselves. The 'new' worker was no longer merely an employee, he or she was also required to assume an identity as a provider whose relationship with the customer was increasingly structured by the technologies that facilitated their interaction. In this sense, management attempts to achieve the real subordination of service labour in the late twentieth century contained sharp contrasts to those adopted by the scientific management school of the earlier twentieth century.

While Taylor and his followers readily acknowledged in the early twentieth century, often in derogatory terms, the conflicting and distinctive interests of labour, a key component of the new US model, in the late twentieth century, was their denial. This was particularly evident in service industries where management consciously adopted strategies aimed at creating a new kind of front-line 'customer-oriented' worker. In the contemporary period, prevailing social values have consigned alternatives to the capitalist market to the history books. These dominant values have been incorporated, via the US model, into the very organization and culture of the workplace. In these circumstances, trade unionism in the UK service industries must address both the ideological and organizational dimensions of restructuring if it is to survive.

Bibliography

Ackers, P., Smith, C. and Smith, P. (eds) (1996) *The New Workplace and Trade Unionism.* London: Routledge.

Ainley, P. (1993) *Class and Skill: Changing Divisions of Knowledge and Labour.* London: Cassell.

Allen, J. and du Gay, P. (1994) The economic identity of services. *Work, Employment and Society,* 8(2), 255–71.

Allen, J. and Henry, N. (1996) Fragments of industry and employment. Contract service work and the shift towards precarious employment. In R. Crompton, D. Gallie and K. Purcell (eds), *Changing Forms of Employment, Organisation, Skills and Gender.* London: Routledge, pp. 65–82.

Allen, J. and Massey, D. (eds) (1988) *Restructuring Britain: The Economy in Question.* London: Open University.

Amin, A. and Thrift, N. (eds) (1994) *Globalisation, Institutions and Regional Development in Europe.* Oxford: Oxford University Press.

Armstrong, P. (1991) The divorce of productive and unproductive management. In C. Smith, D. Knights and H. Willmott (eds), *White Collar Work.* London: Macmillan, pp. 241–61.

Association of British Insurers (1996) *Insurance Facts, Figures and Trends.* London: ABI.

Association of British Insurers (1997) *Insurance Trends, Issue 12.* London: ABI.

Atkinson, J. (1984) Manpower strategies for flexible organisations. *Personnel Management,* August, 28–31.

Atkinson, J. (1985) *Flexibility, Uncertainty and Manpower Management.* IMS Report No. 89. Brighton: University of Sussex, Institute of Manpower Studies.

Bach, S. (1989) Too high a price to pay. A study of competitive tendering for domestic services in the NHS. Warwick Papers in Industrial Relations, Number 25. Coventry: IRRU.

Bacon, N. and Storey, J. (1996) Individualism and collectivism and the changing role of trade unions. In P. Ackers, C. Smith and P. Smith (eds), *The New Workplace and Trade Unionism.* London: Routledge, pp. 77–109.

Bacon, R and Eltis, W. (1976) *Britain's Economic Problem: Too Few Producers.* London: Macmillan.

Bailey, R. (1994) Annual review article 1993: British public sector industrial relations. *British Journal of Industrial Relations,* 32(1), 113–36.

Bain, J. (1993) Budget holding: here to stay? *British Medical Journal*, **306**, 1185–8.

Baker, J. (1996) Less lean but considerably more agile. *Financial Times*, 10 May.

Baldry, C., Bain, P. and Taylor, P. (1998) Bright satanic offices: intensification, control and team Taylorism. In C. Warhurst and P. Thompson (eds), *Workplaces of the Future*. London: Macmillan, pp. 163–83.

Barker, J. and Downing, H. (1985) Word processing and the transformation of patriarchal relations of control in the office. In D. MacKenzie and J. Wajcman (eds), *The Social Shaping of Technology*. Milton Keynes: Open University Press, pp. 147–64.

Beaumont, D. (1992) *Public Sector Industrial Relations*. London: Routledge.

Beaumont, P. (1990) *Change in Industrial Relations*. London: Routledge.

Beauregard, R. (1989) *Economic Restructuring and Political Response*. London: Sage.

Bell, D. (1973) *The Coming of the Post-industrial Society: A Venture in Social Forecasting*. New York: Basic Books.

Bell, D. (1980) The social framework of the information society. In T. Forester (ed.), *The Microelectronics Revolution*. Oxford: Blackwell, pp. 500–49.

Bennett, A. and Smith-Gavine, S. (1988) The percentage utilisation of labour index. In D. Bosworth (ed.), *Working below Capacity*. Basingstoke: Macmillan.

Benyon, H. (1997) The changing practices of work. In R. Brown (ed.), *The Changing Shape of Work*. London: Macmillan, pp. 20–53.

Berg, M. (1980) *The Machinery Question and the Making of Political Economy 1815–1848*. Cambridge: Cambridge University Press.

Beynon, H. (1992) The end of the industrial worker? In N. Abercrombie and A. Wardle (eds), *Social Change in Britain*. Cambridge: Polity Press, 167–83.

BIFU (1988) *The Monopolies and Mergers Commission Enquiry into Credit Card Services: Submission of the Banking, Insurance and Finance Union*. London: BIFU.

BIFU (1992) *History of the Union*. London: BIFU.

BIFU (1995) *Flexible Working*. London: BIFU.

Blackaby, D. and Hunt, L. (1993) An assessment of Britain's productivity record in the 1980s: has there been a miracle? In N. Healey (ed.), *Britain's Economic Miracle: Myth or Reality?* London: Routledge, pp. 109–26.

Bonefeld, W. and Burnham, P. (1996) Britain and the politics of the European Exchange Rate Mechanism. *Capital and Class*, **60**, 5–39.

Braverman, H. (1974) *Labour and Monopoly Capital*. London: Monthly Review Press.

Britton, A. (1993) The economy in the 1980s: a review of the decade. In N. Healey (ed.), *Britain's Economic Miracle: Myth or Reality?* London: Routledge, pp. 43–56.

Brown, R. (ed.) (1997) *The Changing Shape of Work*. London: Macmillan.

Bryan, L. (1991) A blueprint for financial reconstruction. *Harvard Business Review*, May/June, 73–86.

Bryson, C., Jackson, M. and Leopold, J. (1995) The impact of self-governing trusts on trades unions and staff associations in the NHS. *Industrial Relations Journal*, **26**(2), 120–33.

Bullock, P. and Yaffe, D. (1979) Inflation, the crisis and the post-war boom. In *Revolutionary Communist 3/4*, 2nd edn. London: RCP Publications, pp. 5–45.

Burke, G. and Peppard, J. (eds) (1995) *Examining Business Process Re-engineering*. London: Kogan Page.

Burnham, J. (1941) *The Managerial Revolution*. New York: John Day.

Burnham, P. (1996) The recomposition of national states in the global economy: implications for the restructuring of labour/capital relations. Paper presented at the Globalisation of Production and the Regulation of Labour Conference, University of Warwick, 11–13 September.

Calinicos, A. (1989) *Against Post-modernism: A Marxist Critique*. Cambridge: Polity Press.

Capon, N. (1992) *The Marketing of Financial Services: A Book of Cases*. London: Prentice Hall.

Carter, B. (1997) Restructuring state employment. *Capital and Class*, **63**, Autumn, 65–85.

Castells, M. (1993) The informational economy and the new international division of labour. In M. Carnoy, M. Castells, S. Cohen and F. Cardoso (eds), *The New Global Economy in the Information Age*. University Park, PA: Pennsylvania State University Press, pp. 15–44.

Castells, M. (1996) *The Rise of the Network Society*. Oxford: Blackwell.

Castells, M. (1998) *End of Millennium*. Oxford: Blackwell.

Cave, A. (1994) *Managing Change in the Workplace: New Approaches to Employee Relations*. London: Coopers and Lybrand/Kogan Page.

Chandler, A. (1962) *Strategy and Structure*. Boston: MIT Press.

Chandler, A. (1977) *The Visible Hand: The Managerial Revolution in American Business*. Cambridge, MA: Harvard University Press.

Clark, C. (1940) *The Conditions of Economic Progress*. London: Macmillan.

Clark, J. (ed.) (1993) *Human Resource Management and Technical Change*. London: Sage.

Clarke, S. (1988) *Keynesianism, Monetarism and the Crisis of the State*. Aldershot: Edward Elgar.

Clarke, S. (1992) What in the f—'s name is Fordism? In H. Gilbert, R. Burrows and A. Pollert (eds), *Fordism and Flexibility*. London: Macmillan, pp. 13–30.

Clarke, T. (1997) The political economy of the UK privatisation programme: a blueprint for other countries? In T. Clarke and C. Pitelis (eds), *The Political Economy of Privatisation*. London: Routledge, pp. 205–33.

Clegg, H. A. (1972) *The System of Industrial Relations in Britain*. Oxford: Blackwell.

Clegg, H. A. (1979) *The Changing System of Industrial Relations in Britain*. Oxford: Blackwell.

Coakley, J. and Harris, L. (1992) Financial globalisation and deregulation. In J. Michie (ed.), *The Economic Legacy 1979–92*. London: Academic Press, pp. 37–56.

Coddington, D., Palmquist, L. and Trollinger, W. (1985) Strategies for survival in the hospital industry. *Harvard Business Review*, May/June, 129–38.

Cohen, S. and Moody, K. (1998) Unions, strikes and class consciousness today. In L. Panitch and C. Leys (eds), *The Communist Manifesto Now, Socialist Register 1998*. Rendelsham: Merlin, pp. 102–23.

Cohen, S. and Zysman, J. (1987) *Manufacturing Matters: The Myth of the Post Industrial Economy*. New York: Basic Books.

Cooke, P. and Morgan, K. (1994) Growth regions under duress: renewal strategies in Baden Wurttemberg and Emilia Romagna. In A. Amin and N. Thrift (eds), *Globalisation, Institutions and Regional Development in Europe*. Oxford: Oxford University Press.

Cousins, C. (1988) The restructuring of welfare work: the introduction of general management and the contracting out of ancillary services. *Work, Employment and Society*, **2**, 210–28.

Cressey, P. and Scott, P. (1992) Employment, technology and industrial relations in the UK clearing banks: is the honeymoon over? *New Technology, Work and Employment,* **7**(2), 67–71.

Crompton, R., Gallie, D. and Purcell, K. (eds) (1996) *Changing Forms of Employment.* London: Routledge.

Cross, M. (1990) *Changing Job Structures.* London: Heinemann.

Davidow, W. and Malone, M. (1993) *The Virtual Corporation.* New York: Harper Collins.

Day, P. and Klein, R. (1991) Britain's health care experiment. *Health Affairs,* **10**(3), 39–59.

Dent, M. (1991) Autonomy and the medical profession: medical audit and management control. In C. Smith, D. Knights and H. Willmott (eds), *White-Collar Work: The Non-manual Labour Process.* London: Macmillan, pp. 65–88.

Dicken, P. (1992) *Global Shift: The Internationalisation of Economic Activity,* 2nd edn. London: Chapman and Hall.

Dixon, R. (1991) *Banking in Europe.* London: Routledge.

DoH (1989) *Self-governing Hospitals.* Working for Patients Working Paper 1. London: HMSO.

DoH Steering Group (1995) *Interim Report of the Review of Ambulance Performance Standards.* London: HMSO.

Donkin, R. (1996) Management: a bit of an odd fish. Managers face a difficult task when differentiating between mere eccentricity and stressed-out behaviour in the workplace. *Financial Times,* 16 September.

Driver, C. (1992) A legacy of capital shortage. In J. Michie (ed.), *The Economic Legacy 1979–92.* London: Academic Press, pp. 88–90.

Drucker, P. (1991) The new productivity challenge. *Harvard Business Review,* November/December, 69–79.

Dyson, R. (1992) *Changing Patterns of Labour Utilisation in NHS Trusts.* London: NHSME.

Efficiency Unit, Cabinet Office (1994) *The Government's Use of External Consultants.* London: HMSO.

Elger, T. (1979) Valorisation and 'deskilling': a critique of Braverman. *Capital and Class,* **7**, Spring, 58–99.

Elger, T. (1991) Task flexibility and the intensification of labour in UK manufacturing in the 1980s. In A. Pollert (ed.), *A Farewell to Flexibility?* Oxford: Blackwell, pp. 46–68.

Elger, T. and Smith, C. (eds) (1996) *Global Japanisation?* London: Routledge.

Enthoven, A. (1985) *Reflections on the Management of the National Health Service.* Nuffield Provincial Hospitals Trust, Occasional Papers 5. London: Nuffield Provincial Hospitals Trust.

Enthoven, A. (1991) Internal market reform of the British health service. *Health Affairs,* **10**(3), 60–70.

Equal Opportunities Commission (1996) *Call Bank Case Study.* London: EOC.

Fairbrother, P. (1994) *Politics and the State as Employer.* London: Mansell.

Fairbrother, P. (1996) Workplace trade unionism in the state sector. In P. Ackers, C. Smith and P. Smith (eds), *The New Workplace and Trade Unionism.* London: Routledge, pp. 110–48.

Farnham, D. and Horton, S. (eds) (1993) *Managing the New Public Services.* London: Macmillan.

Ferlie, E., Ashburner, L., Fitzgerald, L. and Pettigrew, A. (1996) *The New Public Management in Action*. Oxford: Oxford University Press.

Fincham, R., Fleck, J., Procter, R., Scarborough, H., Tierney, M. and Williams, R. (1994) *Expertise and Innovation Information Technology Strategies in the Financial Services Sector*. Oxford: Clarendon Press.

Fisher, A. (1939) Production: primary, secondary, tertiary. *Economic Record*, 15, 24–38.

Fitzgerald, I. and Stirling, J. (1995) Quality in the emergency services: a preliminary discussion paper. Mimeo, University of Northumbria at Newcastle.

Flanders, A. (1964) *The Fawley Productivity Agreements*. London: Faber and Faber.

Forester, T. (ed.) (1980) *The Microelectronics Revolution*. Oxford: Blackwell.

Forester, T. (ed.) (1985) *The Information Technology Revolution*. Oxford: Blackwell.

Fosh, P. (1993) Membership participation in workplace unionism: the possibility of union renewal. *British Journal of Industrial Relations*, 31(4), 577–92.

Fuchs, V. (1968) *The Service Economy*. New York: Columbia University Press.

Galbraith, J. K. (1967) *The New Industrial State*. London: Hamish Hamilton.

Gall, G. and McKay, S. (1994) Trade union derecognition in Britain 1988–94. *British Journal of Industrial Relations*, 32(3), 433–48.

Gallie, D. (1991) Patterns of skill change: upskilling, de-skilling or the polarisation of skills? *Work, Employment and Society*, 5(3), 319–51.

Gallie, D. (1997) Skill, gender and the quality of employment. In R. Crompton, D. Gallie and K. Purcell (eds), *Changing Forms of Employment*. London: Routledge, pp. 133–59.

Gershuny, J. (1978) *After Industrial Society?* Atlantic Highlands, NJ: Humanities Press.

Glyn, A. (1992) The productivity miracle, profits and investment. In J. Michie (ed.), *The Economic Legacy 1979–1992*. London: Academic Press, pp. 77–87.

Glyn, A. and Sutcliffe, B. (1992) Global but leaderless? The new capitalist order. In R. Miliband and L. Panitch (eds), *Socialist Register 1992*. London: Merlin, pp. 76–95.

Gough, I. (1973) State expenditure in advanced capitalism. *New Left Review*, 92, 72–111.

Gough, J. (1992) Where's the value in 'post Fordism'? In N. Gilbert, R. Burrows and A. Pollert (eds), *Fordism and Flexibility*. London: Macmillan, pp. 31–48.

Graham, L. (1996) How does the Japanese model transfer to the United States? A view from the line. In T. Elger and C. Smith (eds), *Global Japanisation?* London: Routledge, pp. 123–51.

Grant, A. (1983) *Against the Clock*. London: Pluto.

Greenwood, J. and Wilson, D. (1989) *Public Administration in Britain Today*. London: Unwin Hyman.

Gregory, A. (1991) Patterns of working hours in large-scale grocery retailing in Britain and France: convergence after 1992. *Work, Employment and Society*, 5(4), 497–514.

Guest, D. (1990) Have British workers been working harder in Thatcher's Britain? *British Journal of Industrial Relations*, 28(3), 294–310.

Hakim, C. (1987) Trends in the flexible workforce. *Employment Gazette*, 95, November, 549–60.

Hammer, M. (1990) Re-engineering work: don't automate, obliterate. *Harvard Business Review*, July/August, 104–12.

Hammer, M. (1995) *The Re-engineering Revolution: A Handbook*. New York: Harper.

Hammer, M. and Champy, J. (1994) *Re-engineering the Corporation*. New York: Harper.

Harrison, B. (1994) *Lean and Mean: The Changing Landscape of Corporate Power in the Age of Flexibility*. New York: Basic Books.

Harrison, J. (1973) Productive and unproductive labour in Marx's political economy. *Bulletin of the Conference of Socialist Economists*, Autumn, pp. 70–81.

Head, S. (1996) The new ruthless economy. *New York Review of Books*, **43**(4).

Healey, N. (ed.) (1993) *Britain's Economic Miracle: Myth or Reality?* London: Routledge.

Henderson, J. (1989) *The Globalisation of High Technology Production*. London: Routledge.

Heskett, J. (1986) *Managing in the Service Economy*. Boston, MA: Harvard Business School Press.

Hirst, P. and Zeitlin, J. (1989) *Reversing Economic Decline? Industrial Structure and Policy in Britain and Her Competitors*. Oxford: Berg.

Horton, S. (1993) The Civil Service. In D. Farnham and S. Horton (eds), *Managing the New Public Services*. London: Macmillan, pp. 127–49.

Howell, P. (1979) Once again on productive and unproductive labour. In *Revolutionary Communist 3/4*, 2nd edn. London: RCP Publications, pp. 46–68.

Hutton, W. (1996) *The State We're In*. London: Vintage.

Hyman, R. (1991) Plus ça change? The theory of production and the production of theory. In A. Pollert (ed.), *A Farewell to Flexibility?* Oxford: Blackwell, pp. 259–83.

Incomes Data Services (1986) *Flexibility at Work*. IDS Study 360. London: IDS.

Incomes Data Services (1988) *Overtime Working*. IDS Study 413. London: IDS.

Insco (1997) *Annual Report*. London: Insco.

Jackson, T. (1996) Now it's a case of dumbsizing. *Financial Times*, 20 May.

Jenkins, C. and Sherman, B. (1979) *White-Collar Unionism: the Rebellious Salariat*. London: Routledge and Kegan Paul.

Jones, B. (1996) The social constitution of labour markets. In R. Crompton, D. Gallie and K. Purcell (eds), *Changing Forms of Employment*. London: Routledge, pp. 109–32.

Jones, M. (1995) The contradictions of business process re-engineering. In G. Burke and J. Peppard (eds), *Examining Business Process Re-engineering*. London: Kogan Page, pp. 43–59.

Joyce, P. (ed.) (1995) *Class*. Oxford: Oxford University Press.

Keen, M. (1995) BPR: managing the change process – or the process of change managing BPR? In G. Burke and J. Peppard (eds), *Examining Business Process Re-engineering*. London: Kogan Page, pp. 262–75.

Kemp, T. (1990) *The Climax of American Capitalism*. London: Longman.

Kennedy, N. (1991) *The Industrialization of Intelligence*. New York: Random House.

Knights, D. and Morgan, G. (1996) Selling oneself: subjectivity and the labour process in selling life insurance. In C. Smith, D. Knights and H. Willmott (eds), *White Collar Work*, 2nd edn. London: Macmillan, pp. 217–40.

Kochan, L., Katz, H. and McKersie, R. (1986) *The Transformation of American Industrial Relations*. New York: Basic Books.

Krafcik, J. (1986) *Learning from NUMMI, MIT International Motor Vehicles Programme*. Cambridge, MA: MIT.

Kumar, K. (1996) *From Post-industrial to Post-modern Society*. Oxford: Blackwell.

Landes, D. (1969) *The Unbound Prometheus*. Cambridge: Cambridge University Press.

Lash, S. and Urry, J. (1987) *The End of Organized Capitalism*. Cambridge: Polity Press.

Letwin, D. and Redwood, J. (1988) *Britain's Biggest Enterprise: Ideas for Radical Reform of the NHS*. London: Centre for Policy Studies.

Liker, J., Ettlie, J. and Campbell, J. (1995) *Engineered in Japan*. Oxford: Oxford University Press.

Lister, J. (1997) *The Credibility Gap: Rhetoric versus Reality in London's Mental Health Services. An Interim Report for UNISON Greater London Region*. London: London Health Emergency/UNISON.

Lloyd, C. (1997) Decentralisation in the NHS: prospects for workplace unionism. *British Journal of Industrial Relations*, **35**(3), 427–46.

Lloyd, C. and Seifert, R. (1993) Restructuring in the NHS; the impact of the 1990 reforms on the management of labour. Paper presented to Eleventh Annual Labour Process Conference, Aston University.

Locke, R. (1996) *The Collapse of the American Management Mystique*. Oxford: Oxford University Press.

MacKenzie, D. and Wajcman, J. (eds) (1985) *The Social Shaping of Technology*. Milton Keynes: Open University Press.

Maddison, A. (1991) *Dynamic Forces in Capitalist Development*. Oxford: Oxford University Press.

Magdoff, H. (1992) Globalisation to what end? In R. Miliband and L. Panitch (eds), *The Socialist Register*. London: Merlin, pp. 44–75.

Management Consultancies Association (1995) *President's Statement and Annual Report*. London: MCA.

Marshall, G., Newby, H., Rose, D. and Vogler, C. (1988) *Social Class in Modern Britain*. London: Hutchinson.

Martin, R. (1981) *New Technology and Industrial Relations in Fleet Street*. Oxford: Clarendon.

Martin, R. and Rowthorne, B. (1986) *The Geography of De-industrialisation*. London: Macmillan.

Marx, K. (1969) *Theories of Surplus Value, Part One*. London: Lawrence and Wishart.

Marx, K. (1974) *Capital, Volume One*. London: Lawrence and Wishart.

Masuda, Y. (1985) Computopia. In T. Forrester (ed.), *The Information Technology Revolution*. Oxford: Blackwell, pp. 620–34.

Massey, D. (1992) *High Tech Fantasies: Science Parks in Society, Science and Space*. London: Routledge.

May, M. and Brunsdon, E. (1994) Workplace care in the mixed economy of welfare. In *Social Policy Review 6*. London: Social Policy Association, pp. 147–69.

Maynard, G. (1993) Britain's economic recovery. In N. Healey (ed.), *Britain's Economic Miracle: Myth or Reality?* London: Routledge, pp. 57–71.

Meiksins Wood, E. (1986) *The Retreat from Class*. London: Verso.

Metcalf, D. (1988) Trade unions and economic performance: the British evidence. Discussion paper no. 320. London: Centre for Labour Economics, LSE.

Metcalf, D. (1989) Water notes dry up. *British Journal of Industrial Relations*, **27**, 1–31.

Meszaros, I. (1989) *The Power of Ideology*. Brighton: Harvester Wheatsheaf.

Meszaros, I. (1995) *Beyond Capital*. London: Merlin.

Michie, J. (ed.) (1992) *The Economic Legacy*. London: Academic Press.

Michie, J. and Wilkinson, F. (1992) Inflation policy and the restructuring of labour markets. In J. Michie (ed.), *The Economic Legacy 1979–1992*. London: Academic Press, pp. 195–217.

Miliband, R. and Panitch, L. (1992) *Socialist Register*. London: Merlin.

Miller, H. (1991) Academics and their labour process. In C. Smith, D. Knights and H. Willmott (eds), *White Collar Work: The Non-manual Labour Process*. London: Macmillan, pp. 109–38.

Mizen, P. (1994) In and against the training state. *Capital and Class*, **53**, Summer, 99–121.

Mohan, J. (1995) *A National Health Service?* London: St Martins Press.

Moon, G. and Kendall, I. (1993) The National Health Service. In D. Farnham and S. Horton (eds), *Managing the New Public Services*. London: Macmillan, pp. 172–87.

Moore, M. (1996) *Downsize This*. London: Boxtree.

Moore, W. (1993) Rationing the blame. *Health Service Journal*, 18 March, p. 16.

Morris, T. (1986) *Innovations in Banking: Policies, Strategies and Employee Relations*. London: Croom Helm.

Nicholls, T. (1991) Labour intensification, work injuries and the measurement of percentage utilisation of labour (PUL). *British Journal of Industrial Relations*, **29**(3), 569–92.

Nolan, P. (1989) The productivity miracle? In F. Green (ed.), *The Restructuring of the UK Economy*. Brighton: Harvester Press, pp. 101–21.

NUPE (1993) *Skill Mix and Reprofiling in the Health Service: NUPE Guidelines*. London: NUPE.

O'Connell Davidson, J. (1993) *Privatization and Employment Relations*. London: Mansell.

OECD (1993) *Economic Outlook*. Paris: OECD.

O'Reilly, J. (1994) *Banking on Flexibility*. Aldershot: Avebury.

Pakulski, J. and Waters, M. (1996) *The Death of Class*. London: Sage.

Peck, J. (1992) Where's the value in post-Fordism? In N. Gilbert, R. Burrows and A. Pollert (eds), *Fordism and Flexibility*. London: Macmillan, pp. 31–48.

Penn, R., Rose, M. and Rubery, J. (eds) (1994) *Skill and Occupational Change*. Oxford: Oxford University Press.

Piore, M. and Sabel, C. (1984) *The Second Industrial Divide: Possibilities for Prosperity*. New York: Basic Books.

Pollert, A. (1987) *The 'Flexible Firm': A Model in Search of Reality (or a Policy in Search of a Practice)?* Warwick Papers in Industrial Relations No. 19, Coventry: University of Warwick Industrial Relations Research Unit.

Pollert, A. (ed.) (1991) *Farewell to Flexibility?* Oxford: Blackwell.

Poynter, G. (1993) Change in workplace relations: the UK in the 1980s. PhD Thesis, University of Kent at Canterbury.

Poynter, G. (1997) The unions and New Labour. *Soundings*, special issue, The Next Ten Years, September.

Quinn, J. and Gagnon, C. (1986) Will services follow manufacturing into decline? *Harvard Business Review*, November/December, 95–103.

Quinn, J., Doorley, T. and Paquette, P. (1990) Beyond products: service based strategy. *Harvard Business Review*, March/April, 58–68.

Rainnie, A. and Kraithman, D. (1992) Labour market change and the organisation of work. In N. Gilbert, R. Burrows and A. Pollert (eds), *Fordism and Flexibility: Divisions and Change*. London: Macmillan, pp. 49–65.

Riddle, D. (1986) *Service-led Growth: The Role of the Service Sector in World Development*. New York: Praeger.

Riley, B. (1996) Downsizing's dubious dividends. *Financial Times*, 18/19 May.

Rinehart, J., Robertson, D., Huxley, C. and Wareham, J. (1996) Reunifying the conception and execution of work under Japanese production management? A Canadian case study. In T. Elger and C. Smith (eds), *Global Japanisation?* London: Routledge, pp. 152–74.

Ritzer, G. (1993) *The McDonaldization of Society*. London: Sage.

Ritzer, G. (1998) *The McDonaldization Thesis*. London: Sage.

Roach, S. (1991) Services under siege – the restructuring imperative. *Harvard Business Review*, September/October, 71–81.

Robins, K. and Webster, F. (1987) Information as capital: a critique of Daniel Bell. In J. Slack and F. Fejes (eds), *The Ideology of the Information Age*. Norwood, NJ: Ablex Publishing Corporation, pp. 95–117.

Robins, K. and Webster, F. (1989) *The Technical Fix: Education, Computers and Industry*. London: Macmillan.

Rowthorn, B. (1992) Government spending and taxation in the Thatcher era. In J. Michie (ed.), *The Economic Legacy 1979–1992*. London: Academic Press, pp. 261–92.

Rubery, J. (1996) The labour market outlook and the outlook for labour market analysis. In R. Crompton, D. Gallie and K. Purcell (eds), *Changing Forms of Employment*. London: Routledge, pp. 21–39.

Ruigrok, W. and Van Tulder, R. (1995) *The Logic of International Restructuring*. London: Routledge.

Rustin, M. (1989) The politics of post-Fordism, or the trouble with 'new times'. *New Left Review*, **175**, 54–77.

Sayer, A. and Walker, R. (1992) *The New Social Economy*. Oxford: Blackwell.

Schaller, M. (1985) *The American Occupation of Japan*. Oxford: Oxford University Press.

Schiesinger, L. and Heskett, J. (1991) The service-driven service company. *Harvard Business Review*, September/October, 71–81.

Skinner, W. (1974) The focused factory. *Harvard Business Review*, May–June, 105–14.

Slack, J. (1984) The information revolution as ideology. *Media, Culture and Society*, **6**, 247–56.

Slaughter, J. (1989) Charge of the credit card brigade. *Observer*, 19 February.

Smith, C., Knights, D. and Willmott, H. (1991) *The White Collar Labour Process*. London: Macmillan.

Smith, D. (1983) Service workers in the class structure: the case of shopworkers. DPhil thesis, Oxford University.

Smith, S. and Anderson, J. (1992) Over the threshold? Public and private choices in new information technology homeworking. In N. Gilbert, R. Burrow and A. Pollert (eds), *Fordism and Flexibility: Divisions and Change*. London: Macmillan, pp. 170–85.

Stamp, D. (1995) *The Invisible Assembly Line*. New York: American Management Association.

Standing, G. (1986) *Unemployment and Labour Market Flexibility: The United Kingdom*. Geneva: International Labour Organisation.

Stonier, T. (1983) *The Wealth of Information: A Profile of the Post-industrial Economy*. London: Thames Methuen.

Storey, J. and Sisson, K. (1993) *Managing Human Resources and Industrial Relations*. Buckingham: Open University Press.

Storey, J., Cressey, P., Morris, T. and Wilkinson, A. (1996) Changing employment practices in UK banking: case studies. *Personnel Review*, **26**(1/2), 24–42.

Teeling-Smith, G. (1986) *Health: The Politician's Dilemma*. London: Office of Health Economics.

Thompson, P. and Warhurst, C. (1998) *Workplaces of the Future*. London: Macmillan.

Thornley, C. (1996) Segmentation and inequality in the nursing workforce. In R. Crompton, D. Gallie and K. Purcell (eds), *Changing Forms of Employment*. London: Routledge, pp. 160–81.

Thurrow, L. (1993) *Head to Head*. London: Brealey.

Timo, N. and Littler, C. (1996) The routinisation of services: the McDonaldisation of service work? Paper presented to the Globalisation of Production and the Regulation of Labour Conference, University of Warwick, 11–13 September.

Toffler, A. (1981) *The Third Wave*. New York: Bantam Books.

Trapp, R. (1993) Operating prophets. *Independent on Sunday*, 4 April.

Treacy, M. and Wiersema, F. (1995) *The Discipline of Market Leaders*. London: Harper-Collins.

UNISON (1993) *Driven to the Edge: UNISON Evidence to the Nurses Pay Review Body*. London: UNISON.

UNISON (1994) *Nurses on the Production Line*. London: UNISON.

UNISON (1997) *Blueprint for Bluelight Closures*. London: London Health Emergency/UNISON.

Urry, J. (1990) *The Tourist Gaze*. London: Sage.

US Department of Commerce, International Trade Administration (1991) *Trends in International Direct Investment*. Staff Paper No. 91-5. Washington, DC: US Department of Commerce, International Trade Administration.

Waddington, J. (1995) *The Politics of Bargaining: The Merger Process and British Trade Union Structural Development 1892–1987*. London: Mansell.

Waddington, J. and Whitston, C. (1996) Empowerment versus intensification: union perspectives of change in the workplace. In P. Ackers, C. Smith and P. Smith (eds), *The New Workplace and Trade Unionism*. London: Routledge, pp. 149–77.

Walton, R. (1985) From control to commitment in the workplace. *Harvard Business Review*, March/April, 76–84.

Warhurst, P. and Thompson, P. (1998) Hands, hearts and minds: changing work and workers at the end of the twentieth century. In P. Warhurst and P. Thompson (eds) *Workplaces of the Future*. London: Macmillan, pp. 1–24.

Waters, M. (1995) *Globalisation*. London: Routledge.

Webster, F. (1996) *Theories of the Information Society*. London: Routledge.

Whitaker, S. (1998) Investment in the recovery: an assessment. *Bank of England Quarterly Bulletin*, **37**(4), 38–47.

Williams, K. *et al.* (1992) Against lean production. *Economy and Society*, **21**(3), 321–54.

Wolf, M. (1998) Averting the worse. *Financial Times*, 9 September.

Womack, J., Jones, D. and Roos, D. (1991) *The Machine That Changed the World*. New York: First Harper.

INDEX